AA

JUNIOR
ATLAS
OF BRITAIN

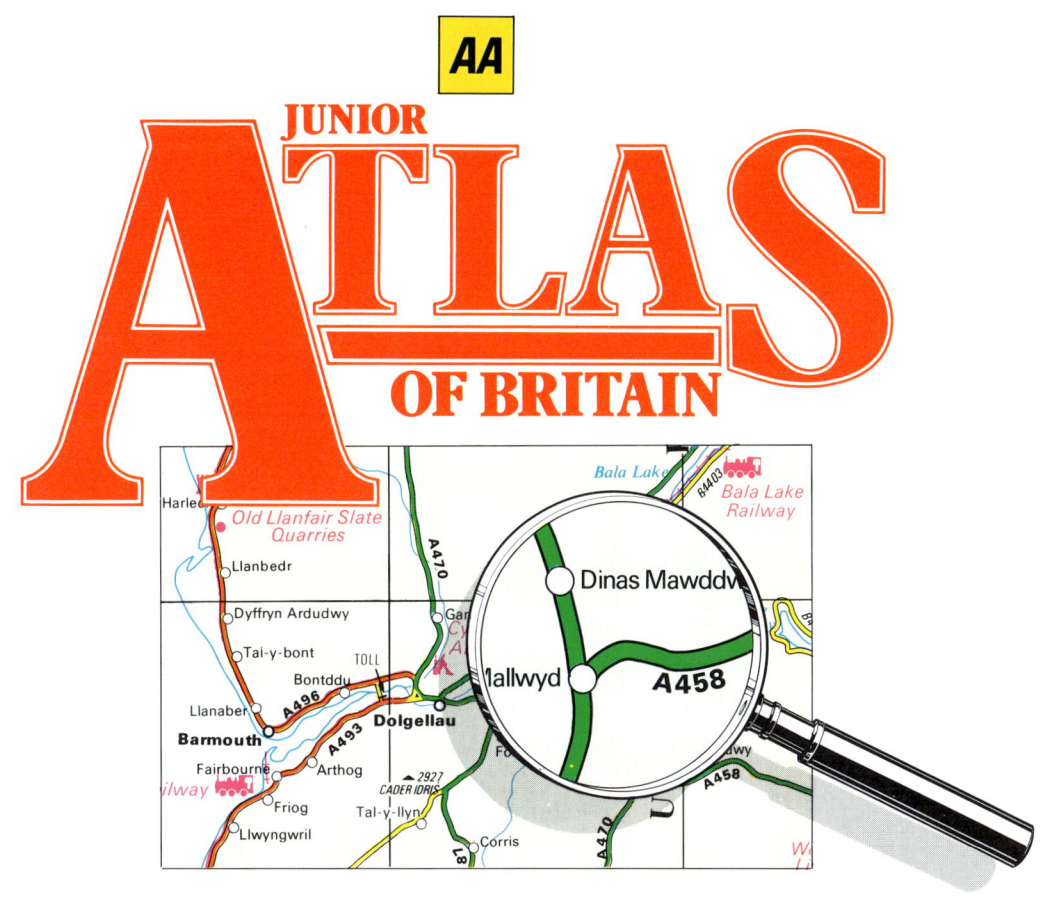

Hamish Hamilton · London

JUNIOR ATLAS OF BRITAIN

AA

Produced jointly by the Publications Division of the
Automobile Association and Hamish Hamilton Ltd.

Text by **Lewis Jones**
Editors: **Julia Brittain, Christine Sandeman**
Art Editor: **Peter Davies**

Illustrations: **Terence Dalley** ARCA, **KAG Design, Joseph Wright**

Maps and town plans produced by the Cartographic Unit of the Automobile
Association.
Road atlas based on the Ordnance Survey maps, with the permission of the
Controller of HM Stationery Office. Crown copyright reserved.

Typeset by Katerprint Co Ltd, Cowley, Oxford
Printed in Belgium by Henri Proost, Turnhout

© **The Automobile Association 1983**
© **Hamish Hamilton Ltd 1983**

ISBN 0241 11041 6   AA Ref 56740

Distributed in the United Kingdom by Hamish Hamilton Ltd.

Published jointly by Hamish Hamilton Ltd, Garden House,
57–59 Long Acre, London WC2E 9JZ, and the Automobile Association,
Fanum House, Basingstoke, Hampshire RG21 2EA.

NOTE
**Because British roads and road speeds are calculated in miles and miles
per hour, the text gives imperial measurements first with their metric
equivalents in brackets immediately afterwards.**

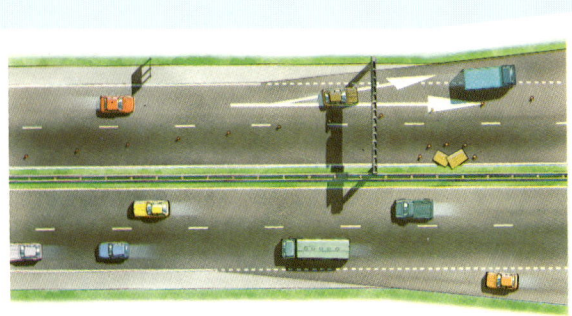

CONTENTS

	page
HOW A MAP IS MADE	8–11
THE SCALE OF A MAP	12–13
SILHOUETTES	14
USING MAP GRIDS	15
THE STORY OF ROADS	16–17
ROADS TODAY	18
MOTORWAYS	19–21
'A' ROADS IN THE COUNTRY	22–23
'A' ROADS IN TOWN	24–25
'B' ROADS	26–27
OTHER ROADS	28–29
VEHICLE MARKS	30–33
MEET THE TRAFFIC POLICE	34–35
EMERGENCY!	36–37
DISTANCE CHART	38
CONVERSION CHARTS	39
HOW TO PLAN YOUR ROUTE	40
ROUTE PLANNING MAP	41–45
ATLAS SYMBOLS	46–47
KEY TO ATLAS PAGES	48
ATLAS	49–79
INDEX AND TOWN PLANS	80–96

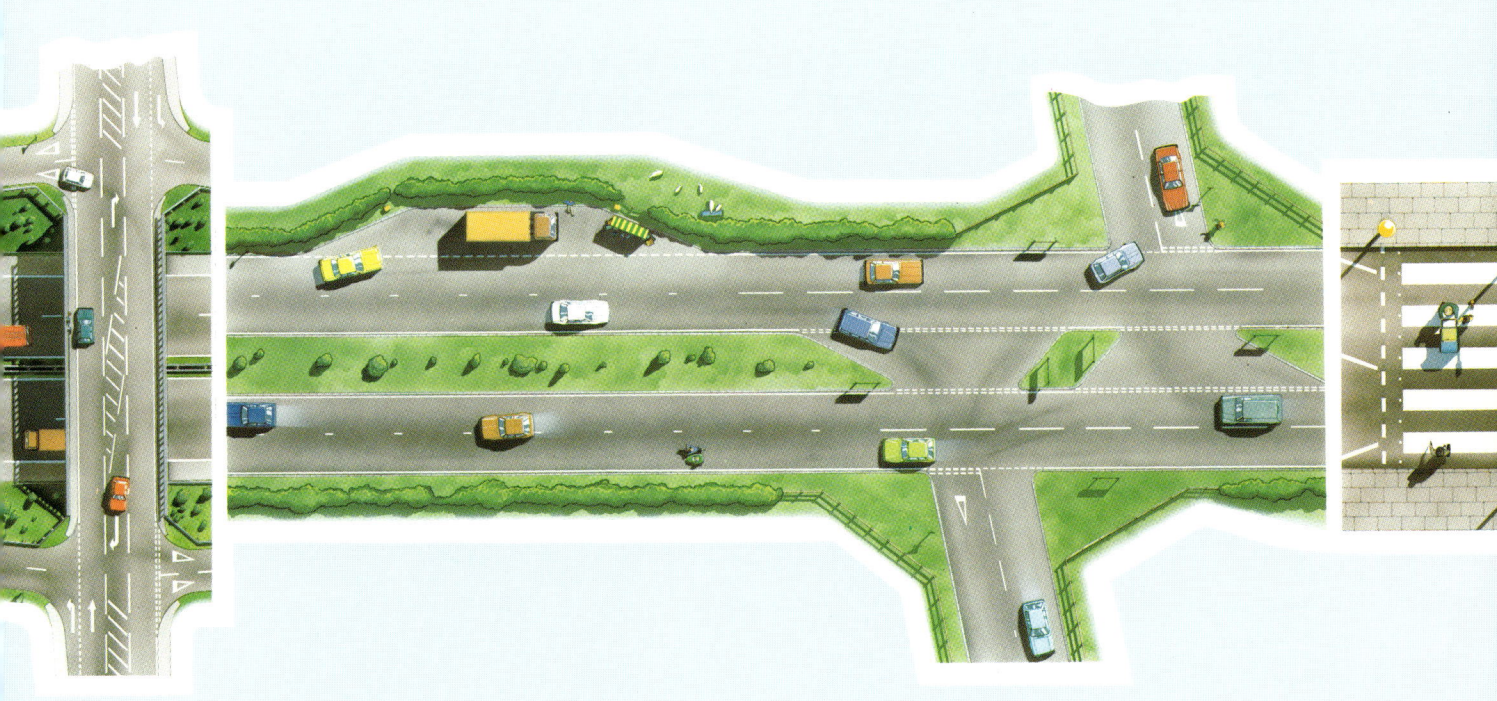

INTRODUCTION

These days nearly everyone who has a car needs a road atlas. But many people don't really know how to use road maps properly.

With this book you can become an expert map-reader almost at a glance. Soon you will be able to plan a route and give directions on family journeys. All of a sudden you'll find you will enjoy travelling in a car far more than you have ever done before.

In a way, this is a very different road atlas from others you have seen, because it has been carefully designed for young people. And young people even helped to design it!

The maps, of course, can be used by everyone. They are clear and easy to follow, showing all the main roads as well as many smaller ones. Counties have been given different colours, and all towns and important villages are marked. So are dozens of interesting places to visit such as zoos, castles and country parks.

Before the map section begins, there are lots of colourful pages explaining how maps work and how to set about planning routes. You will find all kinds of fascinating things to look out for as you go along and plenty of games to test your wits and your patience.

At the end of the book, the names of all the towns and villages shown in the atlas are listed in alphabetical order, so that you can quickly spot the one you want to find on the map.

Now start looking through the book and see how many questions it answers about maps and roads. It may surprise you!

HOW A MAP IS MADE

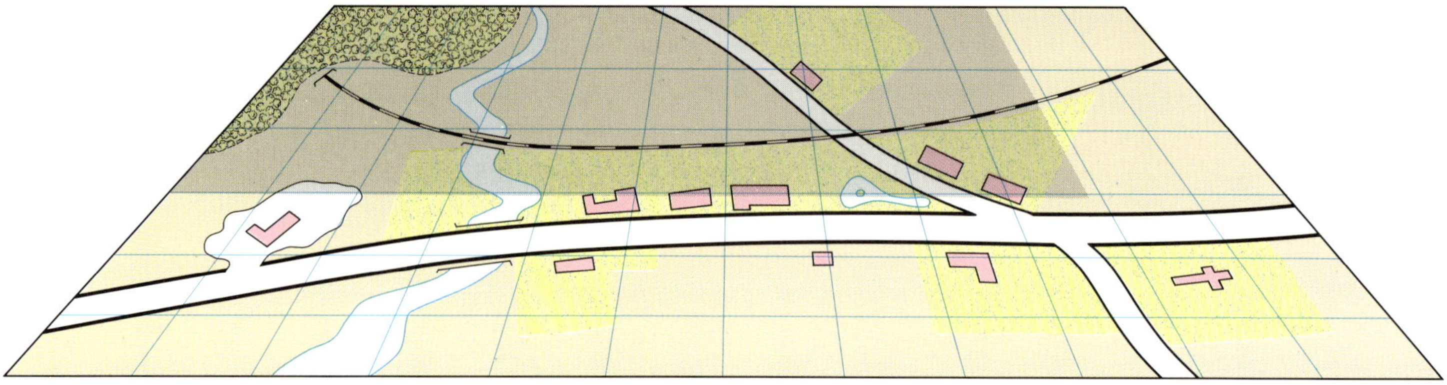

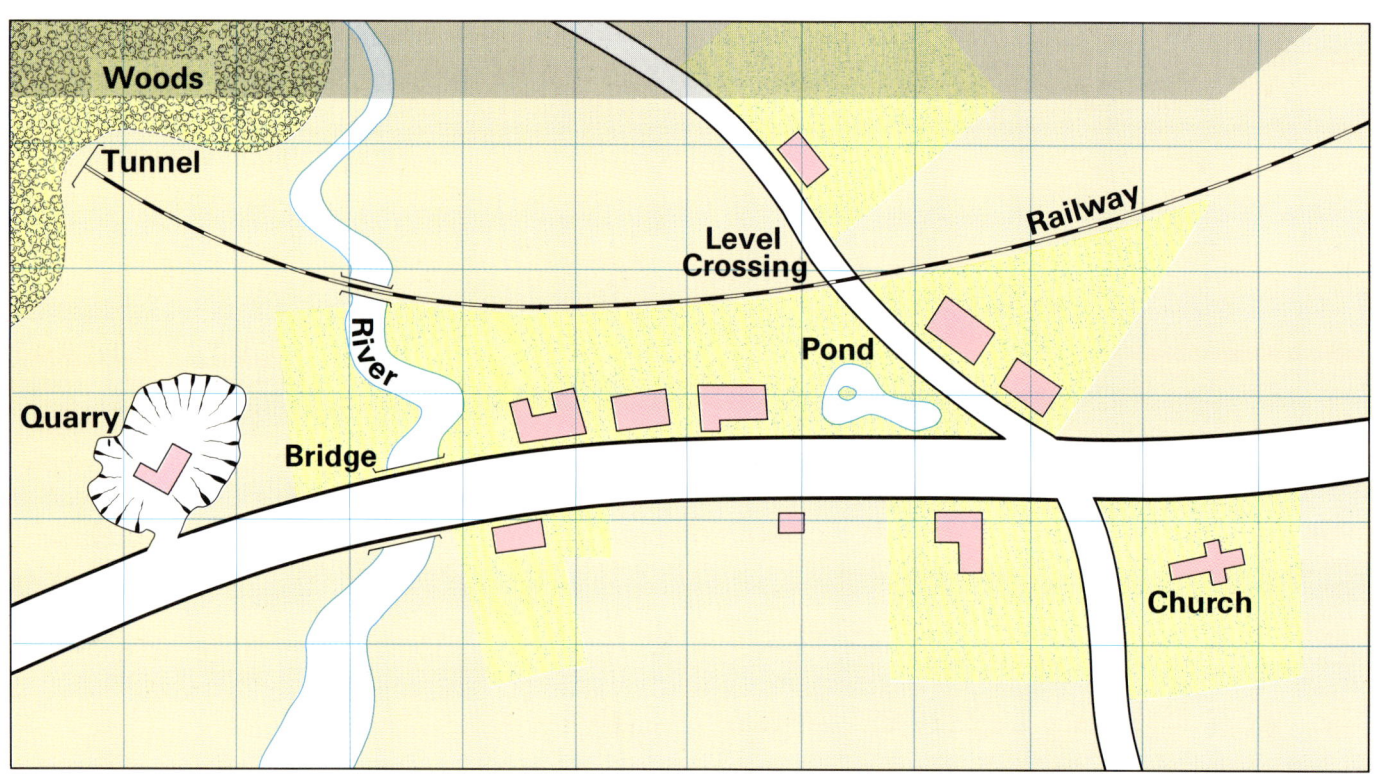

Woods

Tunnel

Railway

Level
Crossing

River

Pond

Quarry

Bridge

Church

The top picture shows a village as you might see it from a helicopter. Suppose you wanted to make a map of it. Which things would you leave in? Which things would you leave out?

First you must decide who the map is for. People in cars want maps to help them find their way. So these maps need to show roads and useful land-marks, but not things like animals and cars. A map like this might include a pond, a church or a river. The middle picture shows your map at this stage.

This picture is not a proper map because it shows the view only from, say, the west. The bottom drawing is like a view straight down from above. The picture has become a map.

Trig points (left) and bench marks (above) are set up by the Ordnance Survey.

The surveyors pictured on the left are making measurements for use in mapping.

If you wanted to make a map showing how far apart two places were, how would you do it? One way would be to measure a chain very carefully and then lay it on the ground in a straight line between the two places, over and over again. If you added all the lengths together, you would find out the distance between the places.

People who make measurements for maps (called *surveyors*) used chains like this for a long time. They also set up special markers, called *trig points*, to help them measure distances. You can sometimes find a trig point (officially called a triangulation pillar) on top of a hill. It's a stone or concrete pillar, about as high as a man's chest, which gets narrower towards the top. From one trig point you can often see a few others. Here are just a few places where you can spot trig points: Box Hill, near Dorking; Butser Hill, overlooking Portsmouth; Beachy Head, near Eastbourne. Many of Britain's highest mountains, such as Snowdon and Ben Nevis, have trig points at the top.

Today, surveyors don't use chains much. They use an instrument called an Electronic Distance Measurer (EDM for short) which sends a beam of light from one place to another. The EDM measures the time it takes for the beam to bounce back. The EDM's computer knows the speed of the beam and does a simple sum: Speed × Time. This gives the distance of the beam's journey

there and back. The computer halves the figure, and shows the answer – which is the distance between the two places.

Another thing to look out for is *bench-marks*. They are often cut into the walls of buildings, not much higher than your knee. They show an upward-pointing arrow head touching a level line. The level line is very useful to road-makers and map-makers because it marks how high somewhere is above sea-level. In towns, you can find bench-marks cut into the walls of buildings (often a church, or a house on the corner of a street). In open country, a bench-mark can be a flat square of concrete in the ground. The head of a bolt marks the exact height above sea-level.

The sea doesn't always stay at exactly the same level, of course. But about 70 years ago, some people went to the little seaside town of Newlyn in Cornwall (page 50 in this atlas) and measured the level of the sea in the harbour there. They did this again and again, once every hour, for six years (it is still checked by machine today). They averaged out all the measurements, and called it sea-level.

On the harbour wall in Newlyn today, you can see a metal bolt-head 15½ feet (about 4·5 m) above sea-level. All over Britain, heights shown on maps as heights above sea-level are really heights above this bolt-head.

The Ordnance Survey

The first proper maps of Britain were made almost 200 years ago to help the army move quickly across country. The word for army stores and guns is 'ordnance' and, today, the part of the government that makes maps of Britain is still called the Ordnance Survey.

HOW A MAP IS MADE

Cartographers draw maps by engraving through a coloured coating on a plastic base. Each colour on the map has its own separate sheet at this stage.

The surveyor makes notes about the work he's done and he passes these notes on to the map-maker, called a *cartographer*. The notes show the distances between places, and the directions.

The cartographer has to decide how big his maps need to be. Every page of an atlas like this is a piece of the map of Britain. The cartographer for this atlas decided that one inch (2.5 cm) of his maps would show about eight miles (13 km) of ground. For example, it's 56 miles (90 km) in a straight line from Scarborough to Leeds, so in this atlas the towns are seven inches (17.5 cm) apart.

The cartographer has to get the direction right as well, so that the network of places on the map matches the real network across Britain. Roads often twist and turn a lot, so the cartographer checks them against aerial photographs of the area shown on the map. Britain is divided into pieces called *counties*, and drivers sometimes like to know which county they are in. So in this atlas the county borders have been drawn, and each county has been given its own colour.

Some atlases (including this one) show you where there are interesting places to visit. The cartographer decides on symbols for things like castles and zoos. Then he draws them and puts them in the right place.

If you try to squeeze too much on to a map, it can be hard to read. So the cartographer has to decide which names and which roads to leave out, as well as which ones to put in.

But maps are not only for people travelling long distances. You may need a map if you are on a bicycle in a small town, or for shopping when you are on holiday in a strange place. Town maps look different from the rest of the atlas. There are some town maps among the index of names, at the back of the book. Look at some of those town maps, then open the atlas at any page. What are the differences between the two sorts of map? What do you find on town maps that are not on the pages of the atlas? What sorts of things in the atlas are not in the town maps? When is it most useful to have a road's name? And when is it more useful to have its number?

Find Durham in the atlas, and find the town plan in the index. Suppose you are in Durham and you want to leave for Newcastle-upon-Tyne. Which map gets you on the right road most easily?

Or suppose you are driving into Stratford-upon-Avon, and you have to meet someone at the bus station. Then you have to take them to the Royal Shakespeare Theatre. Which map is most useful to you?

Who is a map for?

Different people need different kinds of maps. A girl in a canoe doesn't need to find out about roads and level-crossings and town plans. She needs the answers to questions like these:

Where is there a waterfall?
Where is the river very shallow?
Are there any dangerous rocks?
Where can I expect very fast currents?
Are there any sharp bends in the river?

Think of the needs of these different people:

A cross-country walker
An aeroplane pilot
A canal boat owner
A city policeman
A mountain climber

Open this atlas at any page. What extra things would you add to the map for each kind of person? Which of the things on the map would you leave out?

What other kinds of people would be glad of special maps?

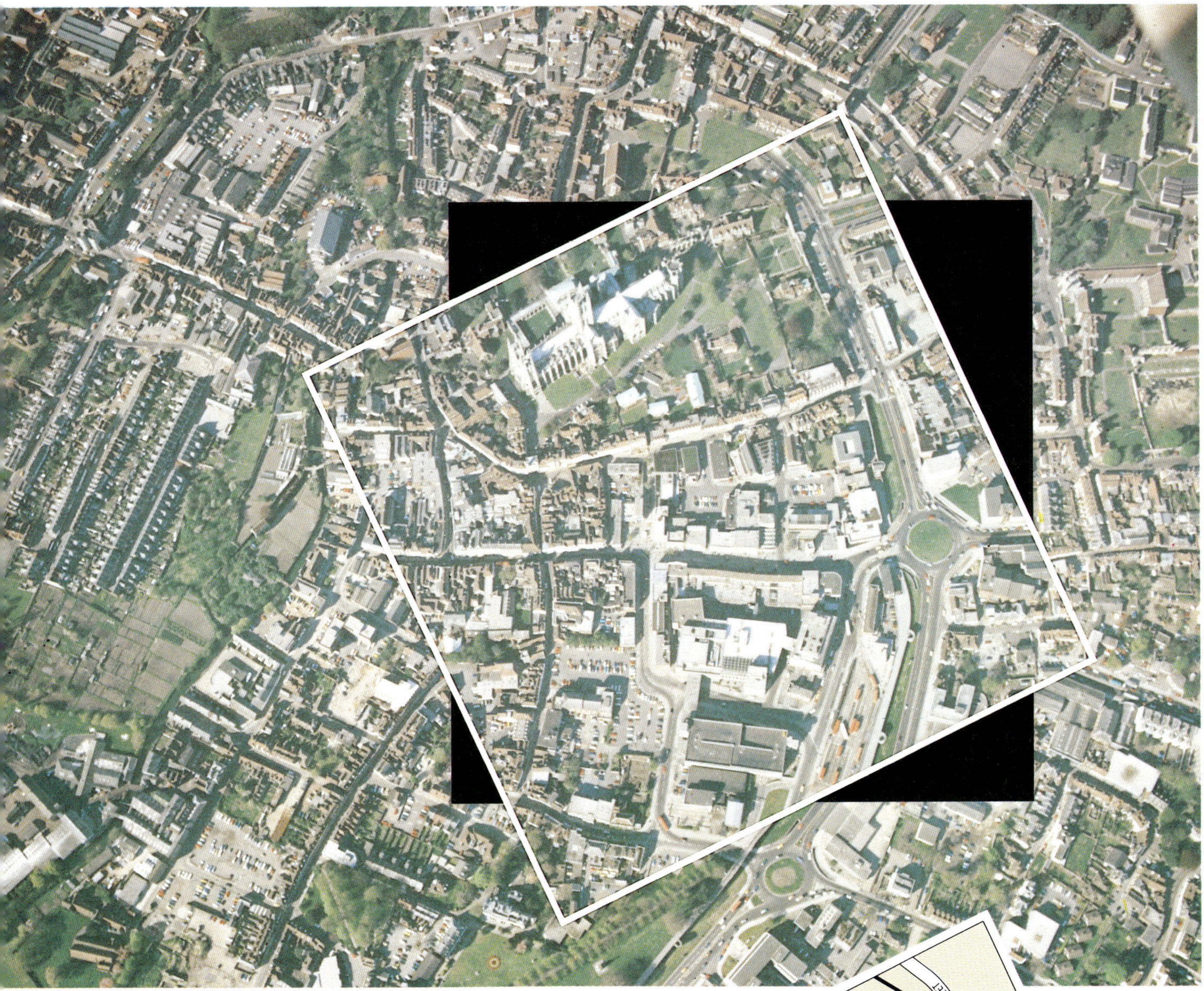

Look at the photograph and the map on this page. The cartographer has decided to leave some things out, and put other things in. Can you spot them? Which things are in both the photo and the map? Which are in the photo only? Which are in the map only? Some things don't appear in either the photo or the map – which ones are these?

To help you to get started, here's a list of some things to think about.

a hill	a car park
a street name	a level-crossing
a post office	a bus station
a church or cathedral	a petrol station
traffic lights	a phone box
a roundabout	a hotel
the old town wall	a tree
a road number	a dual carriageway

Be your own cartographer. Decide which things you want, and don't want, on this map of Canterbury. How would your map be different from the one that's here?

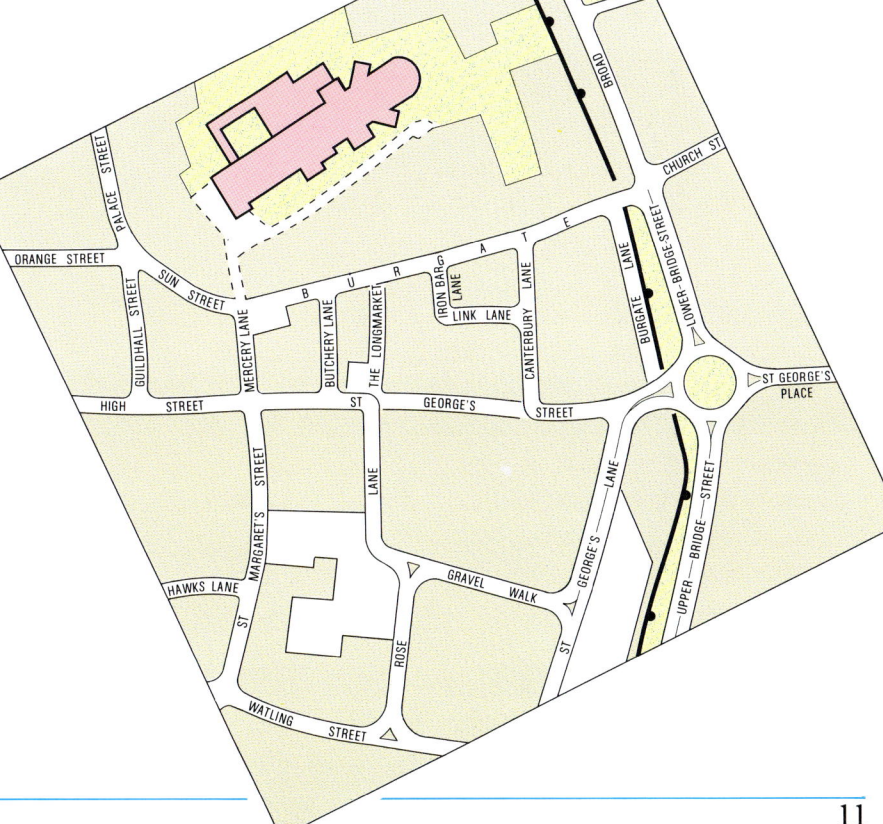

THE SCALE OF A MAP

If you are at home, or at school, open this book and stand it on a table. Then walk to the other side of the room. You will see the shape and colour of the book, and lots of things around it, but you won't be able to read the words.

Move closer, until you can read the words easily. Now you won't see any of the things around the book, unless you look away from it.

Move closer still, until your eye almost touches the page. Now you will see a few letters – useful if you are looking for a printing mistake, but you won't be able to read the words. There's no single right distance for looking at things. Different distances are useful for some things, and useless for others.

It's the same with a map. A weather satellite 600 miles up (nearly 1,000 km) shows the shape of Britain, but it doesn't show any towns or roads. From a plane a mile up (almost 2 km), you can see many more separate things. From the top of a tall building you can see more details still. Which of these views is the best one? It all depends what you want. The view from the tall building can't show the weather over Britain, and the weather satellite can't show the cat in the street. Some maps are like the view from a long way up. They are useful if you want to see a lot of ground on one page. For instance, if you want to see roughly where Inverness is in relation to London, then you could look at the little key map on page 38 of this book. Here the whole of Britain is shown on one small map. Places that are a long way apart can be seen together.

Other maps are like the view from closer to the ground. They are useful if you want to see more things, but they show a smaller piece of ground. A good example of this kind of map is one of the town plans at the back of this book.

When you look at a page of this road atlas, how much of the country are you seeing? The exact *scale* of the atlas is 1 to 500,000 (often written 1:500,000). This means that the distance between any two places is 500,000 times bigger on the ground than it is on the map. In fact, as we've said before, it works out that one inch (2.5 cm) on the map stands for about eight miles (13 km) on the ground. So we would say that this map is at a scale of about eight miles to the inch. The three squares of map on these pages show what maps at different scales look like.

How then do you work out the distance between different places on a map? The *distance bar* (or *scale bar*) will tell you. There is one on page 13 and one on each page of the road atlas.

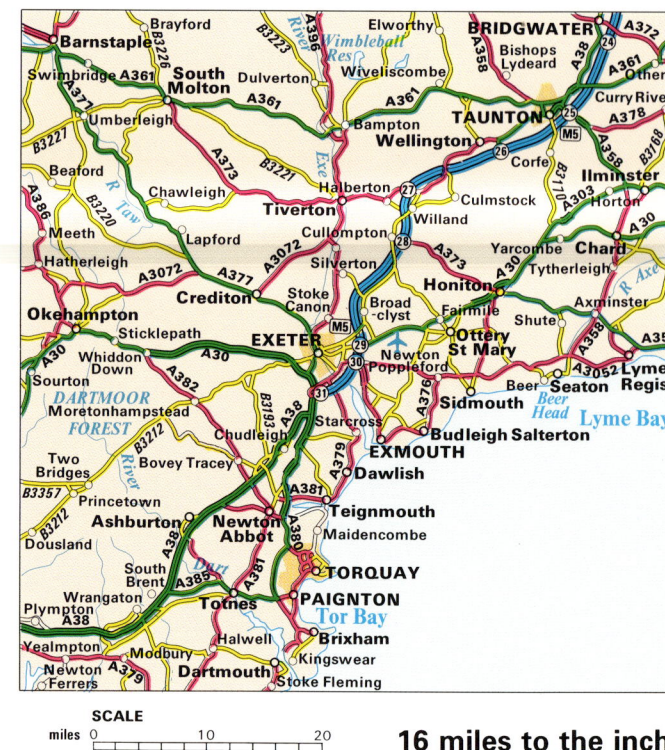

SCALE

16 miles to the inch

This is a map of Exeter and the country around it. It's as if you had gone a long way up in a hot-air balloon, and looked down through a square hole in the floor of the basket.

One inch on this map shows you 16 miles of real country. The map square measures 3½ inches across, so, in other words, you are looking at a square of country measuring 56 miles from side to side.

There are rather a lot of names and road numbers, and not much empty space. You can see a lot of coastline and sea. The M5 motorway can be seen all the way up to Bridgwater. To the right of Exeter, you can see the town of Ottery St Mary. Now look for it on the next map.

Using a scale bar

If you want to find out roughly how far apart two places are, take a piece of paper, or a used envelope, and lay one edge along the scale bar. Put some of the distance marks along the edge of the paper. You can measure your distance in either miles or kilometres – they are both shown on the scale bars in this book. Now put the paper-edge onto the map, to measure the route you want. If the road changes direction, turn the paper to follow it. Real roads don't usually go in a straight line like your paper-edge, so add a bit extra to your measured distance to allow for the curves and bends.

The drawing opposite shows you how to measure distances in this way. With practice, you'll be able to estimate distances on the map simply by looking at the map and the scale bar.

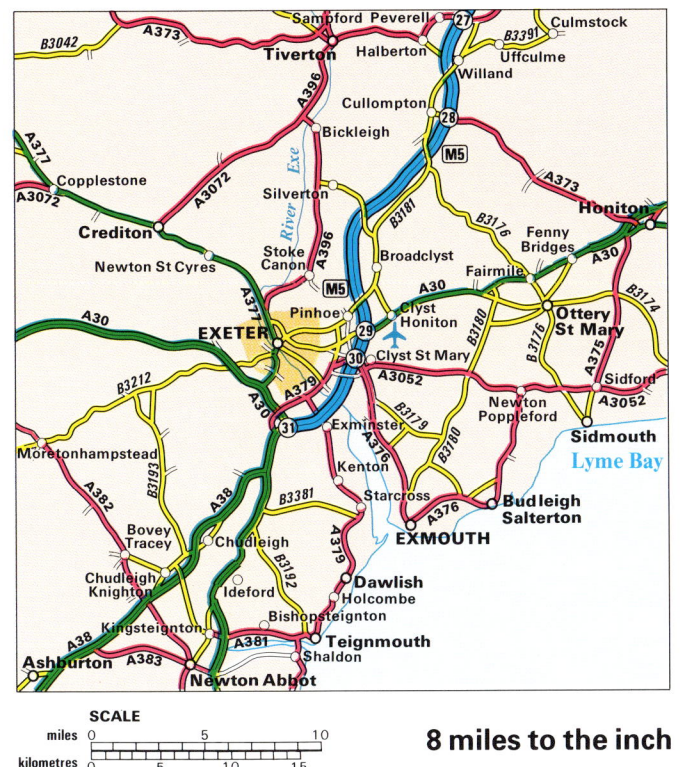

8 miles to the inch

SCALE
miles 0 — 5 — 10
kilometres 0 — 5 — 10 — 15

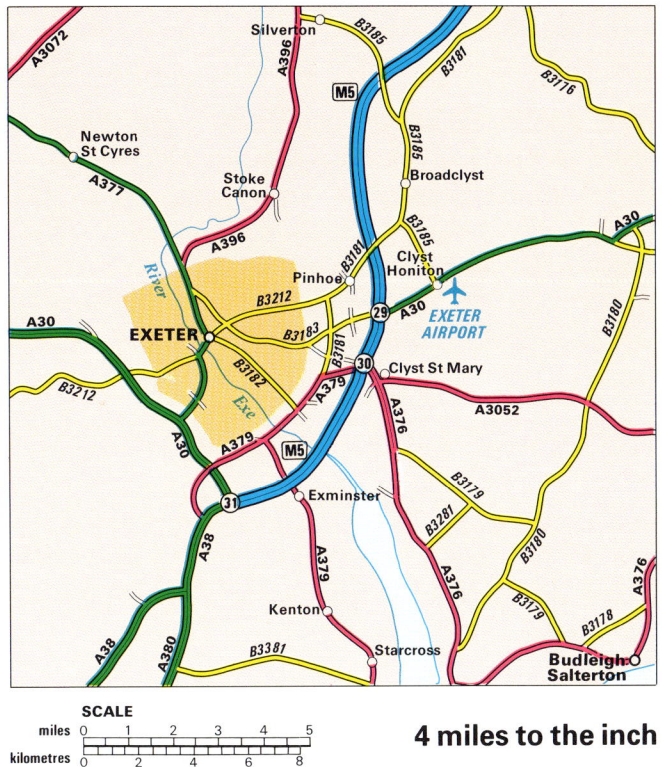

4 miles to the inch

SCALE
miles 0 1 2 3 4 5
kilometres 0 2 4 6 8

Your balloon is lower now. One inch of this map shows only 8 miles of country (the same as this atlas). You are looking at a square 28 miles across.

Ottery St Mary is now near the edge of the map. And some of the places on the first map have disappeared altogether – for example, the seaside towns of Torquay and Paignton. But because this is a closer view, some things are shown that you couldn't see before. Clyst Honiton and Clyst St Mary have appeared between Exeter and Ottery St Mary.

The cartographer has enough room to add some road junctions (look at the B roads on the left of the map). These little *spurs* show motorists where to expect a side road.

Your balloon is now lower still, and 1 inch of this map shows only 4 miles of country. (You are looking at 14 miles across Britain.) Ottery St Mary has disappeared off the right-hand edge of the map. The sea has gone too, except for the mouth of the River Exe.

Notice that the symbol for the airport is the same in all three maps. Symbols are not meant to show the real size of anything. The little drawing only shows you where something is.

An atlas of maps like this one would need four times more pages than the map in the middle; and 16 times more pages than the map at the far left.

Can you spot any other differences between the three maps?

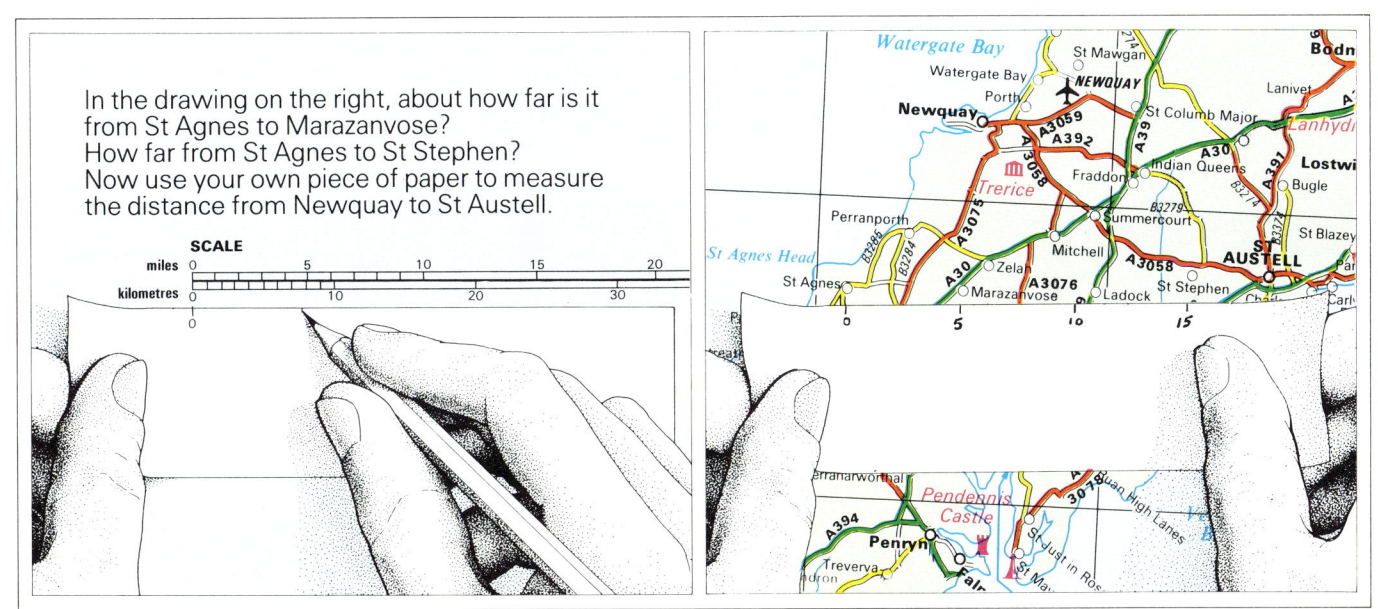

In the drawing on the right, about how far is it from St Agnes to Marazanvose?
How far from St Agnes to St Stephen?
Now use your own piece of paper to measure the distance from Newquay to St Austell.

SCALE
miles 0 5 10 15 20
kilometres 0 10 20 30

SILHOUETTES

Number Silhouettes

This is a game for two. Each player needs a sheet of paper and a pencil. First, look at the grid on the right.

By filling in some of the squares, you can make the figure 3.

In fact you could make any figure:

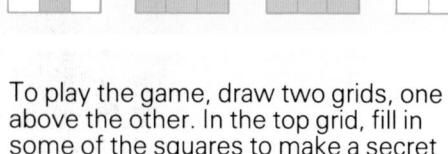

To play the game, draw two grids, one above the other. In the top grid, fill in some of the squares to make a secret figure. The other player does the same.

You must try to find out the other player's secret figure, and she must try and find yours. Notice that each grid has *numbers* along the bottom, and *letters* up the right-hand side.

Decide who starts. If it's you, call out a square by giving its *number* first, then its *letter* (for example, the bottom right square is 3A).

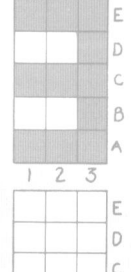

The other player looks at her top grid. If that square is filled in, she says 'Yes'. (And you fill in that square in your bottom grid.)

If that square is blank, she says 'No'. (And you put a small dot in that square in your bottom grid.)

Then it's the other player's turn to call out a square. And so on. The winner is the one who guesses the other player's figure first. But take care – a wrong guess loses.

Here's a bottom grid after only one turn. Already you can tell what the others player's figure is. Only one figure has the square 2D filled in!

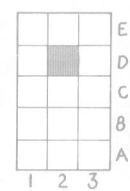

Letter Silhouettes

Use a bigger grid, and you can play the game with capital letters instead of numbers. Like this:

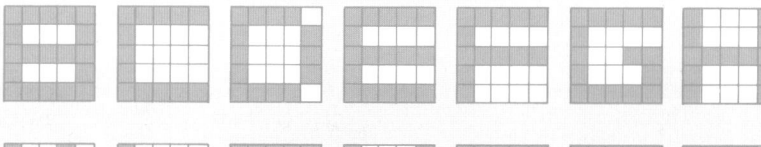

Word Silhouettes

When you get good at the letter game, you can play Silhouettes with words. Draw *three* letter-grids side by side. Think of a three-letter word, and draw one letter in each grid. (Don't forget to draw three more grids underneath, for guessing the other player's word.)

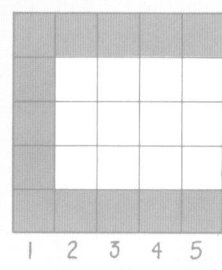
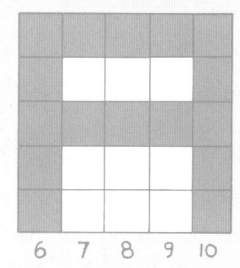
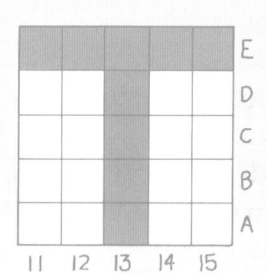

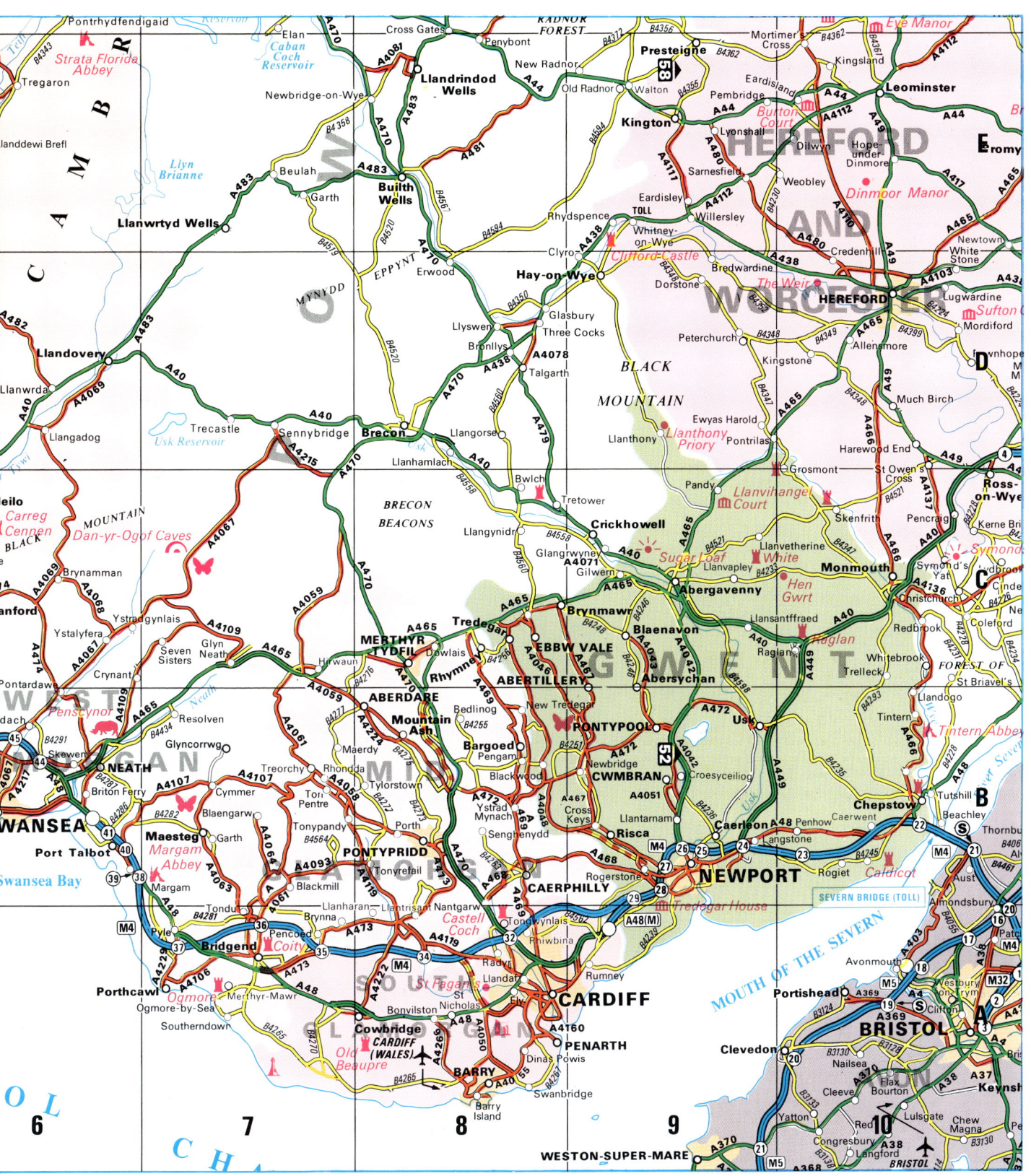

Each page in this atlas has a grid of squares. It makes it easy for you to find the places you want. If you have played the Silhouette games, you will have no trouble with the maps. Every page has a grid with *numbers* along the bottom, and *letters* going up the right-hand side.

If you want to find a place in the atlas, look for its name in the index at the back. That will tell you the page number and the grid square.

For example, the index entry for Aberdare is shown below. Above is part of atlas page 57. You will find Aberdare in grid square 8B.

Place name   Grid square

Aberdare.....................**57**......*8B*

Page number

THE STORY OF ROADS

The oldest tracks and pathways that can be seen in Britain today were made by prehistoric people many thousands of years ago. But it was the Romans who gave Britain its first proper roads, when they invaded about 2,000 years ago. Sometimes their soldiers had to travel long distances to fight Britons who were giving trouble. They built long, straight roads, so they could reach the trouble spots quickly.

The Romans left Britain after a few hundred years, and people began to dig the stones out of

PREHISTORIC

ROMAN

MEDIEVAL

16th–17th CENTURIES

Wrongdoers used to have their legs clamped in stocks as a punishment. Stocks can still be seen in some old villages. The ones in this picture are at Great Tew in Oxfordshire.

Look for milestones by the roadside. This one is at Shrewton in Wiltshire.

Horse-drawn carts are rarely seen today.

18th–19th CENTURIES

Try to spot old or unusual signposts like the one on the left, at Albury.

Unusual pub signs like the one on the right, near Horam, are worth looking for.

RUNT-IN-TUN

the roads. They wanted the stones for building. No-one needed to travel long distances quickly, and the roads became earth and mud again. Sometimes they were used by groups of pilgrims, who travelled to holy places on horseback.

After a long time, people put big gates called turnpikes across the roads at different places. Travellers had to pay a toll before they could get through. The money was collected by a toll-keeper, who often lived in a round or many-sided house so he could see travellers coming from all directions. The money was supposed to pay for mending the roads. But not many people knew enough about road building, so roads didn't get much better. When the horse collar was invented, horses could be used for pulling heavy loads, like coaches, for the first time. The first coaches were bought by people for their own use. Then stage coaches began to carry passengers. People paid a fare for each stage of the journey, and some sat inside, and some sat outside. About every 15 miles (25 km or so), the horses were changed.

Then John Palmer of Bath invented the mail coach. These coaches were light, and carried passengers inside only. They changed horses twice as often as the stage coaches. Soon Britain had the fastest post service in the world. Some coaches could stop, change horses, and be off again, in 45 seconds! The driver and the guard both carried guns to protect the passengers and the letters and parcels. There was always a risk from highwaymen, who would stop coaches in the hope of stealing gold or other valuables.

About 100 years ago, railway trains became travelling post-offices, and the days of the mail coach were over. The railways carried passengers too, and the roads became emptier.

Early cars began to be used in the 1890s. By law, they had to have three people in charge. A man had to walk in front carrying a red flag by day, and a lantern at night. The speed limit was 4 miles an hour (about 6 km an hour) in the country, and 2 miles an hour in town.

As cars became more common, roads improved. The small stones and dust on the road were covered with tar to give a hard surface, and vehicles could go faster. Roads were used more and more by cars, buses and lorries, and soon Britain was covered by a huge network of modern roads, which is still being improved and added to all the time.

1880–1920

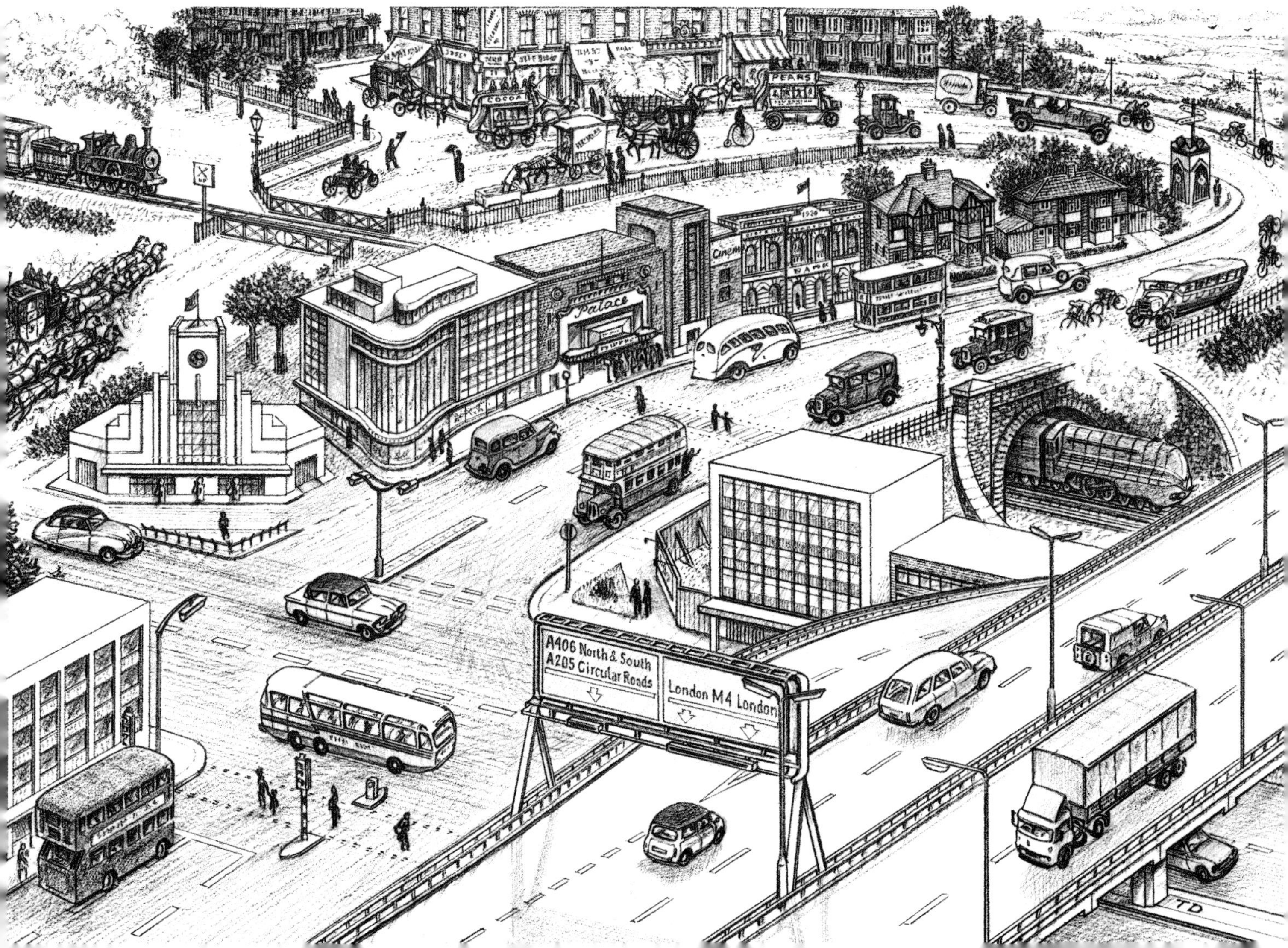

ROADS TODAY

The size of a road came to depend on how many vehicles used it. Some roads had to be widened to take the extra traffic. When these became crowded, new roads had to be built. The only roads that stayed small were in out-of-the-way places where there were few cars.

The biggest roads in the network that covers Britain today are the motorways. The first stretch was 8½ miles (roughly 13 km) of the M6 near Preston, built about thirty years ago. A year later the first part of the M1 was opened. Nowadays, one mile of road in every 200 is motorway, and new motorways are still being built all the time. Apart from motorways, the most important roads are A roads. Instead of names, they have the letter A and a number, like the A59. Next in importance are B roads, like the B6461. The smallest roads have no letters or numbers, and are known by map-makers as unclassified roads. Usually, small signposts point to them, with the names of the places the roads lead to. In this atlas, motorways are coloured blue, A roads are green or red, and B roads are yellow. Each road has its letter and number written on it.

Classes of signs

Three main shapes are used for road signs: triangles, circles and rectangles.

Red triangles warn. Red circles prohibit. Blue circles give positive instructions.

Blue rectangles give general information. Green rectangles are used for directions on primary routes.

Many of Britain's A roads are linked up into a network of *primary routes*. These routes are coloured green on the map. They are specially for long-distance travellers who want to find their way easily across country. Primary routes have their own signposting system. Green signboards direct motorists to the next important place (called a primary town) on their route.

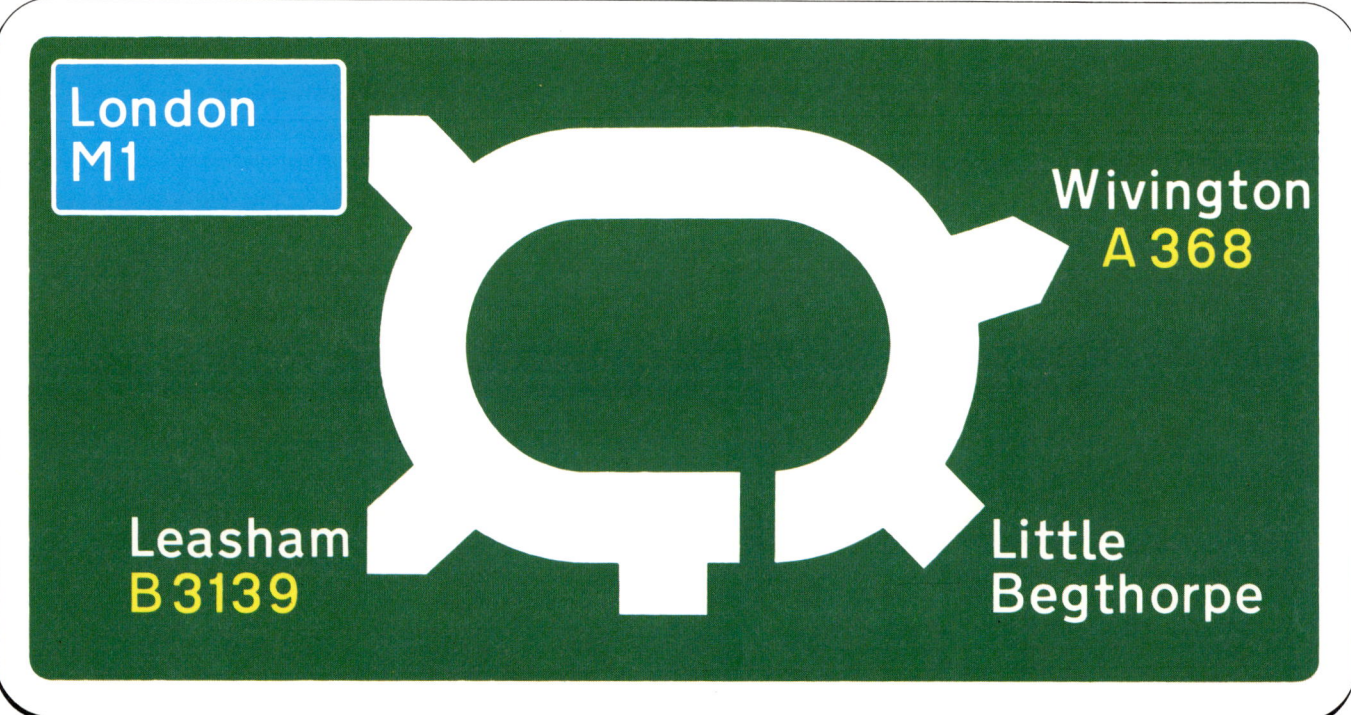

The picture shows a signboard on the approach to a roundabout. You can see how the different sorts of road are signposted – motorways, A roads, B roads and minor roads. The green board tells you that you are on a primary route. Except for London, all the place-names on the sign are imaginary.

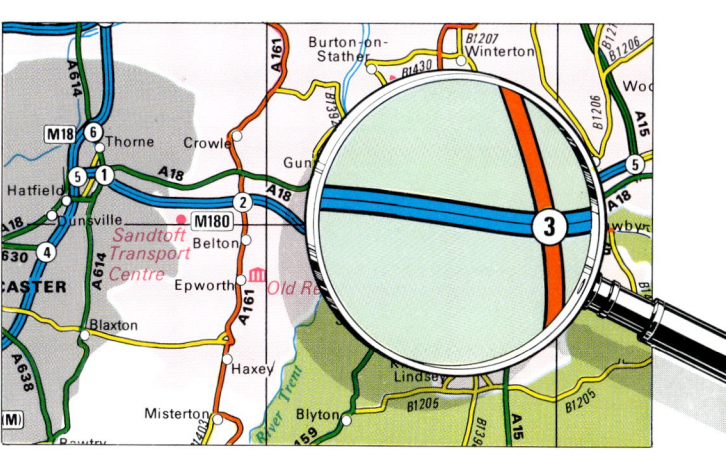

Motorways are built to allow drivers to move quickly from place to place, without being stopped by other traffic. When another road needs to cross the path of a motorway, it has to go over or under it. There are no crossroads or roundabouts.

Motorways have two or three lanes going each way. This is to allow vehicles to overtake each other easily. The two traffic streams are kept apart by a narrow strip of ground called the *central reservation*. Where there are three lanes, caravans and lorries are allowed to use the two lanes on the left only. The speed limit for cars is 70 mph (about 110 kph); heavy lorries mustn't go faster than 60 mph.

Motorways are different from all other public roads in Britain because not everyone is allowed to use them. They must not be used by people on foot, learner-drivers, scooters and small motor-bikes, anything very slow (like farm tractors), bicycles or animals.

Motorways are named by the letter M and a number, such as M1, M3 or M4. Some stretches of road are built as motorways but have a different style of numbering, such as the A1(M).

Lane clear

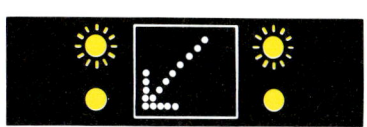

Leave motorway at next exit

Advised maximum speed

Electronic signs on overhead gantries (left) are operated by the police. They can show a speed limit (above), or tell traffic to change lane or leave the motorway (top) if there are roadworks or an accident.

You leave and enter motorways at *junctions*. On most motorways, each junction has its own number. For instance, the M1 begins at London with Junction 1, and ends at Leeds with Junction 47. When you are planning to use a motorway, choose the best junction to join it and the best one to leave it. On the M6, for example, there are five different junctions for different parts of Birmingham. If you leave the motorway at the first junction you see with the name Birmingham, you might have to cross the city through slow, heavy traffic.

All motorway signboards are blue. The number of the junction is in the bottom left-hand corner, in a small black square. It might be written in white paint on the road too (Junction 6 would be J6).

You will see a signboard for your junction when it's still a mile ahead (about 1½ km). There will be another signboard when it's half a mile ahead. When you are 300 yards away (almost 300 metres),

Numbered posts (above) help police to identify any place on a motorway. They also point to emergency telephones (left).

you will see the first of three countdown markers.

If there is an accident, or there are roadworks on a motorway, special signs light up. These may be on a special signboard at the side of the road, or

Start of motorway

The
NORTH WEST
Birmingham

Birmingham
(W & Cen)
A 456
3

You will see signs like the one on the left before you reach a motorway exit. Countdown markers are pictured on the right.

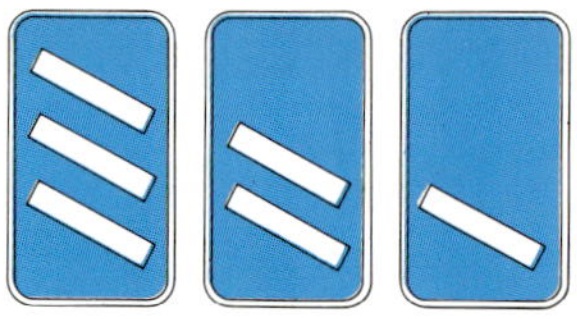

on overhead gantries. The signs direct the traffic to another lane, slow it down, stop it, or make it leave the motorway. The signs are controlled by the police and sometimes operated by computers. The computers keep a record of the days and times when the lighted signs are on, so no-one can forget which signs are on or off.

If it's your car that's in trouble, you can stop on the *hard shoulder* at the side of the road – that's what it's for. There is a white marker post every 110 yards (about every 100 metres). Each marker post has a little picture of a telephone on it, and an arrow that points left or right. The arrow shows which way to go for the nearest telephone. There's a phone every mile, so there's never any need to walk more than half a mile to phone for help. The phones are not locked, and will work without money.

The phones can also be used to report an accident. A call will bring fire engines or ambulances (or both) to the scene. The traffic police are in overall charge. You can find out more about the emergency back-up services on pages 36–37.

End of motorway

'A' ROADS IN THE COUNTRY

A driver who wanted to go quickly from Blackpool to Manchester could use the motorway. But if he wanted to go on from Manchester to Newcastle, there would be no motorway. (Check this on the route planning map on pages 42–43.)

His next best choice would be A roads. Not all A roads are primary routes, but most of them are big and well-made. Some A roads (like the one in the picture) have a strip of ground between the two streams of traffic. These roads are *dual carriageways*.

If a car is in trouble, there's no hard shoulder to stop on. But there are *lay-bys* where drivers can stop in an emergency or just to stretch their legs. People sometimes stop at a lay-by to have something to eat or to take a rest. You may have seen people selling flowers or vegetables or fruit at one.

Traffic can cross an A road. Where a side road

joins an A road, a long white triangle is painted on the ground. This warns drivers to wait until the A road is clear. The white double-dashes are also a warning to give way to traffic on the A road. To cross a dual carriageway, a driver first has to find a gap in the grass strip. Double dashes in the road there tell him to wait until the road is clear.

Short white dashes along the A road separate each side of the carriageway into two lanes. At a junction with a side road, the dashes become longer – a warning to take special care because of danger – in this case from crossing traffic.

At night, drivers can still tell where the lane lines are because of an invention by Percy Shaw. About fifty years ago, he was driving along on a dark, foggy night, when he noticed the eyes of a cat, shining as they reflected the light of his

No U-turns   Quayside or river bank   No stopping (Clearway)   Road works ahead   National speed limit applies   No right turn

Signs like this give directions on primary routes.

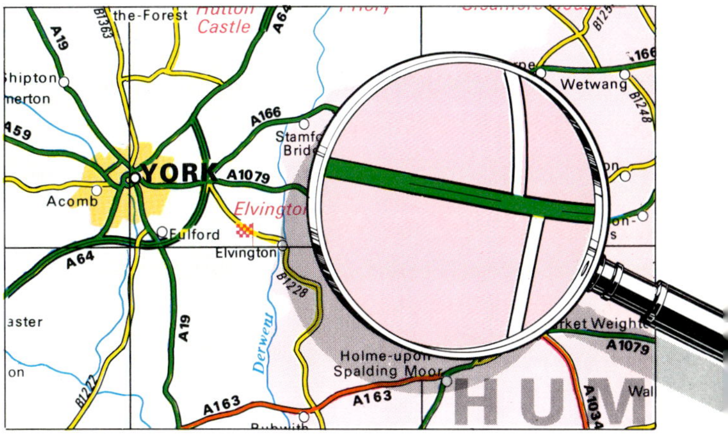

headlamps. They gave him the idea for *cat's eyes* – the little glass reflectors that mark the lane lines at night. When a car wheel runs over them, the eyes are pushed down, and wiped against a rubber lip. This cleans the glass, like an eye-blink, so that they always stay bright.

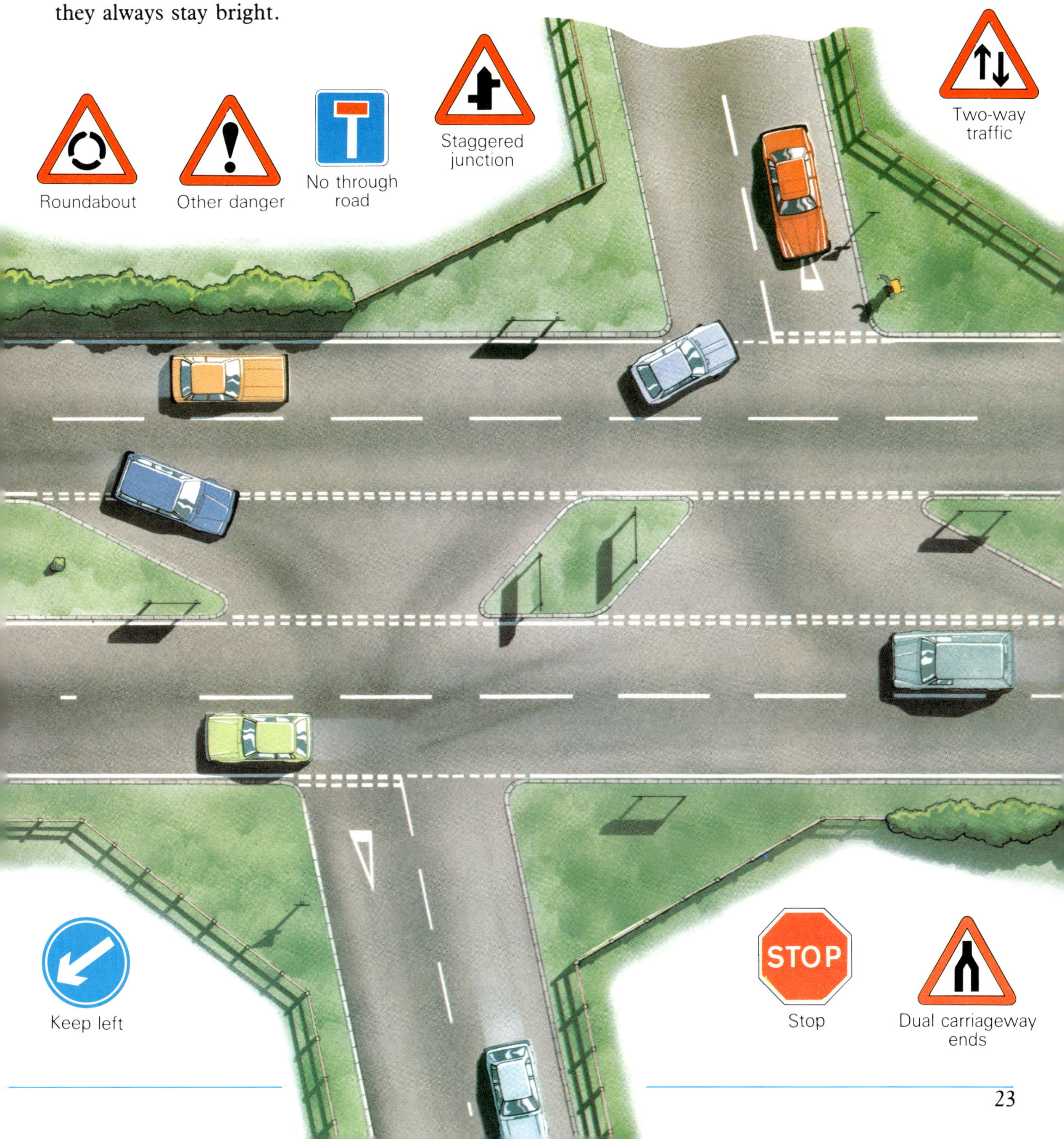

Roundabout

Other danger

No through road

Staggered junction

Two-way traffic

Keep left

Stop

Dual carriageway ends

'A' ROADS IN TOWN

When an A road goes through a town, drivers can sometimes avoid the busy centre by taking a *ring road*. This directs traffic round the outside of the town, and drivers simply follow the sign ®.

But sometimes drivers cannot avoid going through the middle of a busy town. In towns, there are a lot of people on foot, and roads have to help them as well as cars. Pedestrians would find it almost impossible to cross a busy street if there wasn't a special place for crossing. As soon as someone steps onto a zebra crossing, the traffic must stop for them. All ordinary pedestrian crossings have a flashing yellow globe called a *Belisha beacon* at each side, so that drivers can see them at night. Zigzag lines near the crossing mean 'Don't park here'. If cars were parked very close to a zebra crossing, drivers might not see someone on the pavement waiting to cross.

Some crossings are controlled by traffic lights operated by pedestrians themselves. These are called *pelican crossings*. Someone on the pavement can push a button and, after a few moments, the lights will stop the traffic. When the red man on the signal changes to green, it's time to cross the road. Some pelicans give out a beep-beep sound so blind people can tell when the green man is showing.

Drivers need to be particularly aware of pedestrians, whether they are at a crossing or not. A blind person may carry a white stick, or be with a guide dog. Someone who is both blind and deaf may carry a white stick with two red bands.

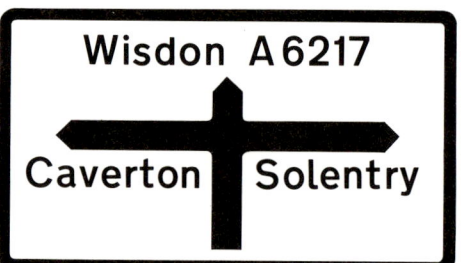

Local direction information is given on signs like this.

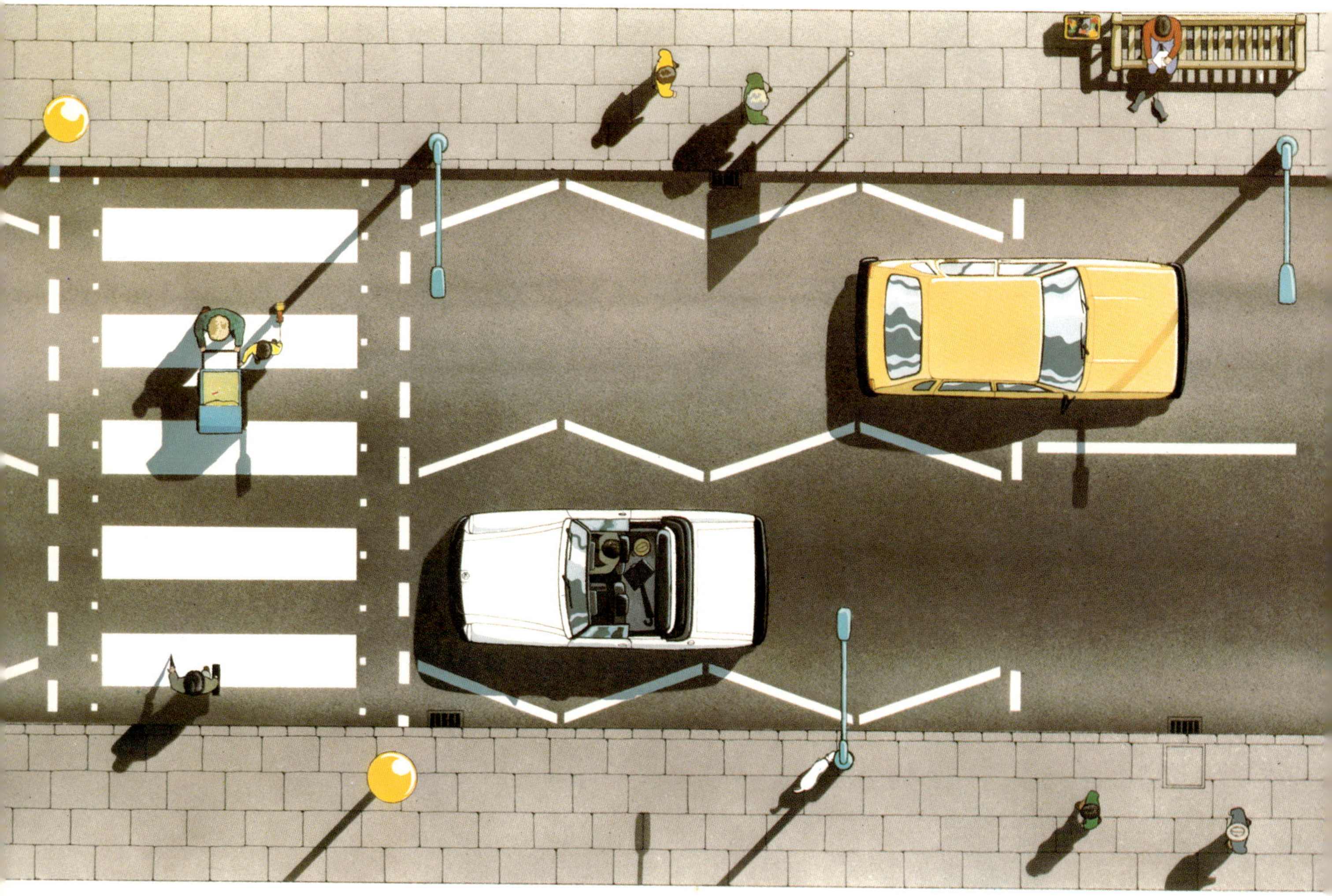

No entry for vehicles

School crossing patrol: vehicles must stop

One way

Maximum speed limit

Turn left ahead

No vehicles

A traffic jam can soon bring a large part of a town to a standstill, so a lot of trouble is taken to keep traffic moving. Cars are not allowed to park on busy roads, and car parks have to be built to take them. Buses may get a special lane of their own, and may sometimes travel in the opposite direction to the traffic on their side of the road. Some roads are made one-way streets. And at busy junctions, there is often a yellow box with criss-cross lines painted on the road, which drivers must not enter unless they are sure of getting to the other side. This is to avoid blocking the junction.

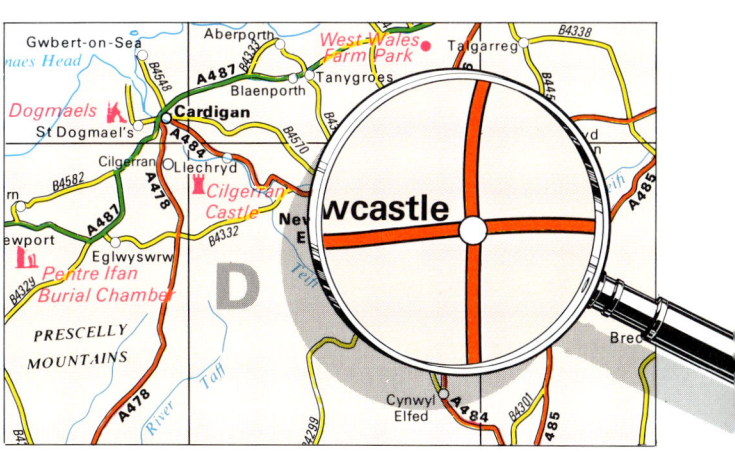

Crossroads

Children

Traffic signals ahead

Pedestrian crossing ahead

'B' ROADS

The road sign B376 tells you that you are on the B road numbered 376. If the road sign says (B376), the brackets show that you are on a road leading to the B376.

It is often impossible to overtake on a B road.

Sometimes, a B road is the best road to take because an A road or a motorway would lead you too far out of your way. Suppose you wanted to drive from Wantage to Newbury. (Find them both in the atlas.) Which road would you use?

Drivers on A roads sometimes look for a B road so that they can avoid heavy traffic. Too many drivers may have taken the same popular route – perhaps they have all followed the Holiday Route sign ⬚HR. The traffic news on the radio may give warnings of traffic jams ahead on the A road.

Since long-distance drivers generally use A roads or motorways, B roads are almost always less busy. But a B road usually has only one lane of traffic going each way. If something as slow as a tractor is on the road, it can be difficult for cars to get past. They may all have to go at the tractor's

No vehicles
Except for access

T-junction

Steep incline

GIVE WAY

Give way

speed for a long time.

In the picture, the tractor has just reached the double lines along the centre of the road. No-one is allowed to cross solid double lines, so no-one can overtake the tractor here.

In the middle of the picture, one of the double lines is dashed. If no traffic was coming the other way, a driver could cross that dashed line to overtake the cyclists, because the dashed line is on his side of the road. But even if the road is clear, traffic coming from the opposite direction must not cross the centre lines – the dashed line is not on their side. The white arrows in the road warn drivers behind the tractor to keep to their own side because they are approaching the double lines.

B roads are often used by horse-riders. They have to ride on the left-hand side of the road, just

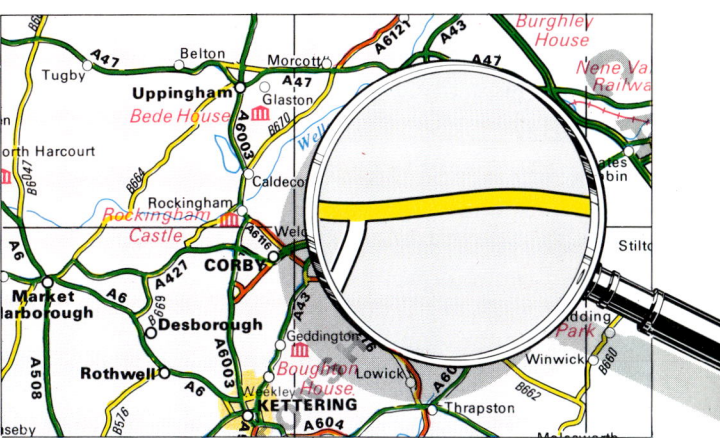

like motorists, and they must obey the same traffic rules. Car drivers should slow down and give them plenty of room, and try not to frighten the horse by sounding the horn or racing the engine.

Side road

Slippery road

No overtaking

Risk of falling rocks

Wild animals

Road narrows on both sides

OTHER ROADS

Roads that are smaller than B roads are usually called unclassified roads by map-makers. They have no letters or numbers on their signposts. They can be very narrow, and they often twist about. Drivers usually have to travel quite slowly along these roads, because they can't be sure what they will meet round the next bend.

Some people prefer to drive on small country roads like this. It gives them a chance to get out of the car, and get away from the traffic for a while.

Steep and winding mountain roads need great care.

Hump bridge

Level crossing without gate or barrier

Level crossing with gate or barrier

Steep decline

Give priority to vehicles from opposite direction

No vehicles over height shown

14'-6"

Uneven road

No vehicles (including load) over weight shown

10 TONS

They can do some bird-watching, enjoy the scenery, or perhaps have a picnic.

Now and again, there may be a gate across the roads to keep cows from wandering. Motorists have to open the gate before they can move on, and then close it behind them. Animals sometimes appear on the road itself. Wild horses or ponies may wander there, and dogs may be loose. A driver could meet a herd of cows being driven for milking, or a shepherd may be moving a flock of sheep from one field to another.

Many little country roads are very old. They were not specially built as roads, but grew from paths between farms and villages, so these roads go up and down as they follow the shape of the land. A road sign warns you each time you are about to go up or down a steep hill. The sign shows a drawing of a hill: if the drawing slopes up to the right, expect to go uphill; if the slope goes

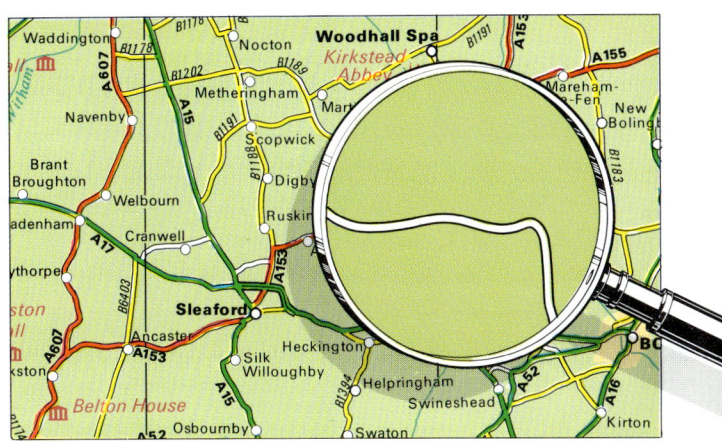

down to the right, expect to go downhill. The road in the picture goes down 10 metres in every 100. This means that the slope is 1 in 10, or 10%. These are two ways of describing the steepness of the slope, or the *gradient*, as it is known.

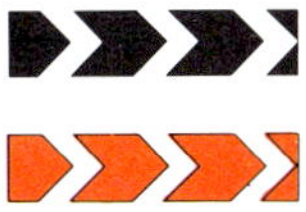

Sharp deviation

Bend to right

Series of bends

Double bend first to left

VEHICLE MARKS

The first *number plates* came into use about 80 years ago. The earliest ones had one or two letters of the alphabet followed by the numbers 1 to 9999. You can still see old number plates like this sometimes. One of the very first – simply A1 – is still around today, and two very old numbers are owned by the AA; these are AA1 and AA2!

When all the numbers of this kind were used up, number plates began to have three letters of the alphabet instead of one or two. They also had numbers from 1 to 999. Sometimes the letters came first and sometimes the numbers, so you might have had either ABC 123 or 123 ABC. You still see number plates like this quite often.

In 1963 a new system began which lasted for the next 20 years. Number plates had three letters, then numbers 1 to 999, then a 'year letter' at the end which showed when the number was first used. The years of issue for this final letter (which, since 1967; has changed on 1 August) are given in the list on the right.

The letters I, O, Q, U and Z are not used as year letters.

A	1963
B	1964
C	1965
D	1966
E	1967
F	1967–68
G	1968–69
H	1969–70
J	1970–71
K	1971–72
L	1972–73
M	1973–74
N	1974–75
P	1975–76
R	1976–77
S	1977–78
T	1978–79
V	1979–80
W	1980–81
X	1981–82
Y	1982–83

See how many foreign or other unusual number plates you can spot. The picture shows some examples.

Not only can a number plate tell you when the vehicle was first registered; it can also tell you *where* it was registered. To find this out, look up the last two letters of the three-letter part in the list on these pages. For example, suppose you see a car with the number LCF 851W. Look up 'CF' in the list. It was registered in Reading. The 'W' tells you that it was registered in 1980–81. If you get to know your local registration letters, then when you go on a journey you can look out for other cars that probably come from the same area as you. Look in the list for the towns near to your home, and make a note of their letters.

Number plates issued after August 1983 have a different system because by then the year letters had all been used up. So new number plates have the order reversed. The year letter starts again with A, but now it comes at the beginning. Next is the number (again between 1 and 999) and at the end is the three-letter part. The last two of these three letters still tell you where the number comes from.

Index Mark	Office	Index Mark	Office	Index Mark	Office	Index Mark	Office
AA	Bournemouth	AV	Peterborough	BP	Portsmouth	CK	Preston
AB	Worcester	AW	Shrewsbury	BR	Newcastle-upon-Tyne	CL	Norwich
AC	Coventry	AX	Cardiff			CM	Liverpool
AD	Gloucester	AY	Leicester	BS	Inverness	CN	Newcastle-upon-Tyne
AE	Bristol	BA	Manchester	BT	Leeds		
AF	Truro	BB	Newcastle-upon-Tyne	BU	Manchester	CO	Exeter
AG	Hull			BV	Preston	CP	Huddersfield
AH	Norwich	BC	Leicester	BW	Oxford	CR	Portsmouth
AJ	Middlesbrough	BD	Northampton	BX	Haverfordwest	CS	Glasgow
AK	Sheffield	BE	Lincoln	BY	London NW	CT	Lincoln
AL	Nottingham	BF	Stoke-on-Trent	CA	Chester	CU	Newcastle-upon-Tyne
AM	Swindon	BG	Liverpool	CB	Manchester		
AN	Reading	BH	Luton	CC	Bangor	CV	Truro
AO	Carlisle	BJ	Ipswich	CD	Brighton	CW	Preston
AP	Brighton	BK	Portsmouth	CE	Peterborough	CX	Huddersfield
AR	Chelmsford	BL	Reading	CF	Reading	CY	Swansea
AS	Inverness	BM	Luton	CG	Bournemouth	DA	Birmingham
AT	Hull	BN	Manchester	CH	Nottingham	DB	Manchester
AU	Nottingham	BO	Cardiff	CJ	Gloucester	DC	Middlesbrough

DD	Gloucester	**ET**	Sheffield	**GH**	London SW	**HW**	Bristol
DE	Haverfordwest	**EU**	Bristol	**GJ**	London SW	**HX**	London (Central)
DF	Gloucester	**EV**	Chelmsford	**GK**	London SW	**HY**	Bristol
DG	Gloucester	**EW**	Peterborough	**GL**	Truro	**JA**	Manchester
DH	Dudley	**EX**	Norwich	**GM**	Reading	**JB**	Reading
DJ	Liverpool	**EY**	Bangor	**GN**	London SW	**JC**	Bangor
DK	Manchester	**FA**	Stoke-on-Trent	**GO**	London SW	**JD**	London (Central)
DL	Portsmouth	**FB**	Bristol	**GP**	London SW	**JE**	Peterborough
DM	Chester	**FC**	Oxford	**GR**	Newcastle-	**JF**	Leicester
DN	Leeds	**FD**	Dudley		upon-Tyne	**JG**	Maidstone
DO	Lincoln	**FE**	Lincoln	**GS**	Luton	**JH**	Reading
DP	Reading	**FF**	Bangor	**GT**	London SW	**JJ**	Maidstone
DR	Exeter	**FG**	Brighton	**GU**	London SE	**JK**	Brighton
DS	Glasgow	**FH**	Gloucester	**GV**	Ipswich	**JL**	Lincoln
DT	Sheffield	**FJ**	Exeter	**GW**	London SE	**JM**	Reading
DU	Coventry	**FK**	Dudley	**GX**	London SE	**JN**	Chelmsford
DV	Exeter	**FL**	Peterborough	**GY**	London SE	**JO**	Oxford
DW	Cardiff	**FM**	Chester	**HA**	Dudley	**JP**	Liverpool
DX	Ipswich	**FN**	Maidstone	**HB**	Cardiff	**JR**	Newcastle-
DY	Brighton	**FO**	Gloucester	**HC**	Brighton		upon-Tyne
EA	Dudley	**FP**	Leicester	**HD**	Huddersfield	**JS**	Inverness
EB	Peterborough	**FR**	Preston	**HE**	Sheffield	**JT**	Bournemouth
EC	Preston	**FS**	Edinburgh	**HF**	Liverpool	**JU**	Leicester
ED	Liverpool	**FT**	Newcastle-	**HG**	Preston	**JV**	Lincoln
EE	Lincoln		upon-Tyne	**HH**	Carlisle	**JW**	Birmingham
EF	Middlesbrough	**FU**	Lincoln	**HJ**	Chelmsford	**JX**	Huddersfield
EG	Peterborough	**FV**	Preston	**HK**	Chelmsford	**JY**	Exeter
EH	Stoke-on-Trent	**FW**	Lincoln	**HL**	Sheffield	**KA**	Liverpool
EJ	Bangor	**FX**	Bournemouth	**HM**	London (Central)	**KB**	Liverpool
EK	Liverpool	**FY**	Liverpool	**HN**	Middlesbrough	**KC**	Liverpool
EL	Bournemouth	**GA**	Glasgow	**HO**	Bournemouth	**KD**	Liverpool
EM	Liverpool	**GB**	Glasgow	**HP**	Coventry	**KE**	Maidstone
EN	Manchester	**GC**	London SW	**HR**	Swindon	**KF**	Liverpool
EO	Preston	**GD**	Glasgow	**HS**	Glasgow	**KG**	Cardiff
EP	Swansea	**GE**	Glasgow	**HT**	Bristol	**KH**	Hull
ER	Peterborough	**GF**	London SW	**HU**	Bristol	**KJ**	Maidstone
ES	Dundee	**GG**	Glasgow	**HV**	London (Central)	**KK**	Maidstone

Vehicles travelling abroad must display an *international distinguishing sign* to show which country the vehicle comes from. This sign is usually a white oval sticker with black letters. The letters for some of the countries you might see are listed here.

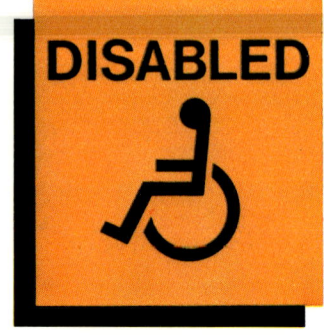

DISABLED

Every vehicle on the road must display a disc (top) to show road tax has been paid. A disabled driver may have an orange badge in his back window.

A	Austria	M	Malta
AND	Andorra	MA	Morocco
AUS	Australia	MC	Monaco
B	Belgium	N	Norway
CDN	Canada	NL	Netherlands
CH	Switzerland	NZ	New Zealand
CS	Czechoslovakia	P	Portugal
D	German Federal Republic	PL	Poland
DDR	German Democratic Republic	RO	Romania
DK	Denmark	RSM	San Marino
E	Spain	S	Sweden
ET	Arab Republic of Egypt	SF	Finland
F	France	SU	Union of Soviet Socialist Republics
FL	Liechtenstein	TR	Turkey
GB	United Kingdom of Great Britain & Northern Ireland	USA	United States of America
GBA	Alderney	V	Holy See (*Vatican City*)
GBG	Guernsey Channel Islands	YU	Yugoslavia
GBJ	Jersey		
GBM	Isle of Man		
GBZ	Gibraltar		
GR	Greece		
H	Hungary		
I	Italy		
IL	Israel		
IRL	Ireland		
L	Luxembourg		

KL	Maidstone	MB	Chester	NR	Leicester	PG	Guildford
KM	Maidstone	MC	London NE	NS	Glasgow	PH	Guildford
KN	Maidstone	MD	London NE	NT	Shrewsbury	PJ	Guildford
KO	Maidstone	ME	London NE	NU	Nottingham	PK	Guildford
KP	Maidstone	MF	London NE	NV	Northampton	PL	Guildford
KR	Maidstone	MG	London NE	NW	Leeds	PM	Guildford
KS	Edinburgh	MH	London NE	NX	Dudley	PN	Brighton
KT	Maidstone	MJ	Luton	NY	Cardiff	PO	Portsmouth
KU	Sheffield	MK	London NE	OA	Birmingham	PP	Luton
KV	Coventry	ML	London NE	OB	Birmingham	PR	Bournemouth
KW	Sheffield	MM	London NE	OC	Birmingham	PS	Aberdeen
KX	Luton	MO	Reading	OD	Exeter	PT	Newcastle-upon-Tyne
KY	Sheffield	MP	London NE	OE	Birmingham	PU	Chelmsford
LA	London NW	MR	Swindon	OF	Birmingham	PV	Ipswich
LB	London NW	MS	Edinburgh	OG	Birmingham	PW	Norwich
LC	London NW	MT	London NE	OH	Birmingham	PX	Portsmouth
LD	London NW	MU	London NE	OJ	Birmingham	PY	Middlesbrough
LE	London NW	MV	London SE	OK	Birmingham	RA	Nottingham
LF	London NW	MW	Swindon	OL	Birmingham	RB	Nottingham
LG	Chester	MX	London SE	OM	Birmingham	RC	Nottingham
LH	London NW	MY	London SE	ON	Birmingham	RD	Reading
LJ	Bournemouth	NA	Manchester	OO	Chelmsford	RE	Stoke-on-Trent
LK	London NW	NB	Manchester	OP	Birmingham	RF	Stoke-on-Trent
LL	London NW	NC	Manchester	OR	Portsmouth	RG	Newcastle-upon-Tyne
LM	London NW	ND	Manchester	OS	Glasgow	RH	Hull
LN	London NW	NE	Manchester	OT	Portsmouth	RJ	Manchester
LO	London NW	NF	Manchester	OU	Bristol	RK	London NW
LP	London NW	NG	Norwich	OV	Birmingham	RL	Truro
LR	London NW	NH	Northampton	OW	Portsmouth	RM	Carlisle
LS	Edinburgh	NJ	Brighton	OX	Birmingham	RN	Preston
LT	London NW	NK	Luton	OY	London NW	RO	Luton
LU	London NW	NL	Newcastle-upon-Tyne	PA	Guildford	RP	Northampton
LV	Liverpool	NM	Luton	PB	Guildford	RR	Nottingham
LW	London NW	NN	Nottingham	PC	Guildford	RS	Aberdeen
LX	London NW	NO	Chelmsford	PD	Guildford	RT	Ipswich
LY	London NW	NP	Worcester	PE	Guildford		
MA	Chester			PF	Guildford		

VEHICLE MARKS

Lorries carrying dangerous substances may display a special panel giving information about their load. You can see one on the lorry pictured above. If the lorry is involved in an accident, the panel tells the police and fire brigade what equipment to use if the load spills, or catches fire. The meaning of the numbers on the panel is explained on the right, and the symbols used for different substances such as poisons, dangerous chemicals or radioactive substances, are pictured at the top.

Box 1: *the number denotes the type of fire appliance and how it should be used; the letters after it stand for the type of chemical and its effect.* **Box 2:** *International Hazard Sign.* **Box 3:** *the United Nations chemical number or its name.*

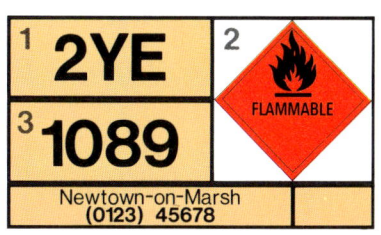

RU	Bournemouth	TK	Exeter
RV	Portsmouth	TL	Lincoln
RW	Coventry	TM	Luton
RX	Reading	TN	Newcastle-upon-Tyne
RY	Leicester		
SA	Aberdeen	TO	Nottingham
SB	Glasgow	TP	Portsmouth
SC	Edinburgh	TR	Portsmouth
SCY	Truro (*Isles of Scilly*)	TS	Dundee
		TT	Exeter
SD	Glasgow	TU	Chester
SE	Aberdeen	TV	Nottingham
SF	Edinburgh	TW	Chelmsford
SG	Edinburgh	TX	Cardiff
SH	Edinburgh	TY	Newcastle-upon-Tyne
SJ	Glasgow		
SK	Inverness	UA	Leeds
SL	Dundee	UB	Leeds
SM	Glasgow	UC	London (Central)
SN	Dundee	UD	Oxford
SO	Aberdeen	UE	Dudley
SP	Dundee	UF	Brighton
SR	Dundee	UG	Leeds
SS	Aberdeen	UH	Cardiff
ST	Inverness	UJ	Shrewsbury
SU	Glasgow	UK	Birmingham
SW	Glasgow	UL	London (Central)
SX	Edinburgh	UM	Leeds
TA	Exeter	UN	Exeter
TB	Liverpool	UO	Exeter
TC	Bristol	UP	Newcastle-upon-Tyne
TD	Manchester		
TE	Manchester	UR	Luton
TF	Reading	US	Glasgow
TG	Cardiff	UT	Leicester
TH	Swansea	UU	London (Central)
TJ	Liverpool	UV	London (Central)

UW	London (Central)	WM	Liverpool
UX	Shrewsbury	WN	Swansea
UY	Worcester	WO	Cardiff
VA	Peterborough	WP	Worcester
VB	Maidstone	WR	Leeds
VC	Coventry	WS	Bristol
VE	Peterborough	WT	Leeds
VF	Norwich	WU	Leeds
VG	Norwich	WV	Brighton
VH	Huddersfield	WW	Leeds
VJ	Gloucester	WX	Leeds
VK	Newcastle-upon-Tyne	WY	Leeds
		YA	Taunton
VL	Lincoln	YB	Taunton
VM	Manchester	YC	Taunton
VN	Middlesbrough	YD	Taunton
VO	Nottingham	YE	London (Central)
VP	Birmingham	YF	London (Central)
VR	Manchester	YG	Leeds
VS	Luton	YH	London (Central)
VT	Stoke-on-Trent	YJ	Brighton
VU	Manchester	YK	London (Central)
VV	Northampton	YL	London (Central)
VW	Chelmsford	YM	London (Central)
VX	Chelmsford	YN	London (Central)
VY	Leeds	YO	London (Central)
WA	Sheffield	YP	London (Central)
WB	Sheffield	YR	London (Central)
WC	Chelmsford	YS	Glasgow
WD	Dudley	YT	London (Central)
WE	Sheffield	YU	London (Central)
WF	Sheffield	YV	London (Central)
WG	Sheffield	YW	London (Central)
WH	Manchester	YX	London (Central)
WJ	Sheffield	YY	London (Central)
WK	Coventry		
WL	Oxford		

33

MEET THE TRAFFIC POLICE

If you put all the cars in Britain on all the roads, there would be one car every 20 yards (18m). It's the job of the traffic police to keep all this traffic moving smoothly and safely.

In a large city like London, there are about 2½ million cars, lorries and cycles on the move every day. If the traffic in just one street comes to a stop the traffic in nearby streets is also quickly brought to a stand-still. And a big traffic jam rapidly gets bigger. The traffic police like to deal with this kind of problem *before* it happens. Day and night, they are on the lookout for signs of trouble. If some traffic lights have stopped working, for example, it's usually not long before the traffic police arrive to give help. But how do they know there is a problem?

In London, a computer at Scotland Yard is connected to about a thousand sets of traffic lights. When one of the lights is not working, the computer knows, and gives a warning. Some roads have detectors just beneath them to keep a check on traffic speeds. When traffic slows down too much, and a jam is likely, the detectors pass the message on to the computer. The computer changes the timing of the traffic lights and gets the traffic moving again.

There are TV cameras on the top of some tall buildings. They look down on the streets, and show a picture of the traffic on TV screens at the traffic control centre. If there are signs of trouble, the control centre passes the news to the BBC and other radio stations. Drivers can hear about traffic jams from their car radios, and change their route to keep away from trouble spots.

If the traffic in one part of the town is getting too thick, or if it's hardly moving, the control centre sends traffic police there. Usually, these police don't travel in cars. They use motorbikes so they can weave in and out of traffic even when it has come to a stop.

If the trouble is something like a broken-down lorry, the police don't usually direct other drivers into the side streets to avoid the blockage. This is because most drivers in a city street are from another part of town and don't know their way around the side streets. The streets would soon fill up with lost motorists. Instead, the police try to move the cause of the trouble, so drivers can continue on their route. If the problem is some-

thing like a burst water-pipe, of course, it can't be moved. Then the police put up diversion signs which lead drivers around the problem and back onto their original route.

Something really big, like a large lorry load, can sometimes block a street. To avoid this, lorry drivers must tell the police if their load is very high, very wide, very long or very heavy. The police may then decide to go with the lorry, and keep other traffic out of the way. Sometimes, big loads are taken through town at night, when there is very little traffic about.

Some roads have more than their fair share of accidents, and the police give these *Accident Black Spots* special treatment. Sometimes, for a week or two, a team of traffic police keeps watch on the Black Spot. If any motorists drive dangerously, the police stop them and explain what they were doing wrong. This simple treatment will some-times cure the problem on its own.

A car can cause accidents even when it's not

Above: London's traffic police have to deal with traffic jams like this every day.

Right: Traffic police on motorcycles can reach the cause of trouble more quickly.

Left: Accident Black Spots are specially signposted to warn drivers to take extra care.

moving – by parking in the wrong place. That's why there are yellow lines at the roadside, with a notice to warn drivers not to park. When a car is parked in a dangerous place, the traffic police may tow it away. The owner has to pay a fine before he can reclaim it. Drivers who park illegally may also be given a 'parking ticket' by a traffic warden, and made to pay a fine.

No accident is pleasant, but an accident is much worse when it happens at high speed. Some of the worst accidents are on motorways. One of the jobs of the motorway police is to make sure that drivers don't exceed the speed limit. A police car with a computer sometimes sits on a bridge over a motorway. The policeman knows the distance between two marks beside the motorway, and he chooses a car to watch. He presses a button when the car passes each mark. The computer divides the distance by the time, and shows the car's speed. If the driver is speeding, he may be taken to court.

EMERGENCY!

The fastest traffic in the country is on the motorways. An accident on one of these is not only dangerous to the people in the crashed cars; it could injure or kill many other people who can't stop in time. So when there's trouble, it must be dealt with fast.

Police cars patrol the motorways all the time. There's a patrol every 10 miles (about 16km) in the countryside, and every 5 miles near the towns. Police in cars are not the only people on the lookout. At junctions near towns, there is often a TV camera on one of the overhead gantries. The police watch the traffic on TV screens in a traffic control centre nearby.

But sometimes accidents happen out of sight of the police. Even then, the nearest traffic control centre usually learns about it fairly quickly. On the TV screen, a busy stretch of road may suddenly become empty. This doesn't tell the control centre where the accident is, but it's a sure sign of trouble. Something is blocking the motorway somewhere, and that could mean an accident.

Some stretches of motorway have detectors under the roads. These keep track of the speed of the traffic, and send their signals to the traffic control centre. When the speed on a motorway drops as low as, say, 20 mph (about 30kph), this is another sign of trouble. The control centre radios to a patrol car to go and find out what's wrong.

Often it's a phone call that gives the control centre the bad news. Most often the call is from one of the motorway telephones. When a motorist picks up one of these, his call goes straight to the traffic control centre. Motorway drivers often don't know where they are (one piece of motorway looks like any other). The control centre knows which phone is being used, and a wall map shows them where it is on the motorway.

Sometimes the problem is only a car that has broken down. The police know one common cause of this. That's why they carry a good supply of water, to fill up the car's radiator. Even on the hard shoulder, a stopped car is too dangerous to leave for very long. So if it won't go, the police ring the AA, or the RAC, or a nearby garage, to come and mend it or tow it away.

But when there has been a crash, a special traffic car arrives. When the police get out of the car, they wear special orange or yellow jackets for safety. These jackets glow brightly in the daytime, and have special strips that shine at night. The traffic police put up accident signs well ahead

of where the accident has happened. Then they place red cones in a long curve around the accident, so the traffic is forced to keep clear.

The traffic-accident car carries a number of things that could be useful. As well as cones, the accident police have plenty of flashing lights to put up around night-time accidents. They have

A police traffic-accident car and its equipment.

Police manning a traffic control centre. Note the closed-circuit TV screens at the top of the picture.

brushes and shovels to clear up broken glass. There's a crowbar for forcing doors open when people are trapped, and fire-extinguishers to put out flames quickly. There are blankets and a first-aid box. All traffic police have to know first aid.

If the accident is a bad one, the control centre asks for an ambulance and the fire brigade. Firemen may have to cut their way through metal to reach people who are trapped. The ambulances take injured people to the nearest hospital.

While all this is going on, the control centre has been busy. It has changed the signals further back along the motorway. These signals are usually about one mile apart (about 1.5km), but near a big town, there may be as many as three to a mile. Some signals have been slowing down the speed of the traffic. Others have been closing some lanes, and moving traffic to different lanes.

If the accident has blocked the motorway completely, the signs make traffic leave the motorway at the junction before the accident. Long-distance travellers may be strangers to this part of the country, and can easily get lost if they don't have help. So the police put up special road signs, with little symbols for different routes – little squares and circles and triangles. A driver who keeps following his route-symbol will find his way back on to the motorway beyond the accident. Then he can continue on his journey.

Drivers who pass the accident spot a few hours later may never know there has been a problem. The police and the signs and the cones and the crashed cars will all be gone. The motorway is clear again.

DISTANCE CHART

This chart shows you the distance between certain towns. Here's how to find the distance between Birmingham and Cardiff.

Put your right forefinger on the name Birmingham, and your left forefinger on the name Cardiff. Move your right finger down the chart, and your left finger along towards the right.

Your two fingers will meet at one of the little squares. The top black number in that square is the distance in miles (107), and the bottom blue number is the distance in kilometres (172).

Distances are given as **miles / kilometres**.

	Aberdeen	Birmingham	Bristol	Cardiff	Dover	Edinburgh	Glasgow	Holyhead	Inverness	London	Manchester	Newcastle-upon-Tyne	Norwich	Penzance	Southampton
Birmingham	430 / 692														
Bristol	511 / 822	85 / 137													
Cardiff	532 / 856	107 / 172	45 / 72												
Dover	595 / 958	203 / 327	198 / 319	233 / 375											
Edinburgh	127 / 204	293 / 472	373 / 600	393 / 632	469 / 755										
Glasgow	149 / 240	291 / 468	372 / 599	393 / 632	490 / 789	45 / 72									
Holyhead	459 / 739	155 / 249	217 / 349	215 / 346	351 / 565	327 / 526	321 / 517								
Inverness	105 / 169	453 / 729	532 / 856	553 / 890	648 / 1043	159 / 256	171 / 275	481 / 774							
London	543 / 874	117 / 188	119 / 192	155 / 249	77 / 124	405 / 652	402 / 647	267 / 430	561 / 903						
Manchester	354 / 570	88 / 142	167 / 269	188 / 303	283 / 455	218 / 351	214 / 344	125 / 201	368 / 592	199 / 320					
Newcastle-upon-Tyne	236 / 380	198 / 319	291 / 468	311 / 501	356 / 573	109 / 175	150 / 241	262 / 422	268 / 431	280 / 451	141 / 227				
Norwich	498 / 801	161 / 259	215 / 346	250 / 402	169 / 272	370 / 595	379 / 610	313 / 504	528 / 850	115 / 185	183 / 295	258 / 415			
Penzance	703 / 1131	278 / 447	202 / 325	241 / 388	365 / 587	567 / 912	563 / 906	409 / 658	728 / 1172	291 / 468	358 / 576	487 / 784	413 / 665		
Southampton	567 / 912	128 / 206	75 / 121	122 / 196	145 / 233	433 / 697	429 / 690	277 / 446	590 / 950	78 / 126	224 / 360	324 / 521	191 / 307	227 / 365	
York	322 / 518	128 / 206	221 / 356	241 / 388	284 / 457	195 / 314	208 / 335	192 / 309	355 / 571	209 / 336	71 / 114	83 / 134	185 / 298	417 / 671	252 / 406

You can use these tables to change metres into feet, kilos into pounds, and so on. Some of these tables have three columns of figures. One of them shows you miles and kilometres. Suppose you know that a distance is 10 miles, or kilometres (it doesn't matter which). Find the number 10 in the middle column. If you want the answer in miles, look in the miles column beside the number 10. The answer is 6·21 m. If you want the answer in kilometres, look in the km column beside the number 10. The answer is 16·09 km. The gradient table is for steep hills. You can find more about them on page 29.

LENGTH: INCHES/CENTIMETRES

cm	in or cm	in
2.54	1	0.39
5.08	2	0.79
7.62	3	1.18
10.16	4	1.57
12.70	5	1.97
25.40	10	3.94
50.60	20	7.87
76.20	30	11.81
101.60	40	15.75
127.00	50	19.68
254.00	100	39.37

LENGTH: FEET/METRES

metres	m or ft	feet
0.30	1	3.28
0.61	2	6.56
0.91	3	9.84
1.22	4	13.12
1.52	5	16.40
3.05	10	32.81
6.10	20	65.62
9.14	30	98.43
12.90	40	131.23
15.24	50	164.04
30.48	100	328.08

LENGTH: MILES/KILOMETRES

km	miles or km	miles
1.61	1	0.62
3.13	2	1.24
4.83	3	1.86
6.44	4	2.48
8.05	5	3.11
9.66	6	3.73
11.27	7	4.35
12.87	8	4.97
14.48	9	5.59
16.09	10	6.21
32.19	20	12.43
48.28	30	18.64
64.37	40	24.85
80.47	50	31.07
160.93	100	62.14
402.34	250	155.34
804.67	500	310.68

TEMPERATURE

°Celsius		°Fahrenheit
0	freezing	+32
+36.9	body temp.	+98.4
+100	boiling	+212

CAPACITY

litres	gallons or litres	gallons
4.55	1	0.22
9.09	2	0.44
13.64	3	0.66
18.18	4	0.88
22.73	5	1.10
27.28	6	1.32
31.82	7	1.54
36.37	8	1.76
40.91	9	1.98
45.46	10	2.2
90.92	20	4.4
136.38	30	6.6
181.84	40	8.8
227.30	50	11.0

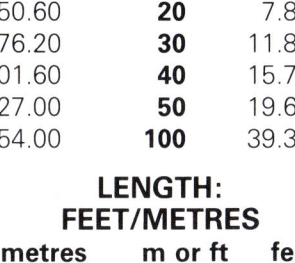

WEIGHT

kg	lb or kg	lb
0.45	1	2.20
0.91	2	4.40
1.36	3	6.61
1.81	4	8.81
2.27	5	11.02
4.54	10	22.05
9.07	20	44.09
13.61	30	66.14
18.14	40	88.18
22.68	50	110.23
45.36	100	220.46

PRESSURE

lb per sq in	kg per sq cm
20	1.41
22	1.55
24	1.69
26	1.83
28	1.97
30	2.11

GRADIENTS

30%	(very steep)	1 in 3	14%		1 in 7
25%		1 in 4	12%		1 in 8
20%		1 in 5	11%		1 in 9
16%		1 in 6	10%	(less steep)	1 in 10

HOW TO PLAN YOUR ROUTE

Here's how you can use different parts of this book together to plan a complete route. Suppose you want to prepare a journey from Gilsland to Tong. (You won't always need all these steps.)

1. Look up Gilsland and Tong in the index at the end of the book. You will find:

Gilsland ....**67**.......*9G*

Tong............................**63**.......*9A*

2. Find Gilsland in the atlas (page 67, grid square 9G), then find a nearby big town: for instance, Carlisle. Find Tong in the atlas (page 63, grid square 9A), then find a nearby big town: for instance, Wolverhampton.

3. Find Carlisle and Wolverhampton in the route planning maps on these pages. (If you can't find them, look at their page-squares – 67 and 63 – on the key map on page 48.)

4. Note down the main roads between these two towns.

5. Follow the whole route from Gilsland to Tong on the atlas. Make a list of the road numbers, the places you go through and whether you turn right or left at junctions. If your route includes a motorway, write down the numbers of the junctions where you join and leave it.

Some things to remember:

1. Where you join another road, write down whether you turn left (L) or right (R). You may like to write down the names of likely places to look for on the road signs. Where you join a motorway, write down the direction (e.g. southbound).

2. Choose the route that suits *you*. Motorways for speed, smaller roads for interest.

3. Look for symbols of places you might like to visit near your route. Make a note of them.

4. Sometimes radio stations give useful news of traffic jams. Be ready to change parts of your route to avoid trouble spots.

5. You may want to know roughly how long it will take to travel part of your route. Estimate the speed you will be travelling at, and the distance you will cover (you may need to use the distance bar).

DISTANCE ÷ SPEED = TIME

Here is one person's route plan for the journey:

Gilsland
B6318
Greenhead. Turn R
A69
Brampton
A69
Warwick
A69
M6 southbound. J43–J12
A5
Gailey
A5
Ivetsey Bank
A5 (about 3 miles, then turn L)
A41
Tong

For example: 200 miles ÷ 50mph = 4 hours
But unless you are on a motorway, it's not easy to keep the same speed for long, so this little sum will only give you a rough answer. Average speeds on most roads are surprisingly low unless there are long stretches of dual carriageway.

Charlie wins the pools

Charlie left Manchester for a holiday at the seaside, but he wouldn't tell us where he was going. While he was away, he won the football pools. We knew the number to ring, but not the town. Then somebody found his notepad, with the road numbers of his route on it:

A6. A623. M1. M18. A1(M). A1. A61. A170

Which town did we ring to give Charlie the good news? (The answer is on page 96.)

Legend	
Motorway	
Motorway under construction	
Primary route	
Other A Roads	

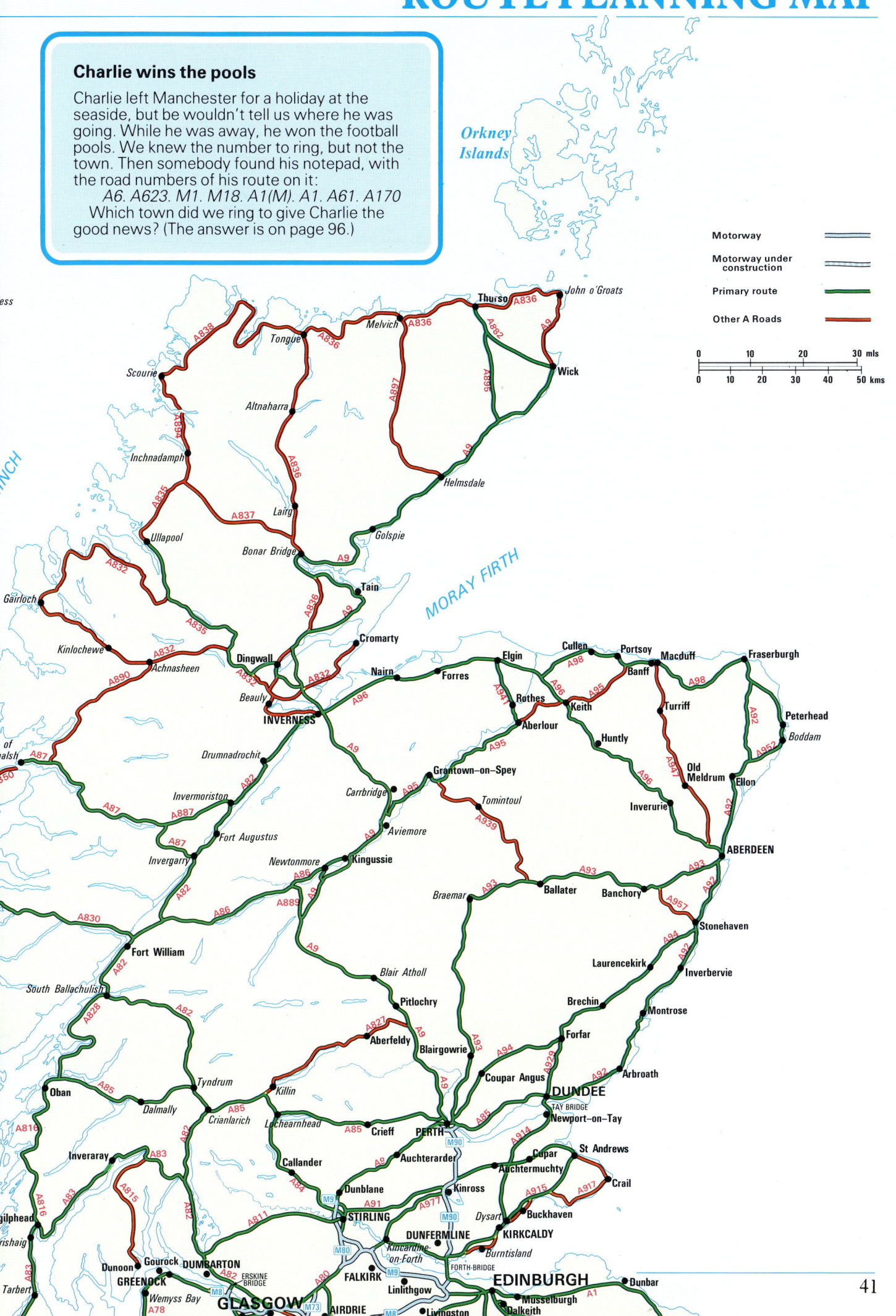

41

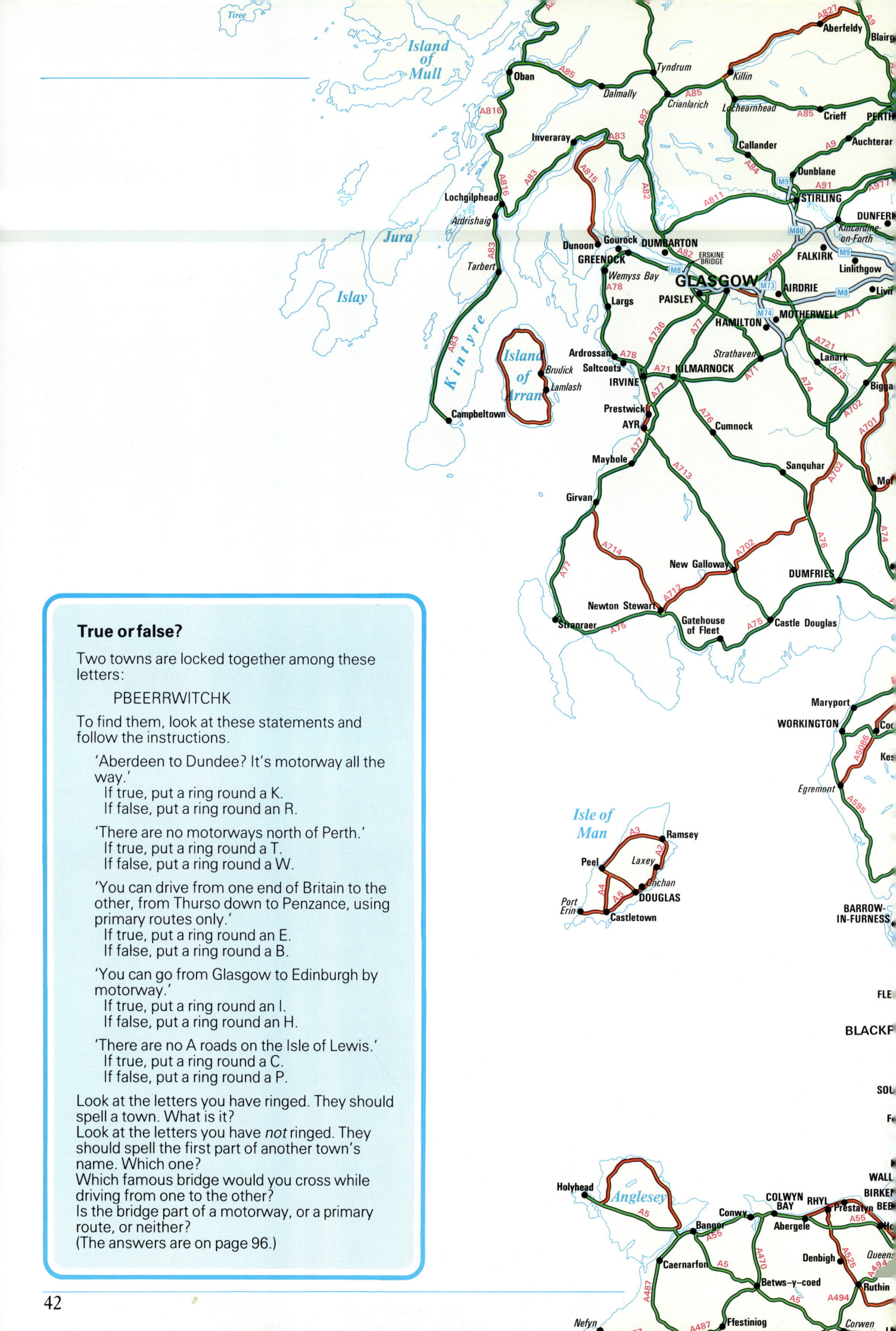

True or false?

Two towns are locked together among these letters:

PBEERRWITCHK

To find them, look at these statements and follow the instructions.

'Aberdeen to Dundee? It's motorway all the way.'
   If true, put a ring round a K.
   If false, put a ring round an R.

'There are no motorways north of Perth.'
   If true, put a ring round a T.
   If false, put a ring round a W.

'You can drive from one end of Britain to the other, from Thurso down to Penzance, using primary routes only.'
   If true, put a ring round an E.
   If false, put a ring round a B.

'You can go from Glasgow to Edinburgh by motorway.'
   If true, put a ring round an I.
   If false, put a ring round an H.

'There are no A roads on the Isle of Lewis.'
   If true, put a ring round a C.
   If false, put a ring round a P.

Look at the letters you have ringed. They should spell a town. What is it?
Look at the letters you have *not* ringed. They should spell the first part of another town's name. Which one?
Which famous bridge would you cross while driving from one to the other?
Is the bridge part of a motorway, or a primary route, or neither?
(The answers are on page 96.)

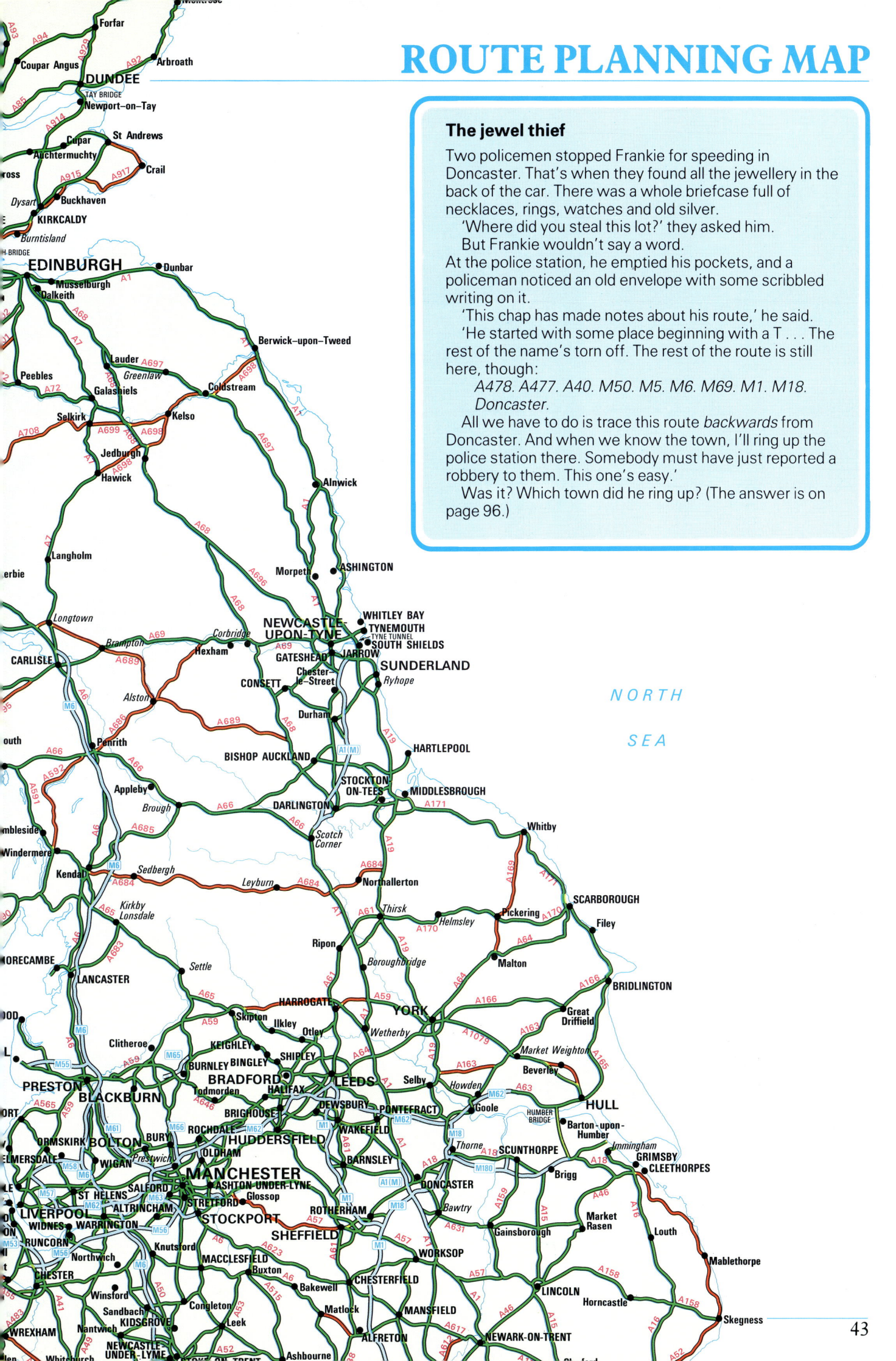

ROUTE PLANNING MAP

The jewel thief

Two policemen stopped Frankie for speeding in Doncaster. That's when they found all the jewellery in the back of the car. There was a whole briefcase full of necklaces, rings, watches and old silver.

'Where did you steal this lot?' they asked him.

But Frankie wouldn't say a word.

At the police station, he emptied his pockets, and a policeman noticed an old envelope with some scribbled writing on it.

'This chap has made notes about his route,' he said.

'He started with some place beginning with a T . . . The rest of the name's torn off. The rest of the route is still here, though:

A478. A477. A40. M50. M5. M6. M69. M1. M18. Doncaster.

All we have to do is trace this route *backwards* from Doncaster. And when we know the town, I'll ring up the police station there. Somebody must have just reported a robbery to them. This one's easy.'

Was it? Which town did he ring up? (The answer is on page 96.)

South to north

'Modern roads are marvellous,' Albert said to his wife as they left Exeter. 'Here we are on the south coast, and we can get all the way back to Glasgow without leaving a motorway. Just look at the atlas, and tell me if I'm right.' So his wife looked at the atlas, and told him . . . what? (The answer is on page 96.)

MAP SYMBOLS

Road numbers and place-names are not the only bits of information people want from a road atlas. There are plenty of interesting things to see besides roads, towns and villages.

Think of a zoo, for instance. There are three reasons why you might like to have it on your map:

1. You might pass it and just be curious about it. You may want to know 'What's that large place on the right, with the big iron gates?'

2. You might like to go in because you enjoy zoos. And if you didn't know what this place was, you would have missed the chance.

3. You might be making a special journey to this zoo, but not know exactly where it is. If it were not shown on the map, you would have to keep stopping to ask people.

These special places are shown on the map by little drawings. Each kind of place has its own kind of drawing. For example, a zoo is always shown in this atlas by a little picture of an elephant. A picture of a butterfly shows a country park. A little drawing used on a map is a *symbol*. In this atlas, you will find 16 different symbols for places to visit. They are printed in red. If you are curious about a symbol near your route on the map, you will find its meaning in the list on this page.

 *A steam train on the North Yorkshire Moors Railway (map reference 69 9A)*

 Abbey or cathedral

 Prehistoric monument

 Ruined abbey or cathedral

 Preserved railway or steam centre

 Castle

 Motor-racing circuit

 House

 Cave

Draw your own symbols

Why don't you invent some symbols of your own? Here's a list of things to try. They don't have to be real pictures of anything. Even a triangle or a square or a circle can be a symbol.

Symbols are quite small on a map, and a lot of detail would be hard to see. So keep each drawing very simple.

ferry
mountain peak
sandy beach
hospital
level-crossing
golf course
airport
race course
cricket ground
football stadium
tunnel
climbing school
television mast
good fishing
museum

Country park

 Zoo

 Dolphinarium or aquarium

 Lighthouse open to public

 Wildlife park (mammals)

 AA viewpoint

 Wildlife park (birds)

 Other place of interest

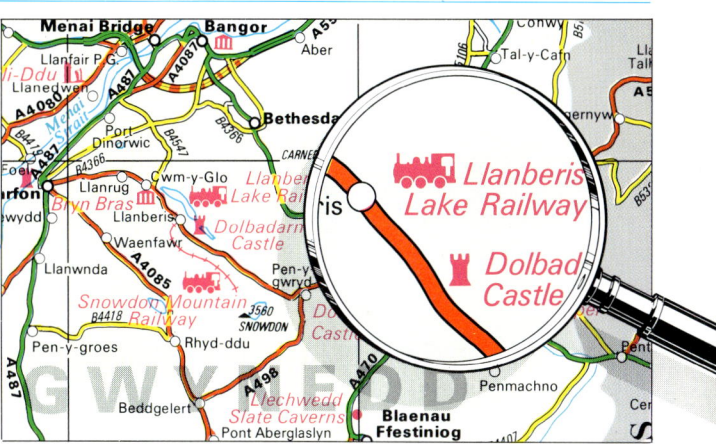

 *Brilliantly coloured parrots of all kinds can be seen at Bird World (map 53 9D)*

 Blenheim Palace is one of Britain's most famous stately homes (map 59 8A)

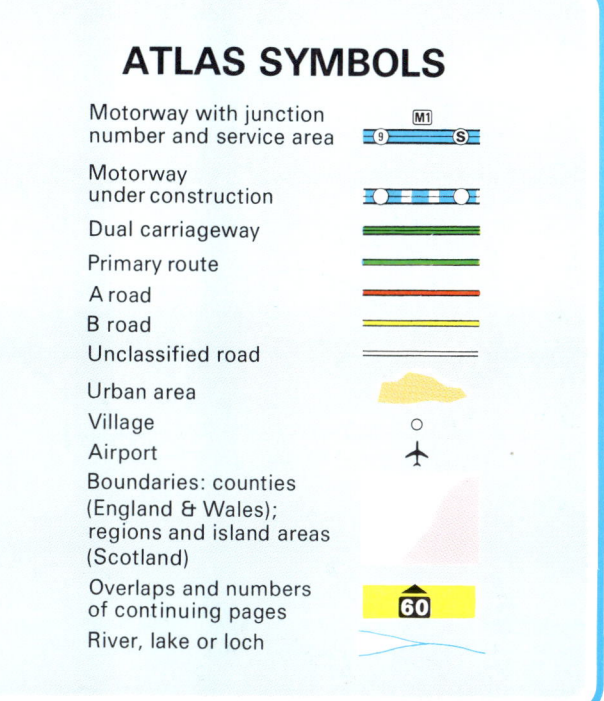

ATLAS SYMBOLS

Motorway with junction number and service area	M1 ⑨ S
Motorway under construction	
Dual carriageway	
Primary route	
A road	
B road	
Unclassified road	
Urban area	
Village	○
Airport	✈
Boundaries: counties (England & Wales); regions and island areas (Scotland)	
Overlaps and numbers of continuing pages	60
River, lake or loch	

KEY TO ATLAS PAGES

This key map shows you which atlas page to turn to for a particular area of the country.

For example, if you are travelling from London, you will begin your map-reading on page 54. If you are in south Wales, you need pages 56–57. If your nearest big town is Carlisle, you could choose either page 67 or page 68.

Each atlas page overlaps slightly with its neighbour. The places and roads in the overlap area are the same on both atlas pages. This means that when you need to turn the page while following a route, you can easily pick up the route exactly where you left it on the page before.

On the atlas pages, the area outside the thick yellow line is the area which overlaps with the next page. The numbers with arrows tell you which page to find next to continue your route.

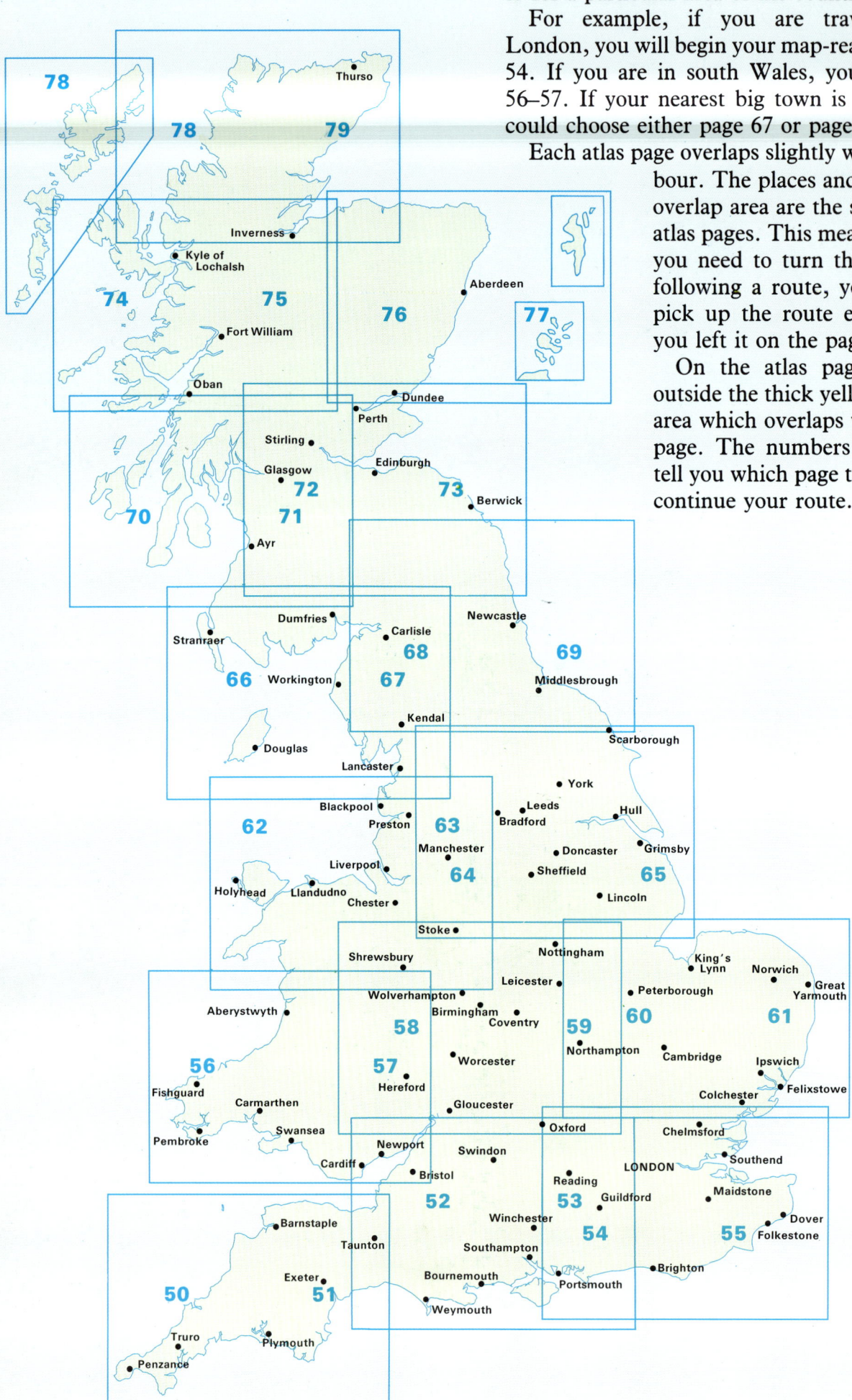

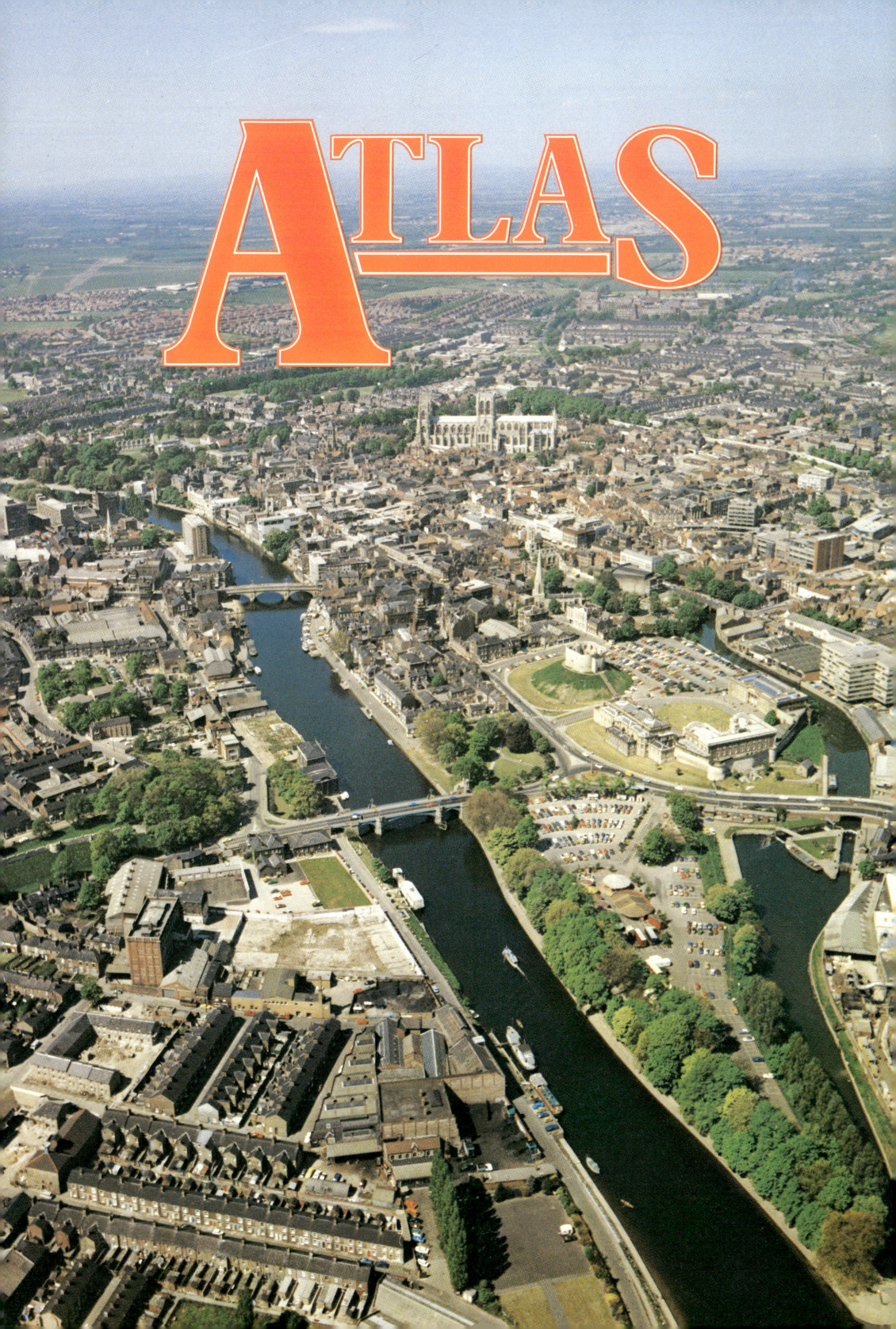

ATLAS

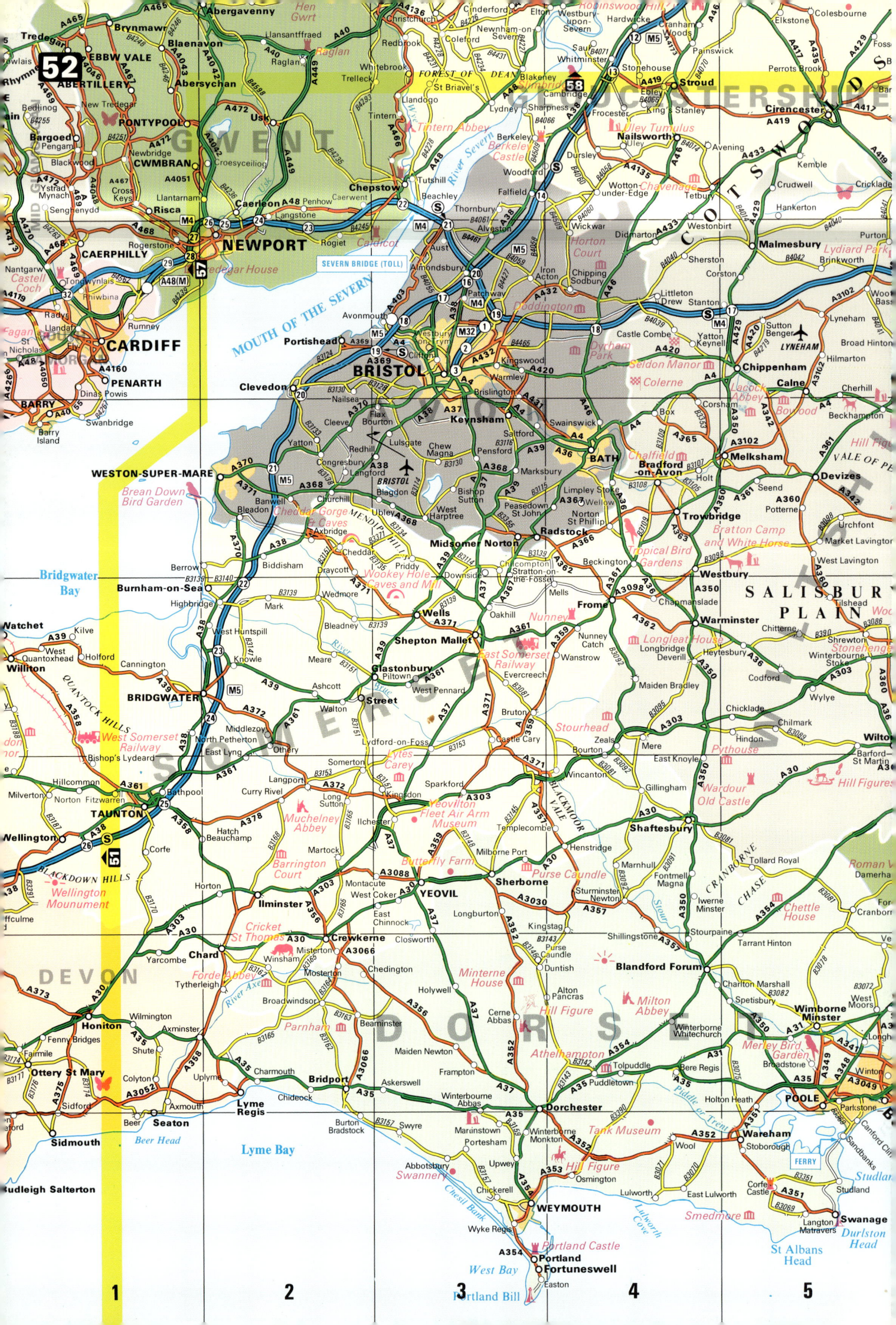

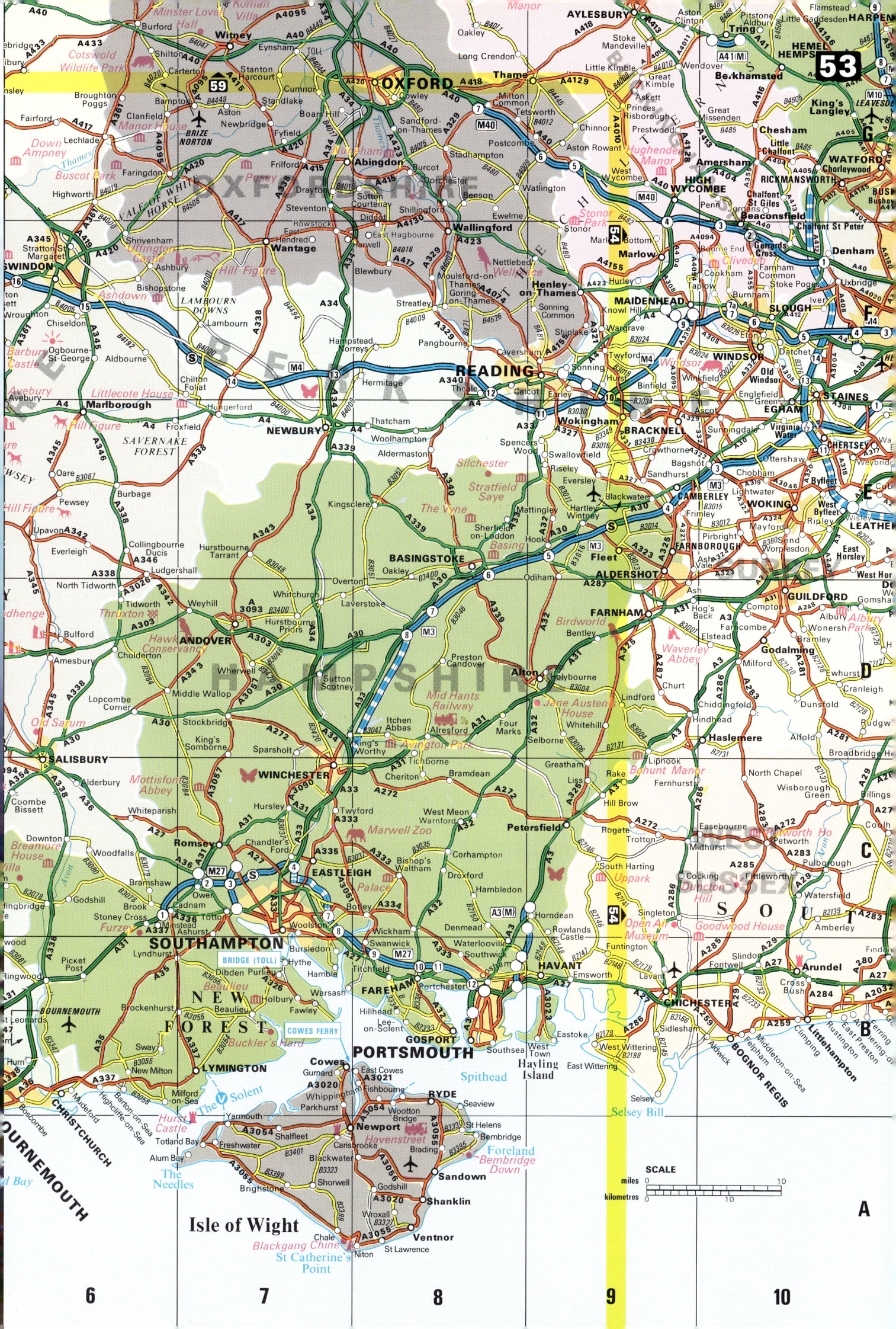

SCALE
miles 0 _____ 10
kilometres 0 _____ 10

C A R D I G A N
B A Y

Tywyn

Aberdov
Aberdyfi
Bar

Bor
Oystermou

Aberystwyth
Vale of Rheidol Railway

Llanfarian

Llanrhystud

Llanstantffraid

Aberarth

Aberaeron

New Quay

A487

A482

B4576

A482

B4342

Llanarth

Synod

A487

A486

Temple Ba

B4338

B4337

A475

La

Llangranog

B4321

B4334

B4342

Aberporth

*West Wales
Farm Park*

Talgarreg

B4459

Rhyd
Owen

Gwbert-on-Sea

Cemaes Head

Blaenporth

Tanygroes

A487

B4570

B4333

Cardigan

Llanybyther

St Dogmaels

St Dogmael's

A484

Llandysul

A486

Llangeler

A486

B4336

Llansa

Strumble Head

*Fishguard
Bay*

Dinas
Head

Cilgerran

Liechryd

*Cilgerran
Castle*

A484

Newcastle
Emlyn

Velindre

A484

A475

A485

Nevern

B4582

A487

A478

B4332

Newport

Goodwick

A487

Dinas

Teifi

D Y F E

Talley Abb

St David's
Head

Fishguard

A487

B4313

*Pentre Ifan
Burial Chamber*

B4329

Eglwyswrw

Brechfa

B4310

PRESCELLY
MOUNTAINS

Letterston

*West
Cleddau*

River Taff

Cynwyl
Elfed

A484

B4301

A485

Ramsey Island

St David's

A487

A40

St Davids

Wolfs
Castle

B4329

B4313

B4299

Gwili Railway

A40

Dryslw

Solva

B4330

Llandissilio

Nantgaredig

A40

Newgale

A487

Roch

Llanarthney

B4310

B4300

A476

St Brides Bay

Llawhaden

*Llawhaden
Castle*

Carmarthen

B4298

Llanddarog

A48

B4297

Haverfordwest

A40

Slebech

Llawhaden

Whitland

A40

A484

A48

Broadhaven

A4076

Robeston
Wathen

B4314

St Clears

Pont Yates

Cross
Hands

A48

49

Skomer I.

B4341

B4327

Narberth

A4075

A478

B4315

Red
Roses

B4314

B4314

A477

*Llanstephan
Castle*

A4066

Laugharne

B4312

B4317

B4309

M4

48

Johnston

BRIDGE (TOLL)

A477

Kidwelly

B4308

Broad Sound

Milford
Haven

B4325

Neyland

Carew

Carew

A477

A478

Saundersfoot

B4318

B4316

Pendine

Pembrey

A484

Pwll

Orseinon

Skokholm I.

Angle

Pembroke
Dock

A4075

St Florence

St Ann's
Head

Dale

Pembroke

A4139

Penally

Tenby

Carmarthen Bay

Burry
Port

LLANELLI

A484

Loughor

Castlemartin

B4320

B4319

Manorbier

Caldey
Island

Bury River

Gowerton

B4296

B4295

*Webbley
Castle*

Linney Head

Bosherston

St Govan's
Head

Llanrhidian

B4271

Blac

B4436

Rhossili

A4118

Pennard

Langla
Bay

Worms Head

B4247

Port Eynon

SWANSEA

B R I

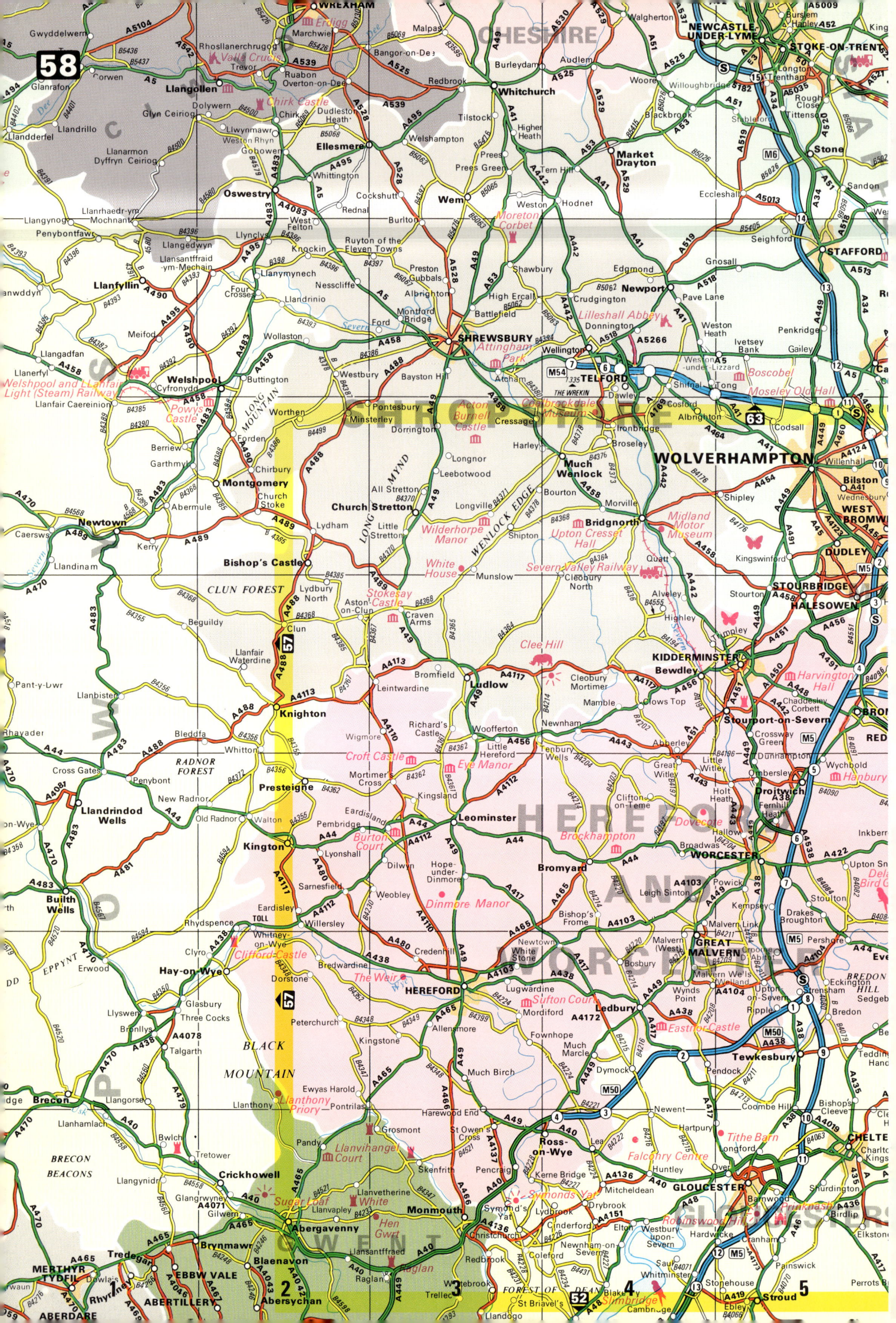

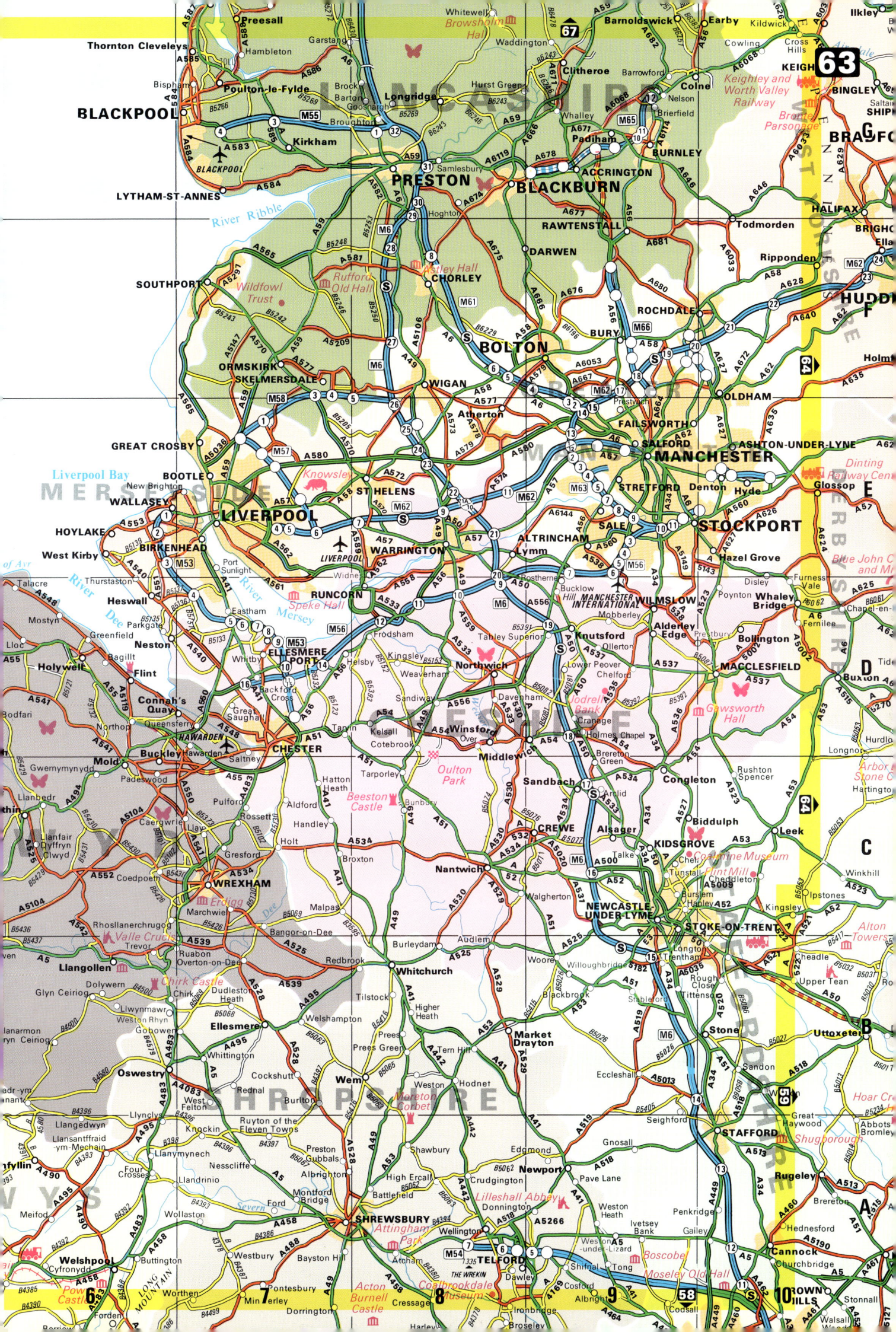

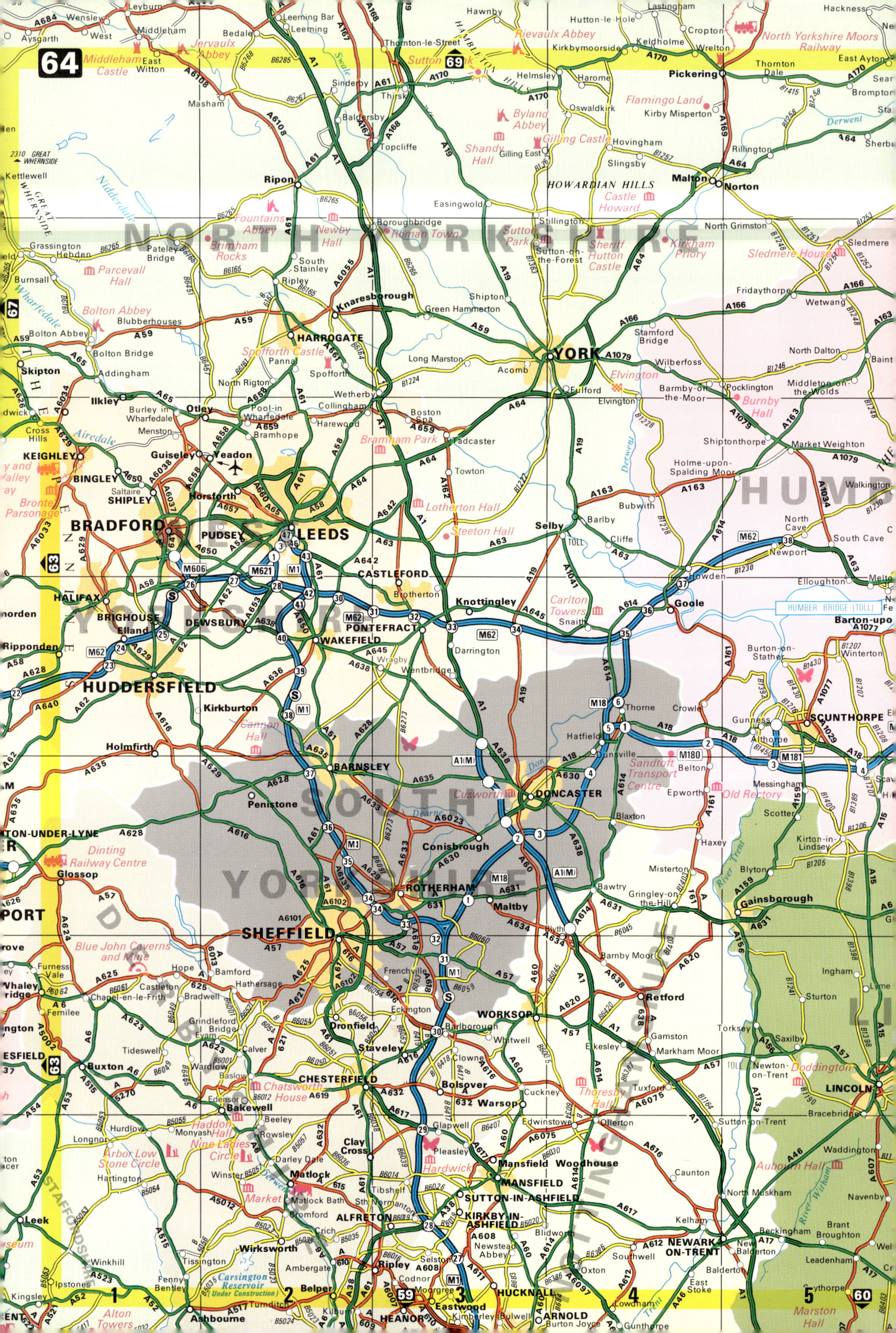

G

SCALE
miles 0   10
kilometres 0   10

Scalby

SCARBOROUGH

Oliver's Mount
69 Cayton
B1261

A1039 Filey
A1039
Flixton B1249 **A166**
Reighton
B1229
Bempton
Flamborough
Flamborough
Head
B1253
B1255

Langtoft
Rudston
Burton Agnes
Hall
B1253
A166 Burton Agnes
Carnaby
BRIDLINGTON
Carnaby

Nafferton
Barmston

Great Driffield
Skipsea
B1242
Beeford
B1249

North
Frodingham **A165**
Atwick

Brandesburton
Hornsea
B1244
Leven
Goxhill
B1243
B1242

Beverley
Aldbrough
A1035
Burton Constable
Hall
Sproatley
B1238
B1242

Willerby
B1240
B1239

Hedon
A1033
Withernsea
HULL
A1033
B1362
A1033
(KINGSTON UPON HULL)

New Holland
Patrington
Easington
Thornton
Abbey
B1445
Wootton
A160
Immingham
Dock
Kilnsea

A180 Immingham
A15 **A180**
Ulceby
Keelby
Spurn Head
5
GRIMSBY
A18
Laceby
CLEETHORPES
HUMBERSIDE
A18

BRIGG
Waltham
Humberston
A1084
B1219
Swallow
Tetney
A46
Caistor
A16
North Cotes
B1201
Grainthorpe
North Somercotes
A1031
Ludborough
A16
Binbrook
Saltfleet

A1103
Tealby
B1203
Market Rasen
A631
Middle Rasen
A6
B1202
A157
Louth
B1200
A1031
Faldingworth
Legbourne
Mablethorpe
Lissington
A153
Withern
A1104
A157
B1373
Sutton-on-Sea
East
Barkwith
A1111
A52
Langworth
Wragby
Cadwell
Park
A153
A158
Alford
B1449
A158
A1104
Baumber
A16
Bilsby
B1196
A1028
Hogsthorpe
B1190
Bardney
Horncastle
Hagworthingham
Ingoldmells
Branston
B1190
B1183
A158 Candlesby
Nocton
A1115
Spilsby
Burgh-le-Marsh
Woodhall Spa
B191
Gunby Hall
A158
Kirkstead
Abbey
A155
A16
Mareham-
le-Fen
Skegness
A52
Metheringham
Martin
New
Stickford
Scopwick
Tattershall
Bolingbroke
Wainfleet
Digby
Coningsby
Stickney
Ruskington
North Kyme
A52
Anwick
South Kyme
Wrangle
A16
B1184
Brancaster Roads
Sleaford
Sibsey
Old Leake
60
A1121
A52
Brancaster
Bay

F

E

D

C

B

A

6   7   8   9   10

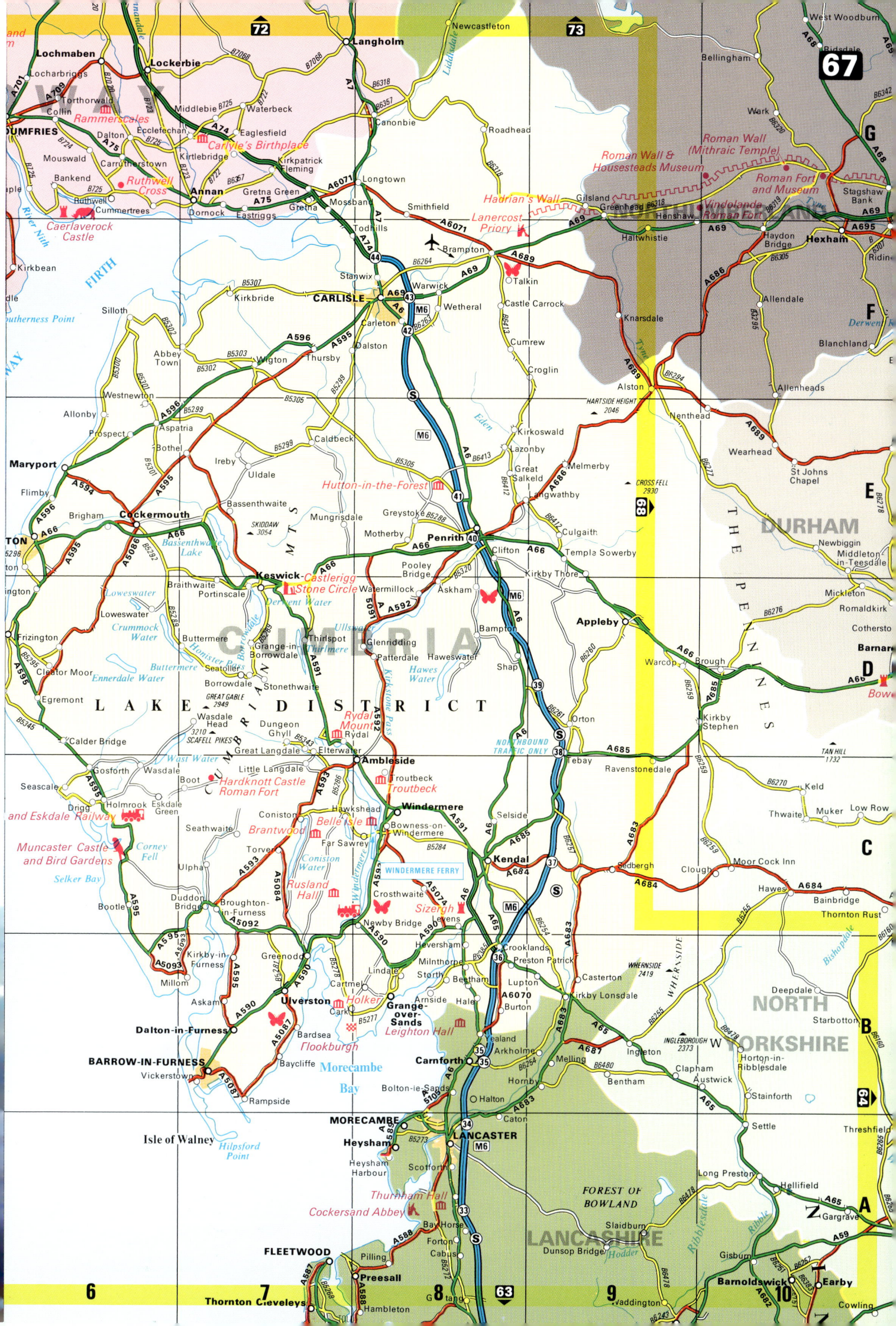

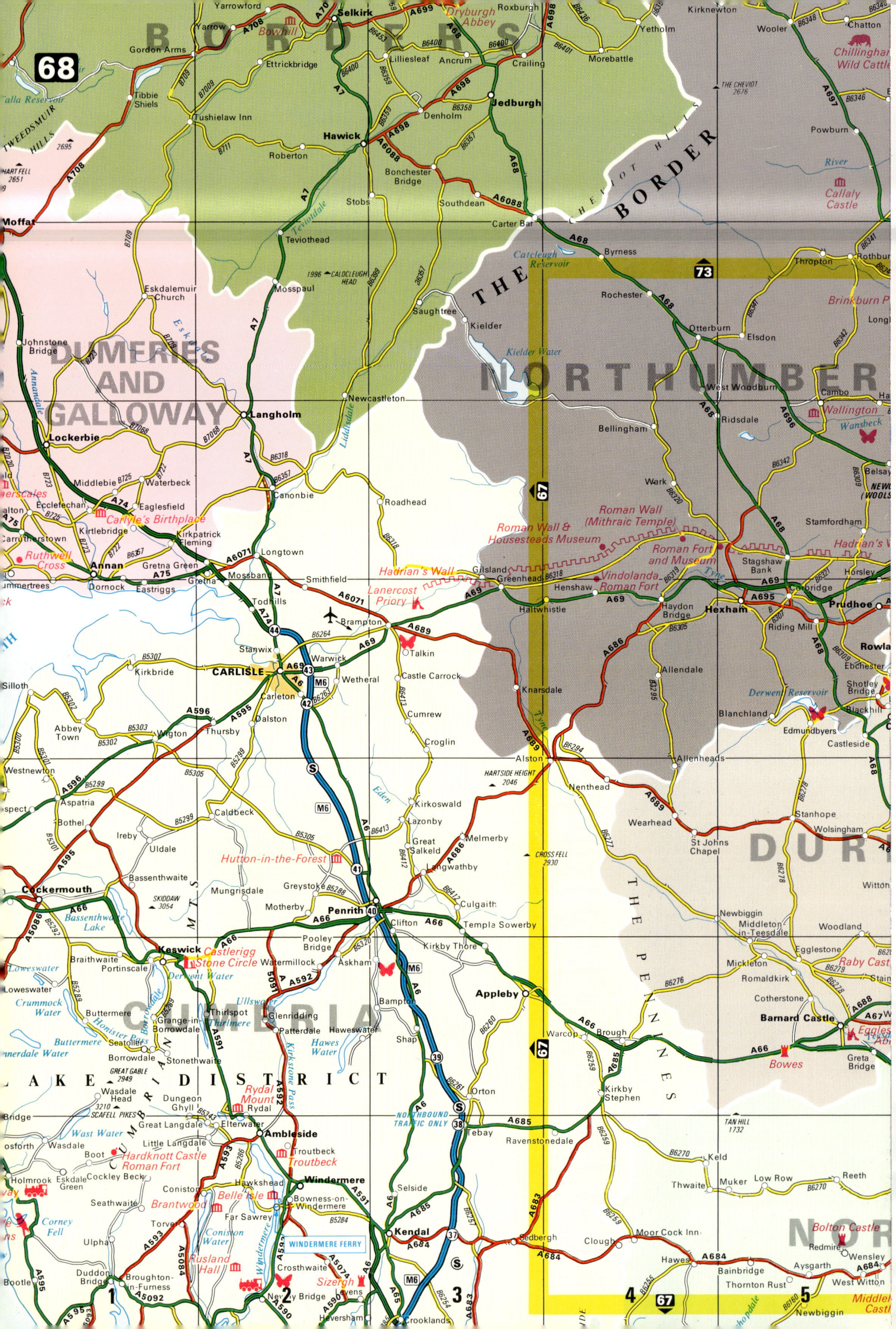

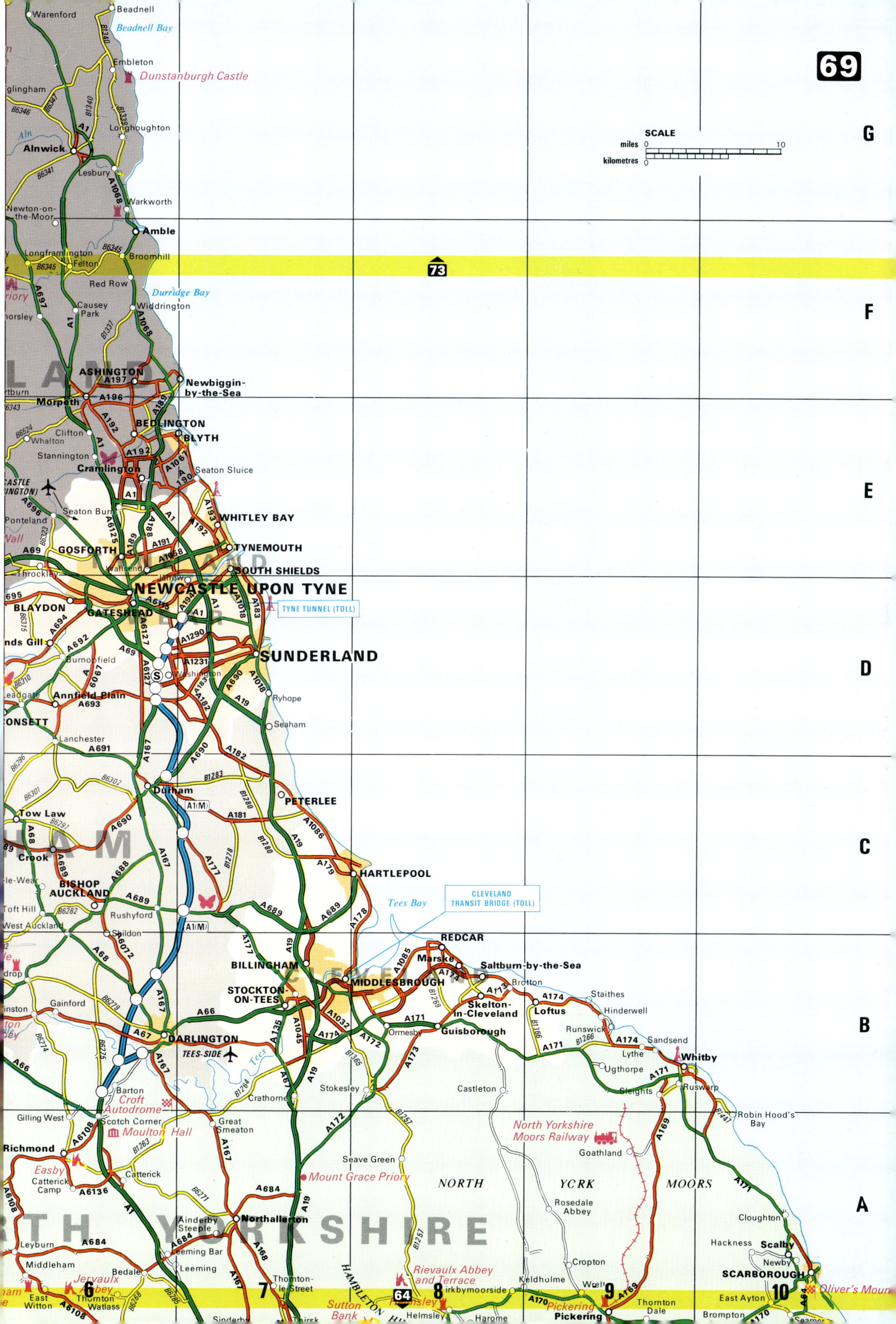

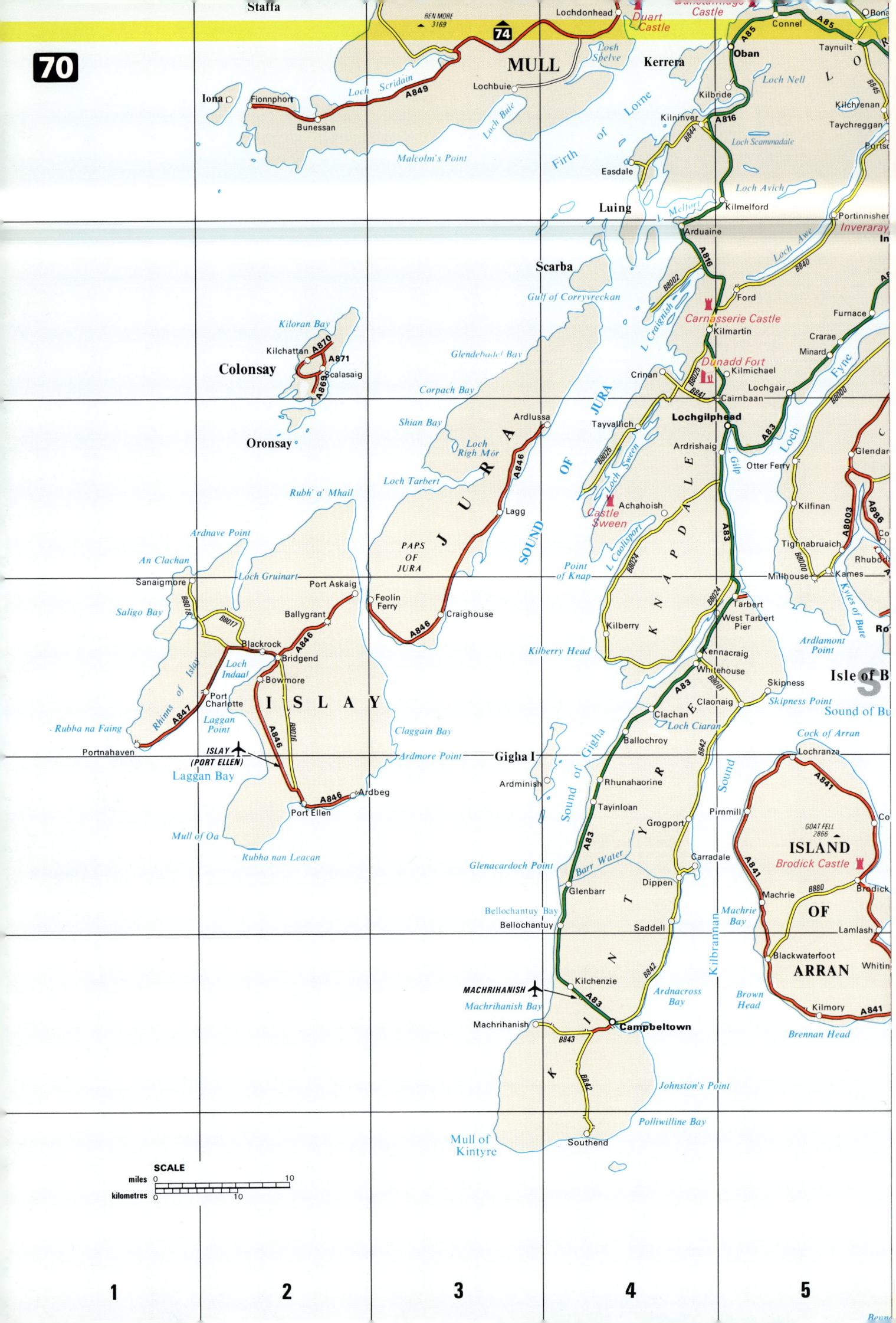

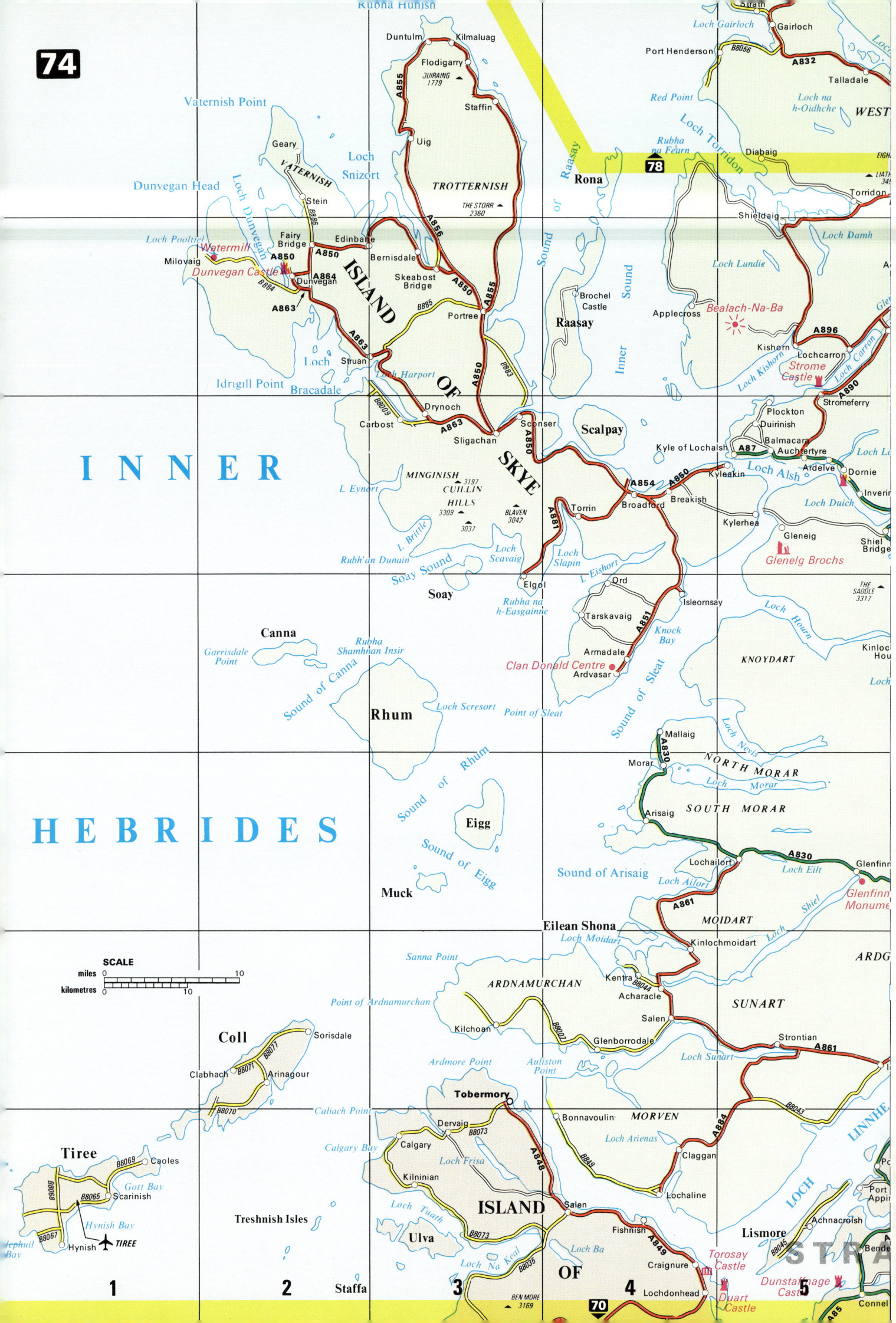

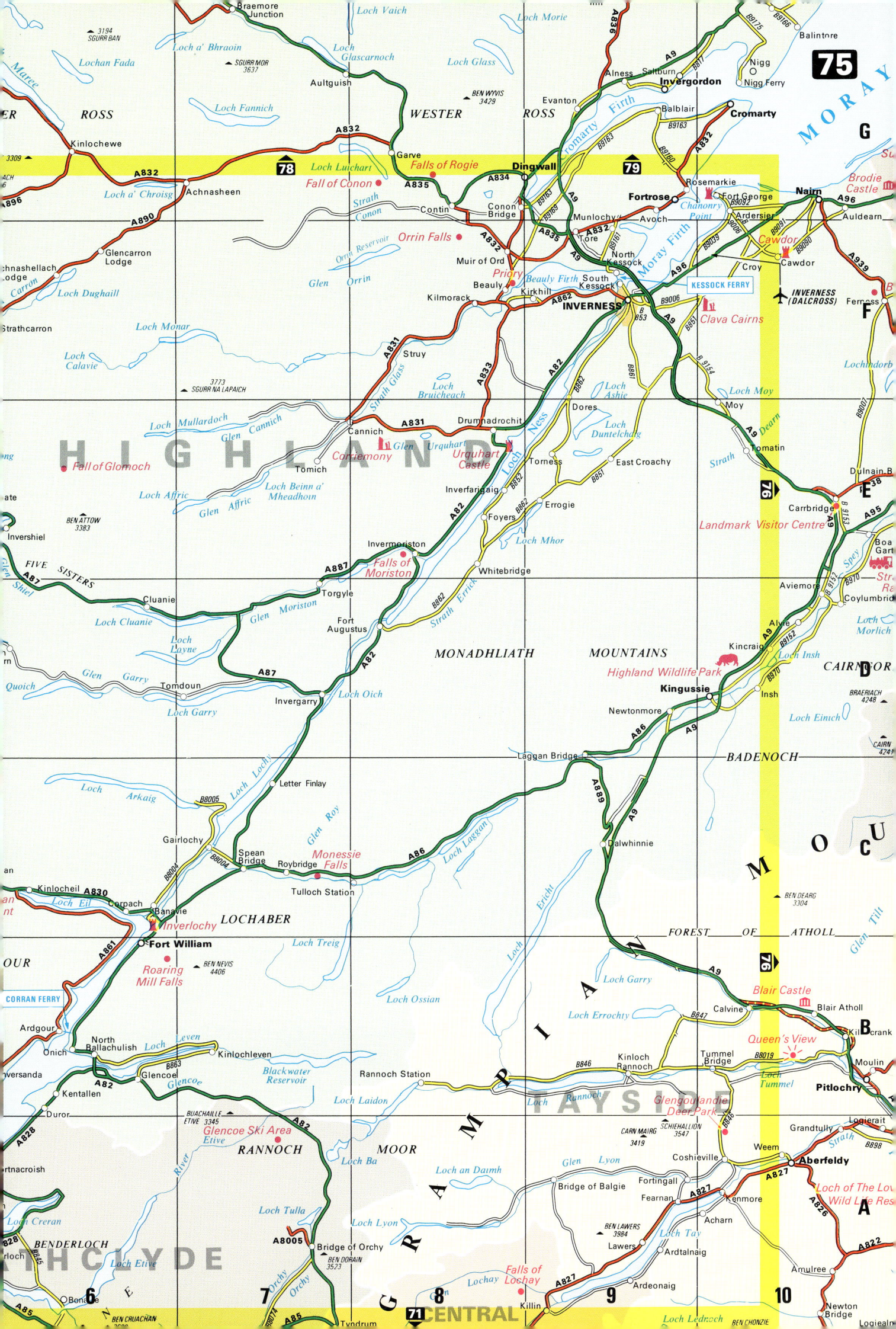

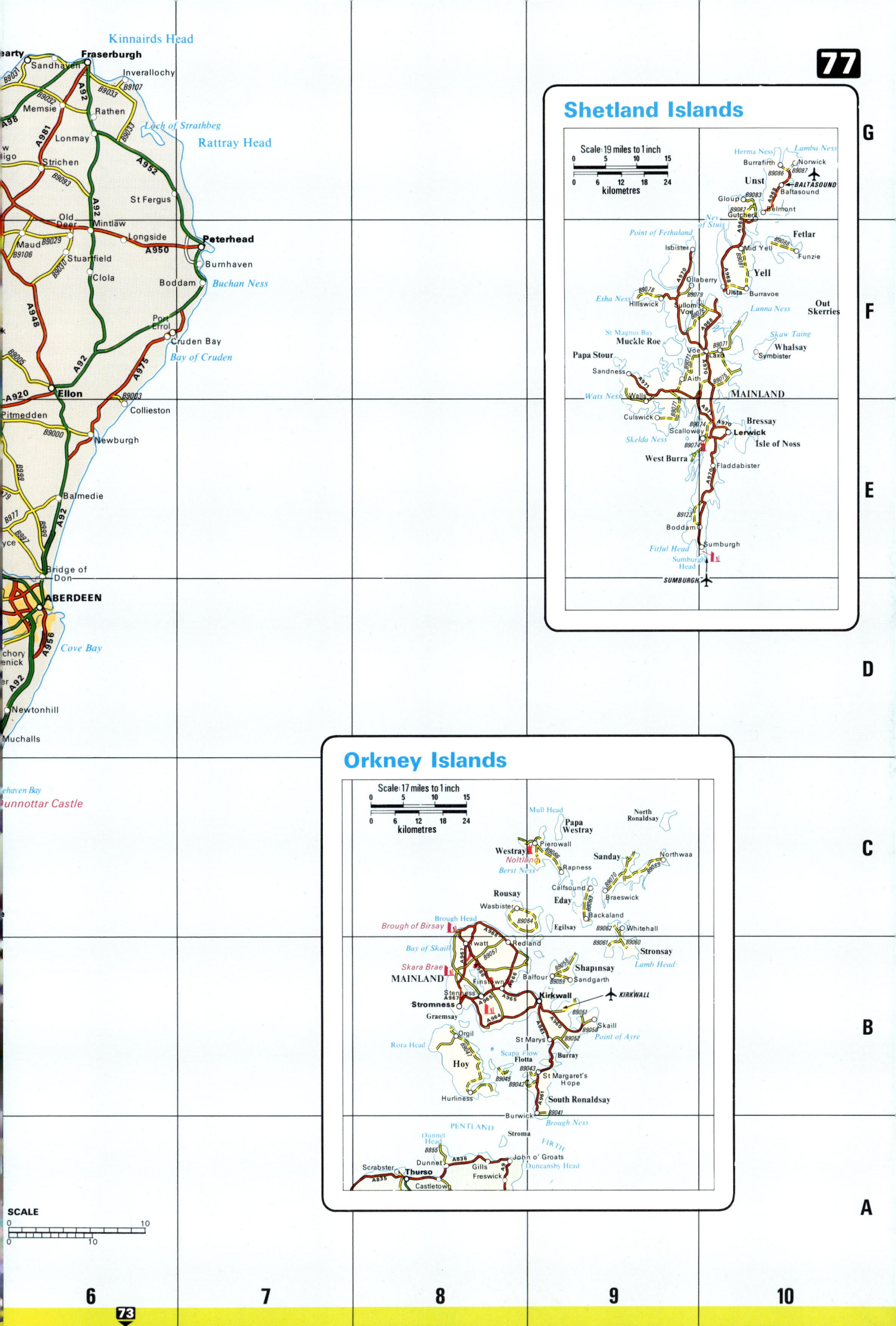

Outer Hebrides

Scale: 22½ miles to 1 inch

0 5 10 15 20

0 8 16 24 32
kilometres

Cape Wrath

Faraid Head

Durness

Keoldale

Sandwood Loch

Kyle of Durness

Kinlochbervie   Badcall

A838

Loch Eriboll

Enboll

Loch Hope

BUTT of LEWIS   Port of Ness

ISLE OF LEWIS

Cellar Head

A867

Barvas   North Tolsta

Dun Carloway Broch

A858   Carloway

Gallan Head

Uig

Breasclète

Stornoway

Tiumpan Head

Broad Bay

Eye Peninsula

A859   Balallan

B8060

STORNOWAY

Husinish

Husinish Point

West Loch Tarbert

CLISHAM 2622   BEINN MHOR 1874

Taransay   Tarbert

Toe Head   Scalpay

Harris

Pabbay   Rodel

Boreray   Bernera

A859

Little Minch

Griminish Point

Tigharry

North Uist   Lochmaddy

A867

A865

BENBECULA   Ronay

Balivanich   Gramsdale

Creagorry   Wiay

B891

Stilligarry   B890

South Uist

Rubha Ardvule

Loch Eynort

Lochboisdale

A865

Scurrival Point   Eriskay

Barra   BARRA

Kisimul   A888

Castlebay

Vatersay

Sandray

Mingulay

Barra Head

WESTERN ISLES

THE SOUND OF THE HEBRIDES

Kinlochbervie   Badcall

Loch Inchard

OINAVEN 2980

Laxford Bridge   BEN ARKLE 2582

Scourie   BEN STACK 2364   A838   Loch Stack

Handa I   Loch More

Badcall   A894   REAY FOREST   BEN HEE 2864

Eddrachillis Bay   Loch Glendhu

Point of Stoer   Clashnessie Bay   Kylesku   Kylestrome   Unapool   Loch Merkland

Drumbeg   B869   Nedd   QUINAG 2653   Loch Glencoul   Loch Fiag

Clashnessie   KYLESKU FERRY   A894   Eas Coul Aulin Falls

Stoer   B869   A837   Loch Assynt   GLASVEN 2541   Overscraig

Lochinver   Inchnadamph   BEN MORE ASSYNT 3273

Loch Inver   Inverkirkaig   SUILVEN 2399   CANISP 2779   A837

Rubha Coigeach   Enard Bay   Loch Veyatie   Cam Loch   Ledmore Junction   Glen Oykell   Loch Ailsh

Reiff   Loch Sionascaig   Knockan   A837

Polbain   Loch Urigill   Loch Oykell

Summer Isles   Achiltibuie   Knockan Cliff   Waterf.

Loch Lurgain   A835   Falls   Strath Oyke

COIGACH   Strathkinnaird

Cailleach Head

Gruinard Bay   Loch Achall   Loch an Daimh

Rubha Reidh   Laide   A832   Little Loch Broom   Ullapool   EASTER RO

Cove   Aultbea   Ardessie   Leckmelm   Loch Broom

Melvaig   Loch Ewe   Dundonnell   AN TEALLACH 3483   BEINN DEARG 3547

B8021   Midtown Brae   Loch na Sealga   A835   Falls of Measach   Loch Vaich

North Erradale   Poolewe   Fionn Loch   Braemore Junction

Strath   3194 SGURR BAN   Loch a' Bhraoin   Loch Glascarnoch

Loch Gairloch   Gairloch   Loch Maree   SGURR MOR 3637

Port Henderson   B8056   A832   Lochan Fada   Aultguish   WESTE

Talladale   Loch Fannich

Red Point   Loch na h-Oidhche   WESTER ROSS   A835

Rubha na Fearn   Kinlochewe   A832   Garve   Falls of R

Kilmaluag   Diabaig   EIGHE 3309   Loch Luichart   A835

Staffin   Torridon   LIATHACH 3456   Achnasheen   Fall of Conon   Contin

THE STORR 2360   A896   Loch a' Chroisg   A890   Carnoch   Strath Conon

Rona   Shieldaig   Glencarron Lodge   Orrin Falls

Loch Lundie   Achnashellach Lodge   Loch Dughaill   Orrin Reservoir

Brochel Castle   Loch Damh   Glen Orrin

Raasay   Bealach-Na-Ba   Glen Carron   Loch Monar   A831

ortree   Applecross   arron   Kilmora

Kishorn   Stra   A896   Struy

Sound of Raasay   Loch Torridon   Sound of Rona

A850   A855

HIGH

74   75
2   3   4   5

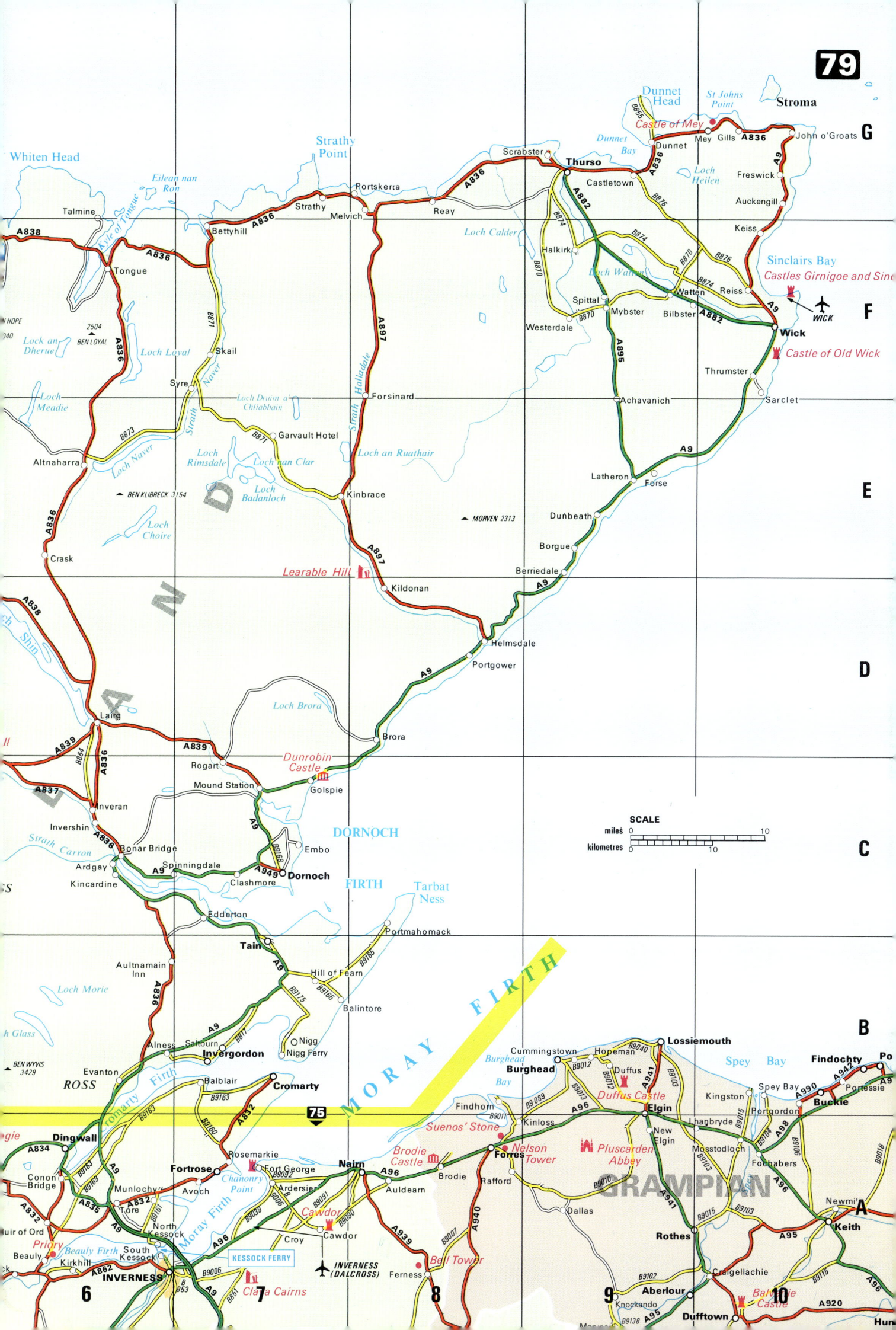

INDEX

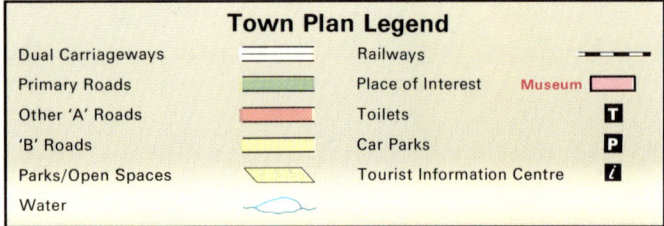

This index will help you to find places in the atlas. Listed on these pages, in alphabetical order, are the names of all the towns and villages that appear in the atlas. For each one, you will find its page number and its grid square. If you need help in using the grid, turn to pages 14–15.

Place name

Grid square

Aberdare...................57......8B

Page number

A

Abberley	58	4D
Abbey Town	67	6F
Abbots Bromley	59	6F
Abbotsbury	52	3A
Aber	62	3D
Aberaeron	56	5E
Aberarth	56	5E
Aberchirder	76	4G
Aberdare	57	8B
Aberdaron	62	1B
Aberdeen	77	6D
Aberdovey	57	6G
Aberfeldy	75	10A
Aberffraw	62	2D
Aberfoyle	71	8F
Abergavenny	58	2A
Abergele	62	5D
Aberlady	73	6E
Aberlour	76	2F
Abermule	57	8G

Abernethy	72	4G
Aberporth	56	4E
Abersoch	62	2B
Abersychan	57	9C
Abertillery	57	9C
Aberystwyth	56	5F
Abingdon	53	7G
Abington (Cambs)	60	5B
Abington (Strath)	72	3B
Ab Kettleby	59	9F
Aboyne	76	4D
Abridge	54	5G
Accrington	63	9G
Achahoish	70	4E
Acharacle	74	4B
Acharn	75	10A
Achavanich	79	9E
Achiltibuie	78	3D
Achnacroish	74	5A
Achnasheen	75	7G
Achnashellach Lodge	75	6F
Acle	61	9F
Acomb	64	3F
Addingham	64	1F
Ainderby Steeple	69	7A
Airdrie	72	2D
Airth	72	3F
Aith	77	9F
Albrighton (Salop)	58	5D
Albrighton (Salop)	63	7A
Albury	54	3D
Alcester	59	6C
Alconbury	60	3D
Aldbourne	53	6F
Aldbrough	65	7E
Aldbury	60	2A
Aldeburgh	61	9C
Aldenham	54	4G
Alderbury	53	6C
Alderley Edge	63	9D
Aldermaston	53	8E
Aldershot	54	2D
Aldford	63	7C
Aldwick	54	3B

Alfold	54	3C
Alford (Grampian)	76	4E
Alford (Lincs)	65	8B
Alfreton	64	3A
Alkham	55	9D
Allanton	73	8D
Allendale	68	4D
Allensmore	58	3B
Allesley	59	7D
Allestree	59	7G
Alloa	72	3F
Allonby	67	6E
Alloway	71	7B
All Stretton	58	3E
Almondsbury	52	3F
Alness	79	6B
Alnwick	73	9B
Alresford	53	8D
Alrewas	59	6F
Alsager	63	9C
Alston	68	4C
Althorpe	64	5D
Altnaharra	79	6E
Alton	53	9D
Alton Pancras	52	4B
Altrincham	63	9E
Alum Bay	53	7A
Alva	72	3F
Alveley	58	4D
Alveston	52	3F
Alvie	75	10D
Alyth	76	2A
Ambergate	64	2A
Amberley	54	3B
Amble	73	10A
Ambleside	67	7C
Amersham	54	3G
Amesbury	53	6D
Amlwch	62	2E
Ammanford	57	6C
Ampthill	60	2B
Amulree	75	10A
Ancaster	60	2G
Ancroft	73	8C
Ancrum	73	6B
Andover	53	7D
Andoversford	59	6A
Andreas	66	3C
Angle	56	2B
Angmering-on-Sea	54	3B
Annan	67	7G
Annfield Plain	69	6D
Anstruther	73	6F
Anwick	65	6A
Appleby	67	9D
Applecross	74	4F
Appledore (Devon)	51	6F
Appledore (Kent)	55	8C
Arbroath	76	4A
Arclid	63	9C
Ardbeg	70	2C
Ardbrecknish	71	6G
Arden	71	7E
Ardentinney	71	6E
Ardeonaig	75	9A
Ardersier	75	10G
Ardessie	78	3C
Ardgay	79	6C
Ardgour	75	6B
Ardleigh	61	7A
Ardley	59	8B
Ardlui	71	7G
Ardlussa	70	4E
Ardminish	70	4C
Ardrishaig	70	5E
Ardrossan	71	6C
Ardtalnaig	75	9A
Arduaine	70	4F
Ardvasar	74	4D
Ardwell	66	1F
Arinagour	74	2B
Arisaig	74	4C
Arkholme	67	9B
Armadale (Highland)	74	4D
Armadale (Lothian)	72	3E
Arnold	59	8G
Arnside	67	8B
Arrington	60	4C
Arrochar	71	7F

ABERYSTWYTH

Police Station

To Cliff Railway

Bath Rocks

yds 0   Scale   220

mtrs 0   200

QUEENS AVENUE

QUEENS ROAD

NORTH ROAD

BRYN ROAD

TREFOR ROAD

Bowls & Tennis Greens

N

Commodore Cinema

Pier

Museum

LOVEDEN ROAD

QUEENS ROAD

NORTH ROAD

CAE MELYN

Pier Pavilion

Library

B4346

MARINE TERRACE

BATH STREET

CORPORATION ST.

PORTLAND STREET

PORTLAND ROAD

EASTGATE

JAYNOR ST.

NORTHGATE STREET

THESPIAN STREET

KINNEAR STREET

POPLAR

TRINITY ROW

PEN-GLAIS ROAD

A487

LLANBADARN

MACHYNLLETH 18ml (29kms)

Rocks

PROMENADE

PIER STREET

LAURA PLACE

KING STREET

NEW STREET

MARKET STREET

NORTH PARADE

CAMBRIAN STREET

CHALYBEATE STREET

TERRACE ROAD

CAMBRIAN ROAD

STANLEY STREET

TRINITY PLACE

EDGE HILL ROAD

BUARTH ROAD

CARADOC ROAD

JORWETH AVENUE

DAVIDS ROAD

A487

A44

LLANGURIG 25ml (40kms)

Castle

NEW

SEA VIEW PLACE

CUSTOMS HOUSE

CASTLE STREET

HIGH STREET

QUEEN STREET

GREAT DARKGATE STREET

UNION ST.

ALEXANDRA ROAD

Station

Vale of Rheidol Railway

Bowling Greens

South Beach

MARINE TERRACE

QUAY ROAD

RHEIDOL TERRACE

SOUTH ROAD

PRINCESS STREET

PROSPECT STREET

VULCAN ST.

GRAYS INN ROAD

GEORGE STREET

POWELL ST.

MILL STREET

BRIDGE STREET

PARK AVENUE

RIVERSIDE TERRACE

GREENFIELD STREET

GLYNGWR ROAD

MAESYRAFON

PLAS CRUG AVENUE

University of Wales Sports Ground

Childrens Playground

Harbour

PONT ABERYSTWYTH

River Rheidol

GLANRAFON TERRACE

SPRING GONS

TREFECHAN

A487

Aberystwyth Football Ground

Fire Station

CARDIGAN 39ml (63kms)

Arthog...62......3A
Arundel...54......3B
Ascog...71......6D
Ash (Kent)...55......10E
Ash (Surrey)...54......2D
Ashbourne...59......6G
Ashburton...51......8C
Ashbury...53......6F
Ashby-de-la-Zouch...59......7F
Ashcott...52......2D
Ashford...55......8D
Ashington (Northumb.)...69......6F
Ashington (Sussex)...54......4C
Ashley...60......5C
Ashtead...54......4E
Ashton...50......2A
Ashton-under-Lyne...63......10E
Ashurst...53......7C
Ash Vale...54......2D
Askam...67......7B
Askerswell...52......3B
Askett...54......2G
Askham...67......8D
Aspatria...67......6E
Aston...53......7G
Aston Clinton...60......1A
Aston-on-Clun...58......2D
Aston Rowant...53......9G
Atcham...63......8A
Atherstone...59......7E
Atherton...63......8E
Attleborough...61......7E
Atwick...65......6F
Auchencairn...66......5F
Auchinleck...71......8B
Auchterarder...72......3G
Auchtermuchty...72......5G
Auchtertyre...74......5E
Auckingill...79......10G
Audlem...63......8B
Auldearn...75......10G
Aultguish...78......5B
Aultbea...78......3C
Aultnamain Inn...79......6B
Aust...52......3F
Austwick...67......10B
Avebury...52......6E
Avening...52......4G
Aveton Gifford...50......7B
Aviemore...75......10D
Avoch...75......9G
Avonmouth...52......3F
Awsworth...59......8G
Axbridge...52......2E
Axminster...52......1B
Axmouth...52......1B
Aylesbury...60......1A
Aylestone...59......8E
Aylsham...61......8F
Aynho...59......8B
Ayot St Lawrence...61......3A
Ayr...71......7B
Aysgarth...68......5A
Ayton...73......8D

B

Backaland...77......9C
Backford Cross...63......7D
Bacton...61......9G
Badcall...78......4E
Badgers Mount...54......5E
Bagillt...63......6D
Baginton...59......7D
Bagshot...54......2E
Bailivanish...78......1E
Bainbridge...68......5A
Bainton...64......5F
Bakewell...64......2B
Bala...62......5B
Balallan...78......2F
Balbeggie...76......2A
Balblair...79......7B
Baldersby...64......2G
Balderton...64......5A
Baldock...60......3B
Balfour...77......9B
Balintore...79......7B

Ballantrae...66......1G
Ballasalla...66......2B
Ballater...76......3D
Ballaugh...66......2C
Ballinluig...76......1B
Ballintuim...76......2B
Balloch...71......7E
Ballochroy...70......4D
Ballygrant...70......2D
Balmacara...75......5E
Balmaclellan...66......4G
Balmedie...77......6E
Balsall Common...59......7D
Balsham...60......5C
Baltasound...77......10G
Bamburgh...73......9C
Bamford...64......2B
Bampton (Cumbria)...67......8D
Bampton (Devon)...51......9F
Bampton (Oxon)...53......7G
Banavie...75......6C
Banbury...59......8B
Banchory...76......4D
Banchory Devenick...76......5D
Banff...76......4G
Bangor...62......3D
Bangor-on-Dee...63......7C
Bankend...67......6G
Bankfoot...76......1A
Bannockburn...72......2F
Banstead...54......4E
Banwell...52......2E
Bardney...65......6B
Bardsea...67......7B
Barford...59......7C
Barford St Martin...52......5D
Bargoed...57......8B
Bargrennan...66......2G
Barham...55......9D
Barkston...60......2G
Barkway...60......4B
Barlborough...64......3B
Barlby...64......4E
Barley...60......4B
Barmby-on-the-Moor...64......4F
Barmouth...62......3A
Barmston...65......6F
Barnard Castle...68......5B
Barnby Moor...64......4B
Barnet...54......4G
Barnoldswick...67......10A
Barnsley (Glos)...52......5G
Barnsley (S. Yorks)...64......2C
Barnstaple...51......7F
Barnwood...58......5A
Barr...71......7A
Barrhill...66......2G
Barrowford...63......9G
Barrow-in-Furness...67......7B
Barry (S. Glam)...57......8A
Barry (Tayside)...76......4A
Barry Island...57......8A
Barton (Cambs)...60......4C
Barton (Lancs)...63......8G
Barton (N. Yorks)...69......6B
Barton-in-the-Clay...60......2B
Barton Mills...61......6D
Barton on Sea...53......6B
Barton Seagrave...60......1D
Barton-upon-Humber...64......6D
Barvas...78......2F
Basildon...55......6F
Basingstoke...53......8E
Baslow...64......2B
Bassenthwaite...67......7E
Baston...60......3F
Bath...52......4E
Bathgate...72......3E
Bathpool...52......1C
Battle...55......7C
Battlefield...63......8A
Battlesbridge...55......7F
Baumber...65......7B
Bawdeswell...61......7F
Bawdsey...61......9B
Bawtry...64......4C
Baycliffe...67......7B
Bay Horse...67......8A
Bayston Hill...63......7A

Beachley...52......3G
Beaconsfield...54......3F
Beadnell...73......9C
Beaford...51......7E
Beal...73......9C
Beaminster...52......2B
Beare Green...54......4D
Bearsted...55......7E
Beaulieu...53......7B
Beauly...75......8F
Beaumaris...62......3D
Beccles...61......9D
Beckford...58......5B
Beckhampton...52......5E
Beckingham...64......5A
Beckington...52......4E
Beck Row...60......5D
Bedale...69......6A
Beddgelert...62......3C
Bedford...60......2B
Bedlington...69......6E
Bedlinog...57......8B
Bedworth...59......7E
Beeford...65......6F
Beeley...64......2A
Beer...52......1A
Beeston...59......8G
Beeswing...66......5G
Beetham...67......8B
Beetley...61......7F
Beguildy...57......8F
Beith...71......7D
Belford...73......9C
Bellingham...68......4E
Bellochantuy...70......4C
Bellshill...72......2D
Belmont (Shetland)...77......10G
Belmont (Surrey)...54......4E
Belper...64......2A
Belsay...68......5E
Belton (Humber)...64......4C
Belton (Leics)...60......1E
Bembridge...53......8A
Bempton...65......6G
Benderloch...74......5A
Benenden...55......7C
Benington...60......3B
Benllech Bay...62......3D
Benmore...71......7G
Benson...53......8G
Bentham...67......9B
Bentley...53......9D
Benwick...60......4E
Bere Regis...52......4B
Berkeley...53......3G
Berkhamsted...54......3G
Bernisdale...74......3F
Berriedale...79......9E
Berriew...57......8G
Berrow...52......2E
Berrynarbor...51......7G
Berwick-upon-Tweed...73......8D
Bethersden...55......8D
Bethesda...62......3D
Bettyhill...79......7F
Betws-y-Coed...62......4C
Betws-yn-Rhos...62......5D
Beulah...57......7E
Beverley...65......6E
Bewdley...58......4D
Bexhill-on-Sea...55......7B
Bexley...54......5E
Bexleyheath...54......5F
Bibury...59......6A
Bicester...59......8A
Bickington...51......7F
Bickleigh...51......9E
Biddenden...55......7D
Biddisham...52......2E
Biddulph...63......9C
Bideford...51......6F
Bidford-on-Avon...59......6C
Bigbury-on-Sea...51......7B
Biggar...72......4C
Biggin Hill...54......5E
Biggleswade...60......3B
Bilbster...79......9F
Bildeston...61......7B
Billericay...55......6F

Billingborough...60......3G
Billingham...69......7B
Billinghay...65......6A
Billingshurst...54......3C
Bilsby...65......8B
Bilston...58......5E
Binbrook...65......7C
Binfield...54......2E
Bingham...59......9G
Bingley...64......1E
Birchington...55......9E
Birdlip...58......5A
Birgham...73......7C
Birkenhead...63......7E
Birmingham...59......6E
Birnam...76......1A
Birstall...59......8F
Bishop Auckland...69......6C
Bishop's Castle...58......2E
Bishop's Cleeve...58......5B
Bishop's Frome...58......4C
Bishop's Lydeard...51......10F
Bishop's Stortford...60......4A
Bishopsteignton...51......9C
Bishopstone...53......6F
Bishop Sutton...52......3E
Bishop's Waltham...53......8C
Bispham...63......7G
Bitchfield...60......2F
Blaby...59......8E
Blackbrook...63......9B
Blackburn (Lancs)...63......8G
Blackburn (Lothian)...72......3D
Blackford...72......3G
Blackhill...68......5D
Blackmill...57......7B
Blackmoor Gate...51......7G
Blackpill...57......6B
Blackpool...63......7G
Blackrock...70......2D
Blackshiels...72......5D
Blackwater (Cornwall)...50......3B
Blackwater (Hants)...54......2E
Blackwater (I.of W.)...53......8A
Blackwaterfoot...70......5B
Blackwood (Gwent)...57......8B
Blackwood (Strath)...72......2C
Bladon...59......8A
Blaenau Ffestiniog...62......4C
Blaenavon...57......9C
Blaengarw...57......7B
Blaenporth...56......4E
Blagdon...52......3E
Blair Atholl...75......10B
Blair Drummond...72......2F
Blairgowrie...76......2A
Blairlogie...72......2F
Blairmore...71......6E
Blakeney (Glos)...58......4A
Blakeney (Norfolk)...61......7G
Blakenham...61......8C
Blanchland...68......5D
Blandford Forum...52......4B
Blaxton...64......4C
Blaydon...69......6D
Blickling...61......8F
Bleadney...52......2D
Bleadon...52......2E
Bleddfa...57......9F
Bletchingley...54......5D
Bletchley...60......1B
Blewbury...53......8F
Blidworth...64......3A
Blindley Heath...54......5D
Blisworth...59......9C
Blofield...61......9E
Bloxham...59......8B
Blubberhouses...64......1F
Blue Anchor...51......9G
Blyth (Northumb)...69......7E
Blyth (Notts)...64......4C
Blyton...64......5C
Boars Hill...53......7G
Boat of Garten...76......1E
Boddam (Grampian)...77......7F
Boddam (Shetland)...77......9E
Bodelwyddan...62......5D
Bodfari...62......5D
Bodfuan...62......2B

Bodmin 50 4C
Bognor Regis 54 3B
Bollington 63 10D
Bolney 54 4C
Bolsover 64 3B
Bolton 63 9F
Bolton Abbey 64 1F
Bolton Bridge 64 1F
Bolton-le-Sands 67 8B
Bolventor 50 5C
Bonar Bridge 79 6C
Bonawe 70 5G
Bonchester Bridge 73 6B
Bo'ness 72 3E
Bonnavoulin 74 4A
Bontddu 62 3A
Bont Newydd 62 2C
Bonvilston 57 8A
Boot 67 7C
Bootle (Cumbria) 67 6C
Bootle (Mersey) 63 7E
Boreham Street 55 6B
Boreham Wood 54 4G
Borgue (Dumf & Gall) 66 4F
Borgue (Highland) 79 9E
Boroughbridge 64 3F
Borrowash 59 8G
Borrowdale 67 7D
Borth 57 6G
Bosbury 58 4B
Boscastle 50 4D
Boscombe 53 6B
Bosherston 56 2B
Boston 60 4G
Boston Spa 64 3E
Botesdale 61 7D
Bothel 67 7E
Bothwell 71 9D
Botley 53 8C
Bottesford 60 1G
Bourne 60 3F
Bourne End 54 2F
Bournemouth 52 5B
Bourton (Dorset) 52 4D
Bourton (Salop) 58 3E
Bourton-on-the-Water 59 6A
Bovey Tracey 51 8D
Bowmore 70 2D
Bowness-on-Windermere 67 8C
Box 52 4E
Boxford 61 7B
Bozeat 60 2C
Bracebridge 64 5B
Brackley 59 8B
Bracknell 54 2E
Braco 72 2G
Bradford 64 1E
Bradford-on-Avon 52 4E
Brading 53 8A
Bradninch 51 9E
Bradwell 64 1B
Bradwell-on-Sea 55 8G
Braemar 76 2D
Braemore Junction 78 4B
Braeswick 77 9C
Braidwood 72 3D
Brailsford 59 7G
Braintree 61 6A
Braithwaite 67 7D
Bramber 54 4B
Bramdean 53 8C
Bramfield 61 9D
Bramhope 64 2E
Bramley 54 3D
Brampton (Cambs) 60 3D
Brampton (Cumbria) 67 8F
Bramshaw 53 6C
Brancaster 61 6G
Brandesburton 65 6F
Brandon (Suffolk) 61 6D
Brandon (Warwicks) 59 7D
Brandon Creek 60 5E
Branston (Lincs) 65 6A
Branston (Staffs) 59 7F
Brant Broughton 64 5A
Brasted 54 5E
Braughing 60 4A
Braunton 51 6F
Brayford 51 7F
Breakish 74 4E
Breasclete 78 2F
Brechfa 56 5D
Brechin 76 4B
Brecon 57 8D
Brede 55 7C
Bredon 58 5B
Bredwardine 58 2B
Brentwood 55 6F
Brenzett 55 8C
Brereton 59 6F
Brereton Green 63 9C
Bressingham 61 7D
Bride 66 3C
Bridestowe 51 7D
Bridgend (Glam) 57 7A
Bridgend (Strath) 70 2D
Bridge of Alford 76 4E
Bridge of Allan 72 2F
Bridge of Balgie 75 9A
Bridge of Cally 76 2B
Bridge of Don 77 6E
Bridge of Earn 72 4G
Bridge of Gairn 76 3D
Bridge of Orchy 75 7A
Bridgnorth 58 4E
Bridgwater 52 2D
Bridlington 65 6F
Bridport 52 2B
Brierfield 63 9G
Brigg 64 6C
Brigham 67 6E
Brighouse 64 1D
Brighstone 53 7A
Brightlingsea 61 7A
Brighton 54 5B
Brigstock 60 2D
Brinkworth 52 5F
Brislington 52 3F
Bristol 52 3F
Brithdir 62 4A
Briton Ferry 57 6B
Brixham 51 9C
Brixworth 59 9D
Broadbridge Heath 54 4C
Broad Clyst 51 9E
Broadford 74 4E
Broadhaven 56 2C
Broad Hinton 53 6F
Broadstairs 55 10E
Broadstone 52 5B
Broadwas 58 4C
Broadwater 60 3A
Broadway 59 6B
Broadwindsor 52 2B
Brochel Castle 74 4F
Brock 63 8G
Brockenhurst 53 6B
Brockford 61 8C
Brodick 70 5C
Brodie 76 1G
Brome 61 8D
Bromfield 58 3D
Brompton 64 5G
Bromsgrove 58 5D
Bromyard 58 4C
Bronllys 57 8D
Brook 53 6C
Brooke 61 8E
Brookland 55 8C
Brookmans Park 54 4G
Broomhill 73 10A
Brora 79 8D
Broseley 58 4E
Brotherton 64 3D
Brotton 69 8B
Brough 68 4B
Broughton (Borders) 72 4C
Broughton (Lancs) 63 8G
Broughton (Northants) 60 1D
Broughton-in-Furness 67 7C
Broughton Poggs 53 6G
Broughty Ferry 76 3A
Brownhills 59 6E
Broxbourne 54 5G
Broxted 60 5A
Broxton 63 7C
Bruton 52 3D
Brynamman 57 6C
Bryncrug 57 6G
Brynmawr 57 8C
Brynna 57 7A
Bubwith 64 4E
Buckfastleigh 51 8C
Buckhaven & Methil 72 5F
Buckhurst Hill 54 5F
Buckie 76 3G
Buckingham 59 9B
Buckland 60 4B
Buckler's Hard 53 7B
Buckley 63 6C
Bucklow Hill 63 9D
Buckminster 60 1F
Bucksburn 76 5E
Bude 50 5E
Budleigh Salterton 51 9D
Bugle 50 4C
Builth Wells 57 8E
Bulford 53 6D
Bull Bay 62 2E
Bulwell 59 8G
Bulwick 60 2E
Bunbury 63 8C
Bunessan 70 2G
Bungay 61 9D
Bunny 59 8G
Buntingford 60 4A
Burbage 53 6E
Burcot 53 8G
Burford 59 7A
Burgess Hill 54 5C
Burghead 76 2G
Burgh Heath 54 4E
Burgh-le-Marsh 65 8A
Burleydam 63 8B
Burlton 63 7B
Burley-in-Wharfedale 64 1E
Burnham 54 3F
Burnham Market 61 6G
Burnham-on-Crouch 55 8G
Burnham-on-Sea 52 2D
Burnhaven 77 7F
Burnley 63 9G
Burnopfield 69 6D
Burnsall 64 1F
Burrafirth 77 10G
Burravoe 77 10F
Burrelton 76 2A
Burry Port 56 5B
Bursledon 53 7B
Burslem 63 9C
Burton 67 8B
Burton Agnes 65 6F
Burton Bradstock 52 2A
Burton Joyce 59 9G
Burton Latimer 60 1D
Burton-on-Stather 64 5D
Burton-upon-Trent 59 7F
Burwash 55 6C
Burwell 60 5C
Burwick 77 9A
Bury 63 9F
Bury St Edmunds 61 6C
Bushey 54 4G
Bushey Heath 54 4F
Butley 61 9C
Buttermere 67 7D
Buttington 63 6A
Buxted 54 5C
Buxton 64 1B
Bwlch 57 8C
Byfield 59 8C
Byfleet 54 3E
Bylchau 62 5C
Byrness 73 7A

C

Cabus 67 8A
Cadnam 53 6C
Caergwrle 63 6C
Caerleon 52 2G
Caernarfon 62 2C
Caerphilly 57 8B
Caersws 57 8G
Caerwent 52 2G
Cairnbaan 70 5B
Cairndow 71 6G
Cairneyhill 72 4F
Cairnryan 66 1G
Caister-on-Sea 61 10F
Caistor 65 6C
Caldbeck 67 7E
Calder Bridge 67 6D
Calfsound 77 9C
Calcot 53 8F
Caldecott 60 1E
Caldercruix 72 2E
Calgary 74 3A
Callander 71 8F
Callington 51 6C
Calne 52 5F
Calver 64 2B
Calvine 75 10B
Camberley 54 2E
Cambo 68 5E
Camborne 50 2B
Cambridge (Cambs) 60 4C
Cambridge (Glos) 52 4G
Cambus o'May 76 3D
Camelford 50 5D
Campbeltown 70 4B
Candlesby 65 8A
Canford Cliffs 52 5A
Cannich 75 8E
Cannington 52 1D
Cannock 63 10A
Canonbie 67 8G
Canterbury 55 9E
Canvey Island 55 7F
Caoles 74 1A
Capel 54 4D
Capel Bangor 57 6F
Capel Curig 62 4C
Caputh 76 1A
Carbis Bay 50 2B
Carbost 74 3E
Cardiff 57 8A
Cardigan 56 3E
Cardross 71 7E
Carew 56 3B
Carfraemill 73 6D
Carhampton 51 9G
Carisbrooke 53 7A
Cark 67 7B
Carleton 67 8F
Carlisle 67 8F
Carloway 78 2F
Carluke 72 3D
Carlyon Bay 50 4B
Carmarthen 56 5C
Carnaby 65 6F
Carnforth 67 8B
Carno 57 7G
Carnon Downs 50 3B
Carnoustie 76 4A
Carnwath 72 3D
Carradale 70 4C
Carrbridge 76 1E
Carrutherstown 67 6G
Carsphairn 71 8A
Carstairs 72 3C
Carter Bar 73 7B
Carterton 59 7A
Cartmel 67 8B
Casterton 67 9B
Castle Acre 61 6F
Castlebay 78 1D
Castle Carrock 67 8F
Castle Cary 52 3D
Castle Combe 52 4F
Castle Donington 59 8G
Castle Douglas 66 4F
Castleford 64 3D
Castle Hedingham 61 6B
Castlemartin 56 2B
Castleside 68 5D
Castleton (Derbys) 64 1B
Castleton (Yorks) 69 8B
Castletown (Highland) 79 9G
Castletown (I. of M.) 66 2B
Caterham 54 5E
Catfield 61 9F
Caton 67 8A

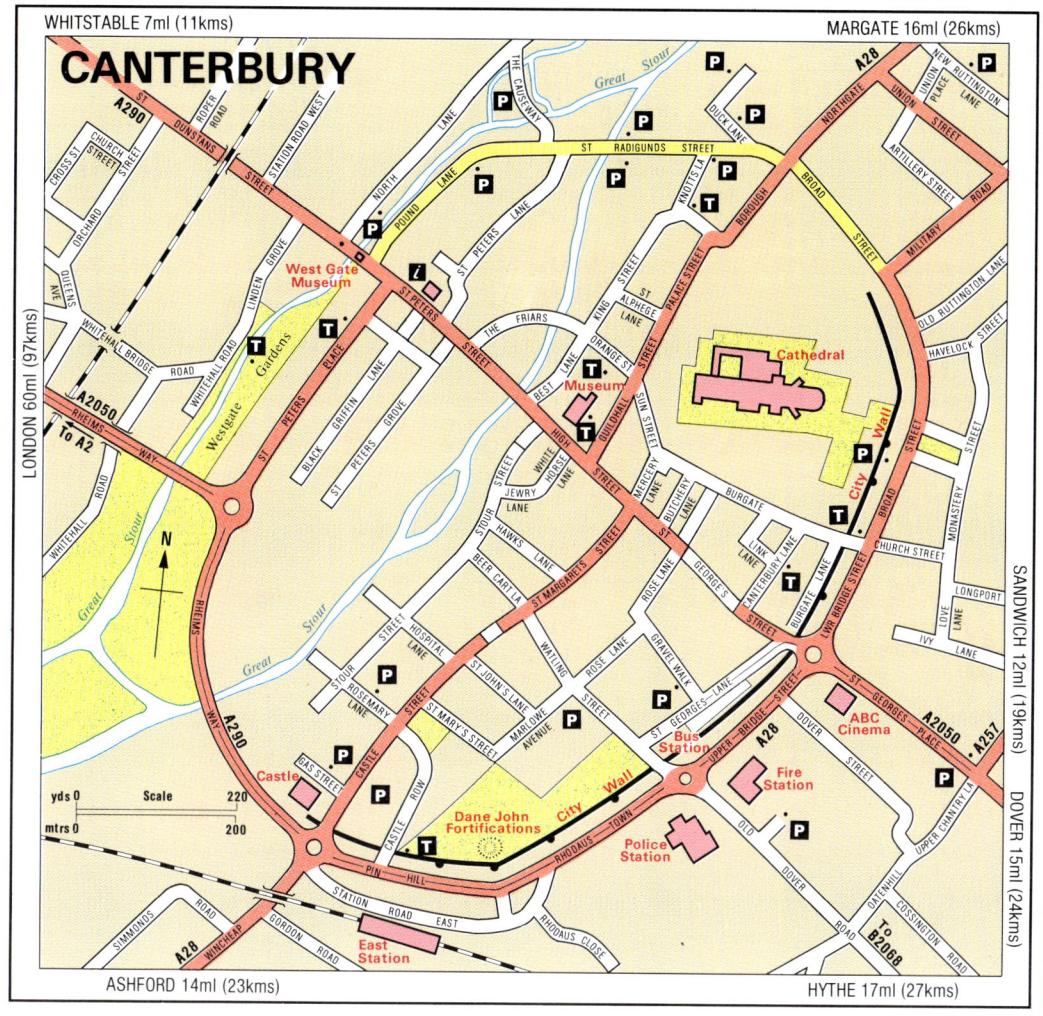

Cleobury North	**58**	4D
Clevedon	**52**	2F
Cley-next-the-Sea	**61**	7G
Cliffe (Kent)	**55**	7F
Cliffe (N. Yorks)	**64**	4E
Clifton (Avon)	**52**	3F
Clifton (Cumbria)	**67**	8E
Clifton (Northumb)	**69**	6E
Clifton-on-Teme	**58**	4C
Cliftonville	**55**	10E
Climping	**54**	3B
Clitheroe	**63**	9G
Clola	**77**	6F
Clophill	**60**	2B
Closworth	**52**	3B
Clough	**68**	4A
Cloughton	**69**	10A
Clova	**76**	3C
Clovelly	**51**	6F
Clovenfords	**73**	6C
Clowne	**64**	3B
Clows Top	**58**	4D
Cluanie	**75**	6D
Clun	**57**	9F
Clydach	**57**	6B
Clydebank	**71**	8D
Clynder	**71**	7E
Clynnogfawr	**62**	2C
Clyro	**57**	9D
Clyst Honiton	**51**	9D
Clyst St Mary	**51**	9D
Coalhall	**71**	8B
Coalville	**59**	8F
Coatbridge	**72**	2D
Cobham (Kent)	**55**	6E
Cobham (Surrey)	**54**	4E
Cockburnspath	**73**	7E
Cockermouth	**67**	6E
Cockfosters	**54**	4G
Cocking	**54**	2C
Cockshutt	**63**	7B
Codford	**52**	5D
Codicote	**60**	3A
Codnor	**64**	3A
Codsall	**58**	5E
Coedpoeth	**63**	6C
Coggeshall	**61**	6A
Colchester	**61**	7A
Cold Ashby	**59**	9D
Coldingham	**73**	8D
Cold Norton	**55**	7G
Coldstream	**73**	7C
Coleford	**58**	3A
Cole Green	**60**	3A
Colesbourne	**58**	6A
Coleshill	**59**	7E
Colintraive	**70**	5E
Collaton St Mary	**51**	8C
Colliers End	**60**	4A
Collieston	**77**	6E
Collin	**67**	6G
Collingbourne Ducis	**53**	6E
Collingham	**64**	3C
Colmonell	**66**	1G
Colne	**63**	9G
Colney Heath	**54**	4G
Colpy	**76**	4F
Colsterworth	**60**	2F
Coltishall	**61**	8F
Colwyn Bay	**62**	4D
Colyton	**52**	1B
Combe Martin	**51**	7G
Compton	**54**	3D
Comrie	**72**	2G
Congleton	**63**	9C
Congresbury	**52**	2E
Coningsby	**65**	7A
Conington	**60**	3D
Conisbrough	**64**	3C
Coniston	**67**	7C
Connah's Quay	**63**	6D
Connel	**74**	5A
Conon Bridge	**75**	8G
Consett	**69**	6D
Contin	**75**	8G
Conwy	**62**	4D
Cooden Beach	**55**	7B
Cookham	**54**	2F
Coolham	**54**	4C

Catrine	**71**	8B	Chawleigh	**51**	8E	Chirnside	**73**	8D
Catsfield	**55**	7B	Cheadle	**59**	6G	Chiseldon	**53**	6F
Catterick	**69**	6A	Cheddar	**52**	2E	Chitterne	**52**	5D
Catterick Camp	**69**	6A	Cheddleton	**63**	10C	Chobham	**54**	3E
Caunton	**64**	4A	Chedington	**52**	2B	Cholderton	**53**	6D
Causewayhead	**72**	2F	Chelford	**63**	9D	Chorley	**63**	8F
Causey Park	**69**	6F	Chell	**63**	9C	Chorleywood	**54**	3G
Cavendish	**61**	6B	Chellaston	**59**	7G	Christchurch (Dorset)	**52**	6B
Caversham	**53**	9F	Chelmsford	**55**	7G	Christchurch (Glos)	**58**	3A
Cawdor	**75**	10F	Chelsham	**54**	5E	Chudleigh	**51**	8D
Cawsand	**51**	6B	Cheltenham	**58**	5A	Chudleigh Knighton	**51**	8D
Cawston	**61**	8F	Chepstow	**52**	3G	Churchbridge	**63**	10A
Caxton	**60**	4C	Cherhill	**52**	5F	Churchill (Avon)	**52**	2E
Caythorpe	**64**	5A	Cheriton	**53**	8C	Churchill (Oxon)	**59**	7A
Cayton	**65**	6G	Chertsey	**54**	3E	Church Stoke	**57**	9G
Cemaes Bay	**62**	2E	Chesham	**54**	3G	Church Stretton	**58**	3E
Cemmaes Road	**62**	4A	Cheshunt	**54**	5G	Churston Ferrers	**51**	9B
Ceres	**72**	5G	Chester	**63**	7D	Churt	**54**	2D
Cerne Abbas	**52**	3B	Chesterfield	**64**	2B	Cilgerran	**56**	3D
Cerrigydrudion	**62**	5C	Chew Magna	**52**	3E	Cinderford	**58**	4A
Chaddesley Corbett	**58**	5D	Chicheley	**60**	2B	Cirencester	**52**	5G
Chadwick End	**59**	7D	Chichester	**54**	2B	Clabhach	**74**	2B
Chale	**53**	7A	Chickerell	**52**	3A	Clachaig	**71**	6E
Chalfont St Giles	**54**	3F	Chicklade	**52**	5D	Clachan	**70**	4D
Chalfont St Peter	**54**	3F	Chiddingfold	**54**	3D	Clacton-on-Sea	**61**	8A
Challacombe	**51**	7G	Chideock	**52**	2B	Cladich	**71**	6G
Challock	**55**	8D	Chigwell	**54**	5F	Claggan	**74**	4A
Chandler's Ford	**53**	7C	Chilcompton	**52**	3E	Clanfield	**53**	6G
Chapel End	**59**	7E	Chillington	**51**	8B	Claonaig	**70**	5D
Chapel-en-le-Frith	**64**	1B	Chilmark	**52**	5D	Clapham (Beds)	**60**	2C
Chapelhall	**72**	2D	Chilton Foliat	**53**	7F	Clapham (N. Yorks)	**67**	9B
Chapmanslade	**52**	4D	Chilwell	**59**	8G	Clare	**61**	6B
Chard	**52**	2B	Chingford	**54**	5F	Clashmore	**79**	7C
Charing	**55**	8D	Chinnor	**53**	9G	Clashnessie	**78**	3E
Charlbury	**59**	7A	Chippenham (Cambs)	**60**	5C	Clavering	**60**	4B
Charlestown	**50**	4B	Chippenham (Wilts)	**52**	5F	Clawton	**51**	6E
Charlton Kings	**58**	5A	Chipping Campden	**59**	6B	Clay Cross	**64**	2A
Charlton Marshall	**52**	4B	Chipping Norton	**59**	7B	Claydon	**61**	8B
Charlwood	**54**	4D	Chipping Sodbury	**52**	4F	Cleator Moor	**67**	6D
Charmouth	**52**	2B	Chipping Warden	**59**	8C	Cleethorpes	**65**	7D
Chatham	**55**	7E	Chipstead	**54**	4E	Cleeve	**52**	2E
Chatteris	**60**	4D	Chirbury	**57**	9G	Cleeve Hill	**58**	5A
Chatton	**73**	9C	Chirk	**63**	6B	Cleobury Mortimer	**58**	4D

Coombe Bissett......**53**......*6C*
Coombe Hill......**58**......*5B*
Copdock......**61**......*8B*
Copplestone......**51**......*8E*
Copthorne......**54**......*5D*
Corbridge......**68**......*5D*
Corby......**60**......*1D*
Corby Glen......**60**......*2F*
Corfe......**52**......*1C*
Corfe Castle......**52**......*5A*
Corgarff......**76**......*2D*
Corhampton......**53**......*8C*
Cornhill-on-Tweed......**73**......*8C*
Corpach......**75**......*6C*
Corrie......**70**......*5C*
Corris......**62**......*4A*
Corsham......**52**......*4E*
Corsock......**66**......*4G*
Corston......**52**......*5F*
Corstorphine......**72**......*4E*
Cortachy......**76**......*3B*
Corwen......**62**......*5B*
Coryton......**55**......*7F*
Cosford......**63**......*9A*
Cosham......**53**......*8B*
Coshieville......**75**......*10A*
Costessey......**61**......*8F*
Cotebrook......**63**......*8D*
Cotherstone......**68**......*5B*
Cottenham......**60**......*4C*
Cottered......**60**......*4A*
Cottesmore......**60**......*1F*
Cottingham......**65**......*6E*
Coughton......**59**......*6C*
Coulport......**71**......*6E*
Coulsdon......**54**......*5E*
Coupar Angus......**76**......*2A*
Cove......**78**......*2C*
Coventry......**59**......*7D*
Coverack......**50**......*3A*
Cowbit......**60**......*3F*
Cowbridge......**57**......*8A*
Cowes......**53**......*7B*
Cowfold......**54**......*4C*
Cowley......**53**......*8G*
Cowling......**63**......*10G*
Coylton......**71**......*7B*
Coylumbridge......**75**......*10D*
Crackington Haven......**50**......*5E*
Crafthole......**51**......*6B*
Craigellachie......**76**......*2F*
Craighouse......**70**......*3D*
Craigmillar......**72**......*5E*
Craigneish......**66**......*2B*
Craignure......**74**......*4A*
Craigrothie......**72**......*5G*
Crail......**73**......*6G*
Crailing......**73**......*7B*
Cramlington......**69**......*6E*
Cramond......**72**......*4E*
Cranage......**63**......*9D*
Cranborne......**52**......*5C*
Cranbrook......**55**......*7D*
Cranham......**58**......*5A*
Cranleigh......**54**......*3D*
Cranshaws......**73**......*7D*
Cranwell......**65**......*6A*
Crarae......**70**......*5F*
Crask......**79**......*6E*
Crathorne......**69**......*7B*
Craven Arms......**58**......*3D*
Crawford......**72**......*3B*
Crawfordjohn......**72**......*3B*
Crawley......**54**......*4D*
Creagorry......**78**......*1E*
Credenhill......**58**......*3B*
Crediton......**51**......*8E*
Creetown......**66**......*3F*
Cressage......**58**......*3E*
Crewe......**63**......*9C*
Crewkerne......**52**......*2B*
Crianlarich......**71**......*7G*
Criccieth......**62**......*2B*
Crich......**64**......*2A*
Crick......**59**......*8D*
Crickhowell......**57**......*9C*
Cricklade......**52**......*5G*
Crieff......**72**......*3G*
Crinan......**70**......*4F*

Cringleford......**61**......*8E*
Crocketford......**66**......*5G*
Croesyceiliog......**52**......*2G*
Croglin......**67**......*8F*
Cromarty......**79**......*7B*
Cromdale......**76**......*1E*
Cromer (Herts)......**60**......*4A*
Cromer (Norfolk)......**61**......*8G*
Cromford......**64**......*2A*
Crook......**69**......*6C*
Crooklands......**67**......*8B*
Crook of Devon......**72**......*4F*
Croome D'Abitot......**58**......*5B*
Cropton......**69**......*9A*
Crosby......**66**......*2B*
Cross Bush......**54**......*3B*
Crossford......**72**......*2D*
Cross Foxes......**62**......*4A*
Cross Gates......**57**......*8F*
Cross Hands......**56**......*5C*
Crosshill......**71**......*7A*
Cross Hills......**63**......*10G*
Cross-in-Hand......**55**......*6C*
Crosshouse......**71**......*7C*
Cross Keys......**57**......*9B*
Crossmichael......**66**......*4G*
Crossway Green......**58**......*5D*
Crosthwaite......**67**......*8C*
Crowborough......**55**......*6C*
Crowland......**60**......*3E*
Crowlas......**50**......*2A*
Crowle......**64**......*4D*
Crown Hill......**51**......*6C*
Crowthorne......**54**......*2E*
Croxton Kerrial......**60**......*1F*
Croy......**75**......*10F*
Croyde......**51**......*6G*
Cruden Bay......**77**......*6F*
Crudgington......**63**......*8A*
Crudwell......**52**......*5G*
Crugybar......**57**......*6D*
Crynant......**57**......*6C*
Cuckfield......**54**......*5C*
Cuckney......**64**......*3B*
Cuffley......**54**......*5G*
Culgaith......**67**......*9E*
Cullen......**76**......*4G*
Cullompton......**51**......*9E*
Culross......**72**......*3F*
Culswick......**77**......*9E*
Culter......**72**......*3C*
Cults......**76**......*5D*
Cumbernauld......**72**......*2E*
Cuminestown......**76**......*5G*
Cummertrees......**67**......*6G*
Cummingstown......**76**......*2G*
Cumnock......**71**......*8B*
Cumnor......**53**......*7G*
Cumrew......**67**......*8F*
Cupar......**72**......*5G*
Curry Rivel......**52**......*2C*
Cwmbran......**57**......*9B*
Cwm-y-Glo......**62**......*3C*
Cwmystwyth......**57**......*6F*
Cyfronydd......**63**......*6A*
Cymmer......**57**......*7B*
Cynwyl Elfed......**56**......*4D*

D

Dagenham......**54**......*5F*
Dailly......**71**......*7A*
Dairsie......**72**......*5G*
Dalbeattie......**66**......*5F*
Dalby......**66**......*2B*
Dale......**56**......*2C*
Dallas......**76**......*2G*
Dalmally......**71**......*6G*
Dalmellington......**71**......*8A*
Dalry (St John's town of)......**66**......*4G*
Dalry......**71**......*7C*
Dalrymple......**71**......*7B*
Dalston......**67**......*7F*
Dalton......**67**......*6G*
Dalton-in-Furness......**67**......*7B*
Dalwhinnie......**75**......*9C*
Damerham......**53**......*6C*
Danbury......**55**......*7G*

Darley Dale......**64**......*2A*
Darlington......**69**......*6B*
Darrington......**64**......*3D*
Darsham......**61**......*9C*
Dartford......**55**......*6E*
Dartmouth......**51**......*8B*
Darvel......**71**......*8C*
Darwen......**63**......*9F*
Datchet......**54**......*3F*
Dava......**76**......*1F*
Davenham......**63**......*8D*
Daventry......**59**......*8C*
Dawley......**63**......*8A*
Dawlish......**51**......*9C*
Deal......**55**......*10D*
Debenham......**61**......*8C*
Deddington......**59**......*8B*
Dedham......**61**......*7B*
Deepdale......**67**......*10B*
Deeping St James......**60**......*3E*
Deganwy......**62**......*4D*
Delabole......**50**......*4D*
Denbigh......**62**......*5D*
Denham......**54**......*3F*
Denholm......**73**......*6B*
Denmead......**53**......*8C*
Dennington......**61**......*8C*
Denny......**72**......*2E*
Densole......**55**......*9D*
Denton......**63**......*10E*
Derby......**59**......*7G*
Derbyhaven......**66**......*2B*
Dereham......**61**......*7F*
Dersingham......**60**......*5F*
Dervaig......**74**......*3A*
Desborough......**60**......*1D*
Desford......**59**......*8E*
Devil's Bridge......**57**......*6F*
Devizes......**52**......*5E*
Devonport......**51**......*6B*
Devoran......**50**......*3B*
Dewsbury......**64**......*2D*
Diabaig......**74**......*5G*
Dial Post......**54**......*4C*
Dibden Purlieu......**53**......*7B*
Didcot......**53**......*8F*
Didmarton......**52**......*4F*
Digby......**65**......*6A*
Dilwyn......**58**......*3C*
Dinas......**56**......*3D*
Dinas Mawddwy......**62**......*4A*
Dinas Powis......**57**......*8A*
Dingwall......**75**......*9G*
Dinnet......**76**......*3D*
Dippen......**70**......*4C*
Dirleton......**73**......*6E*
Disley......**63**......*10E*
Diss......**61**......*8D*
Distington......**67**......*6D*
Ditchling......**54**......*5C*
Dobwalls......**50**......*5C*
Docking......**61**......*6G*
Doddington (Cambs)......**60**......*4D*
Doddington (Northumb)......**73**......*8C*
Dolgellau......**62**......*4A*
Dollar......**72**......*3F*
Dolton......**51**......*7E*
Dolwyddelan......**62**......*4C*
Dolywern......**63**......*6B*
Doncaster......**64**......*3C*
Donington......**60**......*3G*
Donnington......**63**......*9A*
Dorchester (Dorset)......**52**......*3B*
Dorchester (Oxon)......**53**......*8G*
Dordon......**59**......*7E*
Dores......**75**......*9E*
Dorking......**54**......*4D*
Dornie......**74**......*5E*
Dornoch......**79**......*7C*
Dornock......**67**......*7G*
Dorrington......**58**......*3E*
Dorstone......**58**......*2B*
Douglas (I. of M.)......**66**......*3B*
Douglas (Strath)......**72**......*2C*
Doune......**72**......*2F*
Dousland......**51**......*7C*
Dover......**55**......*10D*
Dovercourt......**61**......*8B*

Doveridge......**59**......*6G*
Dowally......**76**......*1A*
Dowlais......**57**......*8C*
Downderry......**51**......*6B*
Downham Market......**60**......*5E*
Downside......**52**......*3E*
Downton......**53**......*6C*
Drakes Broughton......**58**......*5C*
Draycott......**52**......*2E*
Drayton (Norfolk)......**61**......*8F*
Drayton (Oxon)......**53**......*7G*
Dreghorn......**71**......*7C*
Drigg......**67**......*6C*
Droitwich......**58**......*5C*
Dronfield......**64**......*2B*
Droxford......**53**......*8C*
Drumbeg......**78**......*4E*
Drummore......**66**......*1E*
Drumnadrochit......**75**......*8E*
Drybrook......**58**......*4A*
Drynoch......**74**......*3E*
Duddington......**60**......*2E*
Duddon Bridge......**67**......*7C*
Dudley......**58**......*5E*
Dudleston Heath......**63**......*7B*
Duffield......**59**......*7G*
Dufftown......**76**......*3F*
Duffus......**76**......*2G*
Duirinish......**74**......*5E*
Dulnain Bridge......**76**......*1E*
Dulverton......**51**......*9F*
Dumbarton......**71**......*7E*
Dumfries......**67**......*6G*
Dunbar......**73**......*7E*
Dunbeath......**79**......*9E*
Dunblane......**72**......*2F*
Dunchurch......**59**......*8D*
Dundee......**76**......*3A*
Dundonald......**71**......*7C*
Dundonnell......**78**......*4C*
Dundrennan......**66**......*4F*
Dunfermline......**72**......*4F*
Dungeon Ghyll......**67**......*7D*
Dunhampton......**58**......*5C*
Dunipace......**72**......*2E*
Dunkeld......**76**......*1A*
Dunnet......**79**......*9G*
Dunning......**72**......*3G*
Dunoon......**71**......*6E*
Dunragit......**66**......*1F*
Duns......**73**......*7D*
Dunscore......**66**......*5G*
Dunsfold......**54**......*3D*
Dunskeath......**79**......*7B*
Dunstable......**60**......*2A*
Dunster......**51**......*9G*
Dunsville......**64**......*4D*
Duntish......**52**......*3B*
Duntulm......**74**......*3G*
Dunure......**71**......*7B*
Dunvegan......**74**......*2F*
Dunwich......**61**......*9C*
Durham......**69**......*6C*
Durness......**78**......*5G*
Duror......**75**......*6B*
Dursley......**52**......*4G*
Dyce......**76**......*5E*
Dyffryn Ardudwy......**62**......*3A*
Dymchurch......**55**......*9C*
Dymock......**58**......*4B*
Dysart......**72**......*5F*

E

Eaglesfield......**67**......*7G*
Earby......**67**......*10A*
Eardisland......**58**......*3C*
Eardisley......**58**......*2C*
Earith......**60**......*4D*
Earley......**53**......*9F*
Earls Barton......**60**......*1C*
Earl's Colne......**61**......*6A*
Earlsferry......**73**......*6F*
Earl Shilton......**59**......*8E*
Earlston......**73**......*6C*
Earsham......**61**......*9D*
Easdale......**70**......*4G*
Easebourne......**54**......*3C*
Easington......**65**......*8D*

Easingwold.................**64**......*3G*
East Ayton...................**64**......*5G*
East Barkwith..............**65**......*6B*
Eastbourne..................**55**......*6B*
East Bridgford.............**59**......*9G*
East Chinnock.............**52**......*3C*
Eastchurch..................**55**......*8E*
East Cowes..................**53**......*8B*
East Croachy ....**75**......*9E*
Eastdean.....................**55**......*6B*
East Grinstead.............**54**......*5D*
Eastham......................**63**......*7D*
East Hoathly...............**55**......*6C*
East Horndon..............**55**......*6F*
East Horsley................**54**......*3D*
East Knoyle.................**52**......*4C*
Eastleigh.....................**53**......*7C*
East Linton..................**73**......*6E*
East Lulworth..............**52**......*4A*
East Lyng....................**52**......*2C*
Eastoke.......................**53**......*9B*
Easton.........................**52**......*3A*
East Preston................**54**......*3B*
Eastriggs.....................**67**......*7G*
East Rudham...............**61**......*6F*
Eastry..........................**55**......*10D*
East Saltoun................**73**......*6E*
East Stoke...................**64**......*4A*
East Wittering.............**54**......*2B*
East Witton..................**69**......*6A*
Eastwood (Essex)........**55**......*7F*
Eastwood (Notts).........**59**......*8G*
Eathorpe.....................**59**......*7D*
Eaton Socon ....**60**......*3C*
Ebbw Vale..................**57**......*8C*
Ebchester....................**68**......*5D*
Ebley...........................**52**......*4G*
Ecclefechan................**67**......*7G*
Eccles.........................**73**......*7C*
Eccleshall....................**63**......*9B*
Echt.............................**76**......*5D*
Eckington (Derbys).......**64**......*3B*
Eckington (Herefs
  & Worcs)...............**58**......*5B*

Edderton.....................**79**......*7C*
Eddleston....................**72**......*5C*
Edenbridge..................**54**......*5D*
Edensor.......................**64**......*2B*
Edgbaston...................**59**......*6D*
Edgmond.....................**63**......*9A*
Edinbane.....................**74**......*2F*
Edinburgh....................**72**......*5E*
Edmondbyers...............**68**......*5D*
Ednam.........................**73**......*7C*
Ednaston.....................**59**......*7G*
Edwalton.....................**59**......*9G*
Edwinstowe.................**64**......*4A*
Edzell..........................**76**......*4B*
Effingham....................**54**......*4D*
Eggesford....................**51**......*7E*
Egglestone..................**68**......*5B*
Egham.........................**54**......*3E*
Eglingham...................**73**......*9B*
Eglwysfach..................**57**......*6G*
Eglwyswrw...................**56**......*3D*
Egremont.....................**67**......*6D*
Elan.............................**57**......*7F*
Elgin............................**76**......*2G*
Elgol...........................**74**......*3D*
Elham..........................**55**......*9D*
Elie..............................**73**......*6F*
Elkesley.......................**64**......*4B*
Elkstone......................**58**......*5A*
Elland..........................**64**......*1D*
Ellesmere.....................**63**......*7B*
Ellesmere Port.............**63**......*7D*
Ellingham....................**61**......*9E*
Ellon...........................**77**......*6F*
Elloughton...................**64**......*5D*
Elmstead Market..........**61**......*7A*
Elrick...........................**76**......*5D*
Elsdon.........................**68**......*5F*
Elsham........................**65**......*6D*
Elsrickle......................**72**......*4C*
Elstead........................**54**......*3D*
Elstree.........................**54**......*4G*
Elterwater...................**67**......*7D*
Eltisley.......................**60**......*3C*

Elton (Cambs).............**60**......*2E*
Elton (Glos).................**58**......*4A*
Elveden.......................**61**......*6D*
Elvington.....................**64**......*4E*
Elworthy......................**51**......*9F*
Ely (Cambs)................**60**......*5D*
Ely (S. Glam)..............**57**......*8A*
Embleton.....................**73**......*9B*
Embo...........................**79**......*7C*
Empingham..................**60**......*2E*
Emsworth.....................**53**......*9B*
Enfield.........................**54**......*5G*
Englefield Green...........**54**......*3E*
Enstone.......................**59**......*7A*
Epping.........................**54**......*5G*
Epping Forest...............**54**......*5G*
Epsom.........................**54**......*4E*
Epworth.......................**64**......*4C*
Erdington.....................**59**......*6E*
Eriboll..........................**78**......*5F*
Erith............................**55**......*6F*
Errogie........................**75**......*9E*
Errol............................**72**......*5G*
Erwood........................**57**......*8D*
Esher...........................**54**......*4E*
Eskdale Green.............**67**......*6C*
Eskdalemuir Church......**72**......*5A*
Essendine....................**60**......*2F*
Essendon.....................**54**......*4G*
Etal.............................**73**......*8C*
Etchingham..................**55**......*7C*
Eton............................**54**......*3F*
Ettington.....................**59**......*7C*
Ettrickbridge................**72**......*5B*
Evanton.......................**79**......*6B*
Evercreech...................**52**......*3D*
Everleigh.....................**53**......*6E*
Eversley......................**53**......*9E*
Evesham......................**59**......*6B*
Evington......................**59**......*9E*
Ewell...........................**54**......*4E*
Ewelme.......................**53**......*8G*
Ewhurst.......................**54**......*3D*
Ewyas Harold...............**58**......*2B*

Exebridge....................**51**......*9F*
Exeter..........................**51**......*9D*
Exford..........................**51**......*8G*
Exminster....................**51**......*9D*
Exmouth......................**51**......*9D*
Eyam...........................**64**......*2B*
Eye..............................**61**......*8D*
Eyemouth.....................**73**......*8D*
Eynsford......................**55**......*6E*
Eynsham.....................**59**......*8A*

F

Failsworth....................**63**......*9E*
Fairbourne...................**62**......*3A*
Fairford........................**53**......*6G*
Fairlie..........................**71**......*6D*
Fairmile.......................**51**......*9D*
Fairy Bridge.................**74**......*2F*
Fakenham....................**61**......*7F*
Faldingworth................**65**......*6B*
Falfield........................**52**......*3G*
Falkirk.........................**72**......*3E*
Falkland......................**72**......*5G*
Fallin...........................**72**......*2F*
Falmer.........................**54**......*5B*
Falmouth......................**50**......*3A*
Fareham.......................**53**......*8B*
Faringdon.....................**53**......*6G*
Farnborough.................**54**......*2D*
Farncombe...................**54**......*3D*
Farne Islands...............**73**......*9C*
Farnell.........................**76**......*4B*
Farnham.......................**54**......*2D*
Farnham Common.........**54**......*3F*
Farningham..................**55**......*6E*
Far Sawrey...................**67**......*8C*
Farthinghoe..................**59**......*8B*
Fauldhouse...................**72**......*3D*
Faversham....................**55**......*8E*
Fawley.........................**53**......*7B*
Fazeley........................**59**......*7E*
Fearnan........................**75**......*9A*
Felixstowe....................**61**......*9B*
Felpham.......................**54**......*3B*
Felsted.........................**60**......*5A*
Felton...........................**73**......*9A*
Feltwell........................**61**......*6E*
Fenny Bentley ....**64**......*1A*
Fenny Bridges ....**51**......*10E*
Fenny Drayton.............**59**......*7E*
Fenny Stratford............**60**......*1B*
Feolin Ferry.................**70**......*3D*
Ferness........................**76**......*1F*
Fernhill Heath..............**58**......*5C*
Fernilee.......................**63**......*10D*
Fernhurst.....................**54**......*2C*
Ferring.........................**54**......*3B*
Fettercairn...................**76**......*4C*
Ffestiniog....................**62**......*4B*
Filby............................**61**......*9F*
Filey............................**65**......*6G*
Fincham.......................**60**......*5E*
Finchingfield................**60**......*5B*
Findhorn......................**76**......*1G*
Findochty.....................**76**......*3G*
Findon.........................**54**......*4B*
Finedon........................**60**......*2D*
Finningham..................**61**......*7C*
Finstown......................**77**......*8B*
Fionphort.....................**70**......*2G*
Fishbourne...................**53**......*8B*
Fishguard.....................**56**......*2D*
Fishnish.......................**74**......*4A*
Fittleworth....................**54**......*3C*
Fladdabister.................**77**......*10E*
Flamborough................**65**......*7G*
Flamstead....................**60**......*2A*
Flax Bourton................**52**......*3E*
Fleet............................**54**......*2D*
Fleetwood....................**67**......*7A*
Flimby.........................**67**......*6E*
Flint............................**63**......*6D*
Flitwick.......................**60**......*2B*
Flixton.........................**65**......*6G*
Flore...........................**59**......*9C*
Fochabers....................**76**......*3G*
Foel.............................**62**......*2D*
Folkestone....................**55**......*9D*

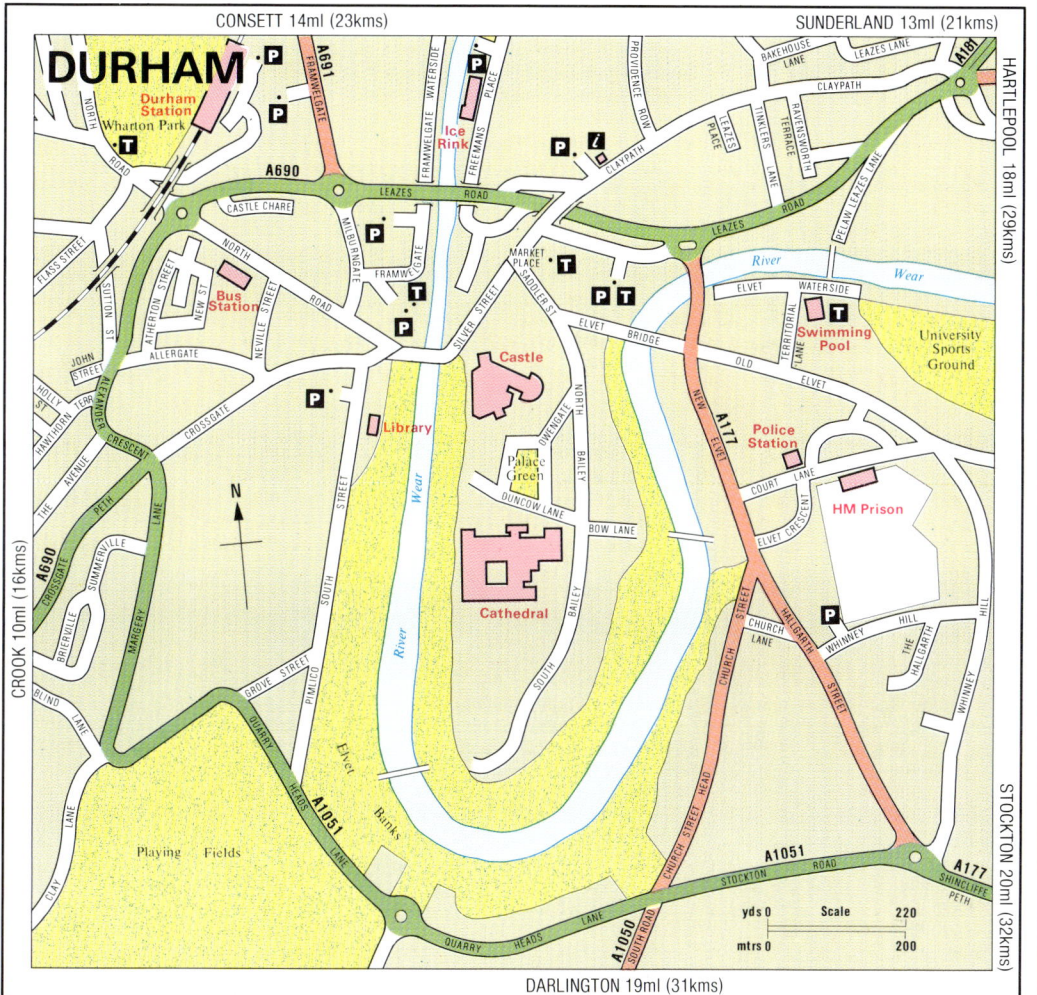

Folkingham **60** *2G*
Fontmell Magna **52** *4C*
Fontwell **54** *3B*
Ford (Northumb) **73** *8C*
Ford (Salop) **63** *7A*
Ford (Strath) **70** *5F*
Fordcombe **55** *6D*
Forden **57** *9G*
Fordoun **76** *5C*
Forfar **76** *3B*
Fordingbridge **53** *6C*
Fordwich **55** *9E*
Forest Row **54** *5C*
Forres **76** *1G*
Forse **79** *9E*
Forsinard **79** *8F*
Fort Augustus **75** *8D*
Forteviot **72** *4G*
Fort George **75** *10G*
Forth **72** *3D*
Fortingall **75** *9A*
Forton **67** *8A*
Fortrose **75** *9G*
Fortuneswell **52** *3A*
Fort William **75** *6B*
Fossebridge **59** *6A*
Foston (Derbys) **59** *6G*
Foston (Lincs) **60** *1G*
Four Crosses **63** *6A*
Four Marks **53** *8D*
Fowey **50** *5B*
Fownhope **58** *3B*
Foxdale **66** *2B*
Foyers **75** *8E*
Fraddon **50** *4C*
Framlingham **61** *8C*
Frampton **52** *3B*
Frant **55** *6D*
Fraserburgh **77** *6G*
Freckenham **60** *5D*
Frenchville **64** *3B*
Freshwater **53** *7A*
Fressingfield **61** *8D*
Freswick **79** *10G*
Fridaythorpe **64** *5F*
Frilford **53** *7G*
Frimley **54** *2E*
Frinton-on-Sea **61** *8A*
Friockheim **76** *4B*
Friog **62** *3A*
Fritton **61** *9E*
Frizington **67** *6D*
Frocester **52** *4G*
Frodsham **63** *8D*
Frome **52** *4D*
Froxfield **53** *6E*
Fulford **64** *4F*
Funtington **53** *9B*
Funzie **77** *10F*
Furnace **70** *5F*
Furnace End **59** *7E*
Furness Vale **63** *10D*
Fyfield (Essex) **55** *6G*
Fyfield (Oxon) **53** *7G*
Fyvie **76** *5F*

G

Gailey **63** *10A*
Gainford **69** *6B*
Gainsborough **64** *5C*
Gairloch **78** *2B*
Gairlochy **75** *7C*
Galashiels **73** *6C*
Galston **71** *8C*
Gamlingay **60** *3C*
Gamston **64** *4B*
Garboldisham **61** *7D*
Garelochhead **71** *6F*
Gargrave **67** *10A*
Garlieston **66** *3F*
Garlogie **76** *5D*
Garstang **63** *7G*
Garston **54** *4G*
Garth (Mid Glam) **57** *7B*
Garth (Powys) **57** *7E*
Garthmyl **57** *8G*
Garvault Hotel **79** *7E*
Gatehouse of Fleet **66** *4F*
Gateshead **69** *6D*
Gaydon **59** *7C*
Gayton **61** *6F*
Geary **74** *2G*
Geddington **60** *1D*
Gedney Drove End **60** *4F*
Georgeham **51** *6G*
Gerrards Cross **54** *3F*
Gidea Park **55** *6F*
Gifford **73** *6E*
Gilling East **64** *4G*
Gillingham (Dorset) **52** *4C*
Gillingham (Kent) **55** *7E*
Gillingham (Norfolk) **61** *9E*
Gilling West **69** *6A*
Gills **79** *10G*
Gilmerton **72** *3G*
Gilsland **67** *9G*
Gilwern **57** *9C*
Girvan **71** *6A*
Gisburn **67** *10A*
Glamis **76** *3A*
Glan Conwy **62** *4D*
Glangrwyney **57** *9C*
Glanrafon **62** *5B*
Glapwell **64** *3A*
Glasbury **57** *8D*
Glasgow **71** *8D*
Glaston **60** *1E*
Glastonbury **52** *3D*
Glemsford **61** *6B*
Glenbarr **70** *4C*
Glenbarry **76** *4G*
Glenborrodale **74** *4B*
Glencaple **67** *6G*
Glencarron Lodge **75** *6F*
Glencoe **75** *6B*
Glendaruel **70** *5E*
Glendevon **72** *3F*
Gleneagles Hotel **72** *3G*
Glenelg **74** *5E*
Glenfarg **72** *4G*
Glenfinnan **74** *5C*
Glenkindie **76** *3E*
Glenlivet **76** *2E*
Glenluce **66** *2F*
Glenmaye **66** *2B*
Glenridding **67** *8D*
Glenrothes **72** *5F*
Glenshee (Spittal of) **76** *2C*
Glentham **65** *6C*
Glossop **64** *1C*
Gloucester **58** *5A*
Gloup **77** *10G*
Glyn Ceiriog **63** *6B*
Glyncorrwg **57** *7B*
Glynde **54** *5B*
Glyn Neath **57** *7C*
Gnosall **63** *9A*
Gobowen **63** *7B*
Godalming **54** *3D*
Godmanchester **60** *3D*
Godshill (Hants) **53** *6C*
Godshill (I. of W.) **53** *8A*
Godstone **54** *5D*
Golspie **79** *7C*
Gomshall **54** *3D*
Goodmayes **54** *5F*
Goodrington **51** *8C*
Goodwick **56** *2D*
Goole **64** *4D*
Goosnargh **63** *8G*
Gordon **73** *7C*
Gordon Arms **72** *5B*
Gorebridge **72** *5D*
Goring-by-Sea **54** *4B*
Goring-on-Thames **53** *8F*
Gorleston-on-Sea **61** *10E*
Gorseinon **56** *5B*
Gosberton **60** *3G*
Gosberton Clough **60** *3F*
Gosforth (Cumbria) **67** *6C*
Gosforth (Tyne & Wear) **69** *6E*
Gosport **53** *8B*
Goudhurst **55** *7D*
Gourock **71** *7E*
Gowerton **56** *5B*
Goxhill **65** *6E*
Grain **55** *7F*
Grainthorpe **65** *7C*
Gramisdale **78** *1E*
Grampound **50** *4B*
Grandtully **75** *10A*
Grange-in-Borrowdale **67** *7D*
Grangemouth **72** *3E*
Grange-over-Sands **67** *8B*
Grantham **60** *2G*
Grantown-on-Spey **76** *1E*
Grantshouse **73** *7D*
Grassington **64** *1F*
Graveley **60** *3A*
Gravesend **55** *6E*
Grays **55** *6F*
Great Baddow **55** *7G*
Great Bardfield **60** *5A*
Great Barford **60** *3C*
Great Bircham **61** *6G*
Great Bookham **54** *4D*
Great Casterton **60** *2E*
Great Chesterford **60** *5B*
Great Crosby **63** *7E*
Great Dalby **59** *9F*
Great Driffield **65** *6F*
Great Dunmow **60** *5A*
Great Gidding **60** *3D*
Great Glen **59** *9E*
Great Gransden **60** *3C*
Greatham **53** *9C*
Great Haywood **63** *10A*
Great Kimble **54** *2G*
Great Langdale **67** *7D*
Great Malvern **58** *4B*
Great Missenden **54** *2G*
Great Offley **60** *3A*
Great Ponton **60** *2F*
Great Salkeld **67** *8E*
Great Sampford **60** *5B*
Great Saughall **63** *7D*
Great Shelford **60** *4C*
Great Smeaton **69** *7A*
Great Staughton **60** *3C*
Greatstone-on-Sea **55** *8C*
Great Tew **59** *7B*
Great Wakering **55** *8F*
Great Waltham **60** *5A*
Great Witley **58** *4C*
Great Yarmouth **61** *10E*
Great Yeldham **61** *6B*
Greenfield **63** *6D*
Green Hammerton **64** *3F*
Greenhead **67** *9G*
Greenlaw **73** *7C*
Greenloaning **72** *2G*
Greenock **71** *7E*
Greenodd **67** *7B*
Greetham **60** *2F*
Gresford **63** *7C*
Greta Bridge **68** *5B*
Gretna **67** *7G*
Gretna Green **67** *7G*
Greystoke **67** *8E*
Grimsby **65** *7D*
Grimsthorpe **60** *2F*
Grindleford Bridge **64** *2B*
Gringley-on-the-Hill **64** *4C*
Grogport **70** *4C*
Groombridge **55** *6D*
Grosmont **58** *3A*
Guard Bridge **73** *6G*
Guildford **54** *3D*
Guisborough **69** *8B*
Guiseley **64** *1E*
Guist **61** *7F*
Gullane **73** *6E*
Gunness **64** *5D*
Gunnislake **51** *6C*
Gunthorpe **59** *9G*
Gurnard **53** *7B*
Gutcher **77** *10G*
Guyhirne **60** *4E*
Guy's Cliffe **59** *7D*
Gwbert-on-Sea **56** *3E*
Gweek **50** *3A*
Gwernymynydd **63** *6C*
Gwithian **50** *2B*
Gwyddelwern **62** *5C*

H

Hackness **69** *10A*
Haddenham **60** *4D*
Haddington **73** *6E*
Haddiscoe **61** *9E*
Hadleigh (Essex) **55** *7F*
Hadleigh (Suffolk) **61** *7B*
Hadley Wood **54** *4G*
Hagworthingham **65** *7B*
Hailey **60** *4A*
Hailsham **55** *6B*
Hainault **54** *5F*
Halberton **51** *9E*
Hale **67** *8B*
Hales **61** *9E*
Halesowen **58** *5D*
Halesworth **61** *9D*
Halifax **64** *1D*
Halkirk **79** *9F*
Halland **54** *5C*
Hallow **58** *5C*
Hallworthy **50** *5D*
Halstead (Essex) **61** *6B*
Halstead (Kent) **54** *5E*
Halton **67** *8A*
Haltwhistle **68** *4D*
Halwell **51** *8B*
Halwill Junction **51** *6E*
Hamble **53** *7B*
Hambledon **53** *8C*
Hambleton **63** *7G*
Hamilton **72** *2D*
Hampstead Norreys **53** *8F*
Ham Street **55** *8C*
Handcross **54** *4C*
Handley **63** *7C*
Hankerton **52** *5G*
Hanley **63** *9C*
Happendon **72** *2C*
Happisburgh **61** *9G*
Harbertonford **51** *8B*
Harborne **59** *6D*
Hardwicke **58** *5A*
Hare Street **60** *4A*
Harewood **64** *2E*
Harewood End **58** *3A*
Harlech **62** *3B*
Harleston **61** *8D*
Harley **58** *3E*
Harlow **54** *5G*
Harlyn Bay **50** *3C*
Harold Wood **55** *6F*
Harpenden **60** *3A*
Harrington **67** *6E*
Harrogate **64** *2F*
Harston **60** *4B*
Hartburn **68** *5E*
Hartest **61** *6C*
Hartfield **54** *5D*
Hartington **64** *1A*
Hartland **50** *5F*
Hartlepool **69** *8C*
Hartley Wintney **53** *9E*
Hartpury **58** *4A*
Harvington **59** *6C*
Harwell **53** *7F*
Harwich **61** *8B*
Haslemere **54** *3C*
Hassocks **54** *4C*
Hastings **55** *7B*
Hatch Beauchamp **52** *2C*
Hatfield (Herts) **54** *4G*
Hatfield (S. Yorks) **64** *4D*
Hatfield Broad Oak **60** *5A*
Hatfield Heath **60** *5A*
Hatfield Peverel **61** *6A*
Hatherleigh **51** *7E*
Hathern **59** *8F*
Hathersage **64** *2B*
Hatton Heath **63** *7C*
Havant **53** *9B*
Haverfordwest **56** *2C*
Haverhill **60** *5B*
Hawarden **63** *7D*
Hawes **68** *4A*
Haweswater **67** *8D*
Hawick **73** *6B*
Hawkedon **61** *6C*

INDEX

Hawkhurst 55 7C
Hawkinge 55 9D
Hawkshead 67 7C
Haxey 64 4C
Haydon Bridge 68 4D
Hayle 50 2B
Hay-on-Wye 57 9D
Haywards Heath 54 5C
Hazel Grove 63 10E
Headcorn 55 7D
Heanor 59 8G
Heathfield 55 6C
Hebden 64 1F
Heckington 60 3G
Hednesford 63 10A
Hedon 65 6E
Helensburgh 71 7E
Hellifield 67 10A
Helmingham 61 8C
Helmsdale 79 8D
Helmsley 64 4G
Helpringham 60 3G
Helsby 63 7D
Helston 50 2A
Hemel Hempstead 54 3G
Hemingford Abbots 60 3D
Hempnall 61 8E
Hemsby 61 9F
Hendy 56 5B
Henfield 54 4C
Henley-in-Arden 59 6C
Henley-on-Thames 53 9F
Henllan 62 5D
Henlow 60 3B
Henshaw 68 4D
Henstead 61 9D
Henstridge 52 4C
Hereford 58 3B
Hermitage 53 8F
Herne 55 9E
Herne Bay 55 9E
Hersden 55 9E
Herstmonceux 55 6B
Hertford 60 4A
Hessle 65 6D
Heswall 63 6D
Hethersett 61 8E
Heversham 67 8B
Hexham 68 5D
Heysham 67 8A
Heysham Harbour 67 8A
Heytesbury 52 5D
Hibaldstow 64 5C
Hickstead 54 4C
Higham Ferrers 60 2C
Highampton 51 6E
High Blantyre 71 9D
Highbridge 52 2D
Highcliffe-on-Sea 53 6B
High Ercall 63 8A
Higher Heath 63 8B
High Halden 55 8D
Highley 58 4D
High Roding 60 5A
Highworth 53 6G
High Wycombe 54 2F
Hildenborough 55 6D
Hilgay 60 5E
Hill Brow 53 9C
Hillcommon 51 10F
Hillhead 53 8B
Hill of Fearn 79 7B
Hillswick 77 9F
Hilmarton 52 5F
Hilton 59 7G
Hinckley 59 8E
Hinderwell 69 9B
Hindhead 54 2D
Hindon 52 5D
Hingham 61 7E
Hirwaun 57 7C
Histon 60 4C
Hitcham 61 7C
Hitchin 60 3A
Hockham 61 7E
Hockliffe 60 2A
Hoddesdon 54 5G
Hodnet 63 8B
Hoghton 63 8G
Hog's Back 54 2D
Hogsthorpe 65 8B
Holbeach 60 4F
Holbrook 61 8B
Holbury 53 7B
Holcombe 51 9C
Holford 51 10G
Holland Arms 62 2D
Holland-on-Sea 61 8A
Hollingbourne 55 7E
Hollybush 71 7B
Holmbury St Mary 54 4D
Holmes Chapel 63 9D
Holme-upon-Spalding Moor 64 5E
Holmfirth 64 1D
Holmrook 67 6C
Holsworthy 51 6E
Holt (Cheshire) 63 7C
Holt (Norfolk) 61 7G
Holt (Wilts) 52 4E
Holt Heath 58 5C
Holton Heath 52 5B
Holybourne 53 9D
Holyhead 62 1D
Holy Island 73 9C
Holytown 72 2D
Holywell (Clwyd) 63 6D
Holywell (Dorset) 52 3B
Homersfield 61 8D
Honington 61 7D
Honiton 51 10E
Hook 53 9E
Hope 64 1B
Hopeman 76 2G
Hope-under-Dinmore 58 3C
Hopton-on-Sea 61 10E
Horam 55 6C
Horley 54 4D
Hornby 67 9B
Horncastle 65 7B
Horndean 53 9C
Horning 61 9F
Horns Cross 51 6F
Hornsea 65 6F
Horrabridge 51 7C
Horringer 61 6C
Horsey 61 9F
Horsforth 64 2E
Horsham 54 4C
Horsham St Faith 61 8F
Horsley 68 5D
Horton 52 2C
Horton-in-Ribblesdale 67 10B
Hoton 59 8F
Houghton St Giles 61 7G
Hove 54 4B
Hovingham 64 4G
Howden 64 4E
Howgate 72 5D
Hoxne 61 8D
Hoylake 63 6E
Hucknall 64 3A
Huddersfield 64 1D
Hull 65 6E
Humberston 65 7C
Humbie 73 6D
Hume 73 7C
Hungerford 53 7E
Hunstanton 60 5G
Hunters Quay 71 6E
Huntingdon 60 3D
Huntley 58 4A
Huntly 76 4F
Hurdlow 64 1A
Hurliness 77 8B
Hurn 53 6B
Hursley 53 7C
Hurst 53 9F
Hurstbourne Priors 53 7D
Hurstbourne Tarrant 53 7E
Hurst Green (Lancs) 63 8G
Hurst Green (Sussex) 55 7C
Hurstpierpoint 54 4C
Husbands Bosworth 59 9D
Husborne Crawley 60 2B
Husinish 78 2F
Hutton 55 6G
Hyde 63 10E
Hynish 74 1A
Hythe (Hants) 53 7B
Hythe (Kent) 55 9C

I

Ideford 51 8C
Ightham 55 6E
Ilchester 52 3C
Ilfracombe 51 7G
Ilkeston 59 8G
Ilkley 64 1E
Ilminster 52 2C
Immingham 65 6D
Immingham Dock 65 6E
Inchnadamph 78 4D
Indian Queens 50 4C
Ingatestone 55 6G
Ingham 64 5B
Ingleton 67 9B
Ingoldisthorpe 60 5G
Ingoldmells 65 8B
Inkberrow 59 6C
Innellan 71 6D
Innerleithen 72 5C
Insch 76 4E
Insh 75 10D
Instow 51 6F
Inverallochy 77 6G
Inveran 79 6C
Inveraray 71 6F
Inverbeg 71 7F
Inverbervie 76 5C
Inverey 76 1C
Inverfarigaig 75 8E
Invergarry 75 7D
Invergordon 79 7B
Invergowrie 76 3A
Inverinate 74 5E
Inverkeilor 76 4A
Inverkip 71 6E
Inverkirkaig 78 4D
Invermoriston 75 8E
Inverness 75 9F
Inversanda 74 5B
Invershiel 75 6E
Invershin 79 6C
Inversnaid 71 7F
Inverurie 76 5E
Iona 70 2G
Ipstones 63 10C
Ipswich 61 8B
Irchester 60 2C
Ireby 67 7E
Iron Acton 52 3F
Ironbridge 58 4E
Irthlingborough 60 2D
Irvine 71 7C
Isbister 77 9F
Isle of Whithorn 66 3E
Isle Ornsay 74 4D
Itchen Abbas 53 8D
Iver 54 3F
Ivetsey Bank 63 9A
Ivinghoe 60 2A
Ivybridge 51 7B
Ivychurch 55 8C
Iwade 55 7E
Iwerne Minster 52 4C
Ixworth 61 7D

J

Jarrow 69 7D
Jedburgh 73 7B
John O'Groats 79 10G
Johns Cross 55 7C
Johnshaven 76 5B
Johnston 56 2C
Johnstone Bridge 72 4A
Jordans 54 3F
Jurby 66 2C

K

Kames 70 5E
Kates Cabin 60 3E
Keelby 65 6D
Kegworth 59 8G
Keighley 64 1E
Keiss 79 10F
Keith 76 3G
Keld 68 4A
Keldholme 69 9A
Kelham 64 4A
Kelsale 61 9C
Kelsall 63 8D
Kelso 73 7C
Kelvedon 61 6A
Kemble 52 5G
Kemnay 76 5E
Kempsey 58 5C
Kempston 60 2B
Kendal 67 8C
Kenilworth 59 7D
Kenley 54 5E
Kenmore 75 10A
Kennacraig 70 4D
Kenninghall 61 7D
Kennington 55 8D
Kentallen 75 6B
Kentford 61 6C
Kenton 51 9D
Kentra 74 4B
Keoldale 78 5G
Kerne Bridge 58 3A
Kerry 57 8G
Kesgrave 61 8B
Kessingland 61 10D
Keswick 67 7D
Kettering 60 1D
Ketton 60 2E
Keynsham 52 3E
Key Street 55 7E
Keyston 60 2D
Kibworth Harcourt 59 9E
Kidderminster 58 5D
Kidsgrove 63 9C
Kidwelly 56 5C
Kielder 73 6A
Kilbarchan 71 7D
Kilberry 70 4D
Kilbirnie 71 7D
Kilbride 70 5G
Kilburn 59 7G
Kilchattan (Strath) 71 6D
Kilchatton (Strath) 70 2F
Kilchenzie 70 4B
Kilchoan 74 3B
Kilchrenan 70 5G
Kilcreggan 71 6E
Kildonan 79 8D
Kildrummy 76 3E
Kildwick 64 1E
Kilfinan 70 5E
Kilkhampton 50 5E
Killiecrankie 75 10B
Kilmacolm 71 7D
Kilmaluaig 74 3G
Kilmany 72 5G
Kilmarnock 71 7C
Kilmartin 70 4F
Kilmaurs 71 7C
Kilmelford 70 5G
Kilmichael 70 5F
Kilmorack 75 8F
Kilmory 70 5B
Kilninian 74 3A
Kilninver 70 4G
Kilnsea 65 8D
Kilrenny 73 6F
Kilsby 59 8D
Kilsyth 72 2E
Kilve 51 10G
Kilwinning 71 7C
Kimberley (Norfolk) 61 7E
Kimberley (Notts) 59 8G
Kimbolton 60 2C
Kinbrace 79 7E
Kincardine 79 6C
Kincardine-on-Forth 72 3F
Kincraig 75 10D
Kineton 59 7C
Kingsbarns 73 6G
Kingsbridge 51 8B
Kingsbury 59 7E
Kingsclere 53 8E
Kingsdon 52 3C

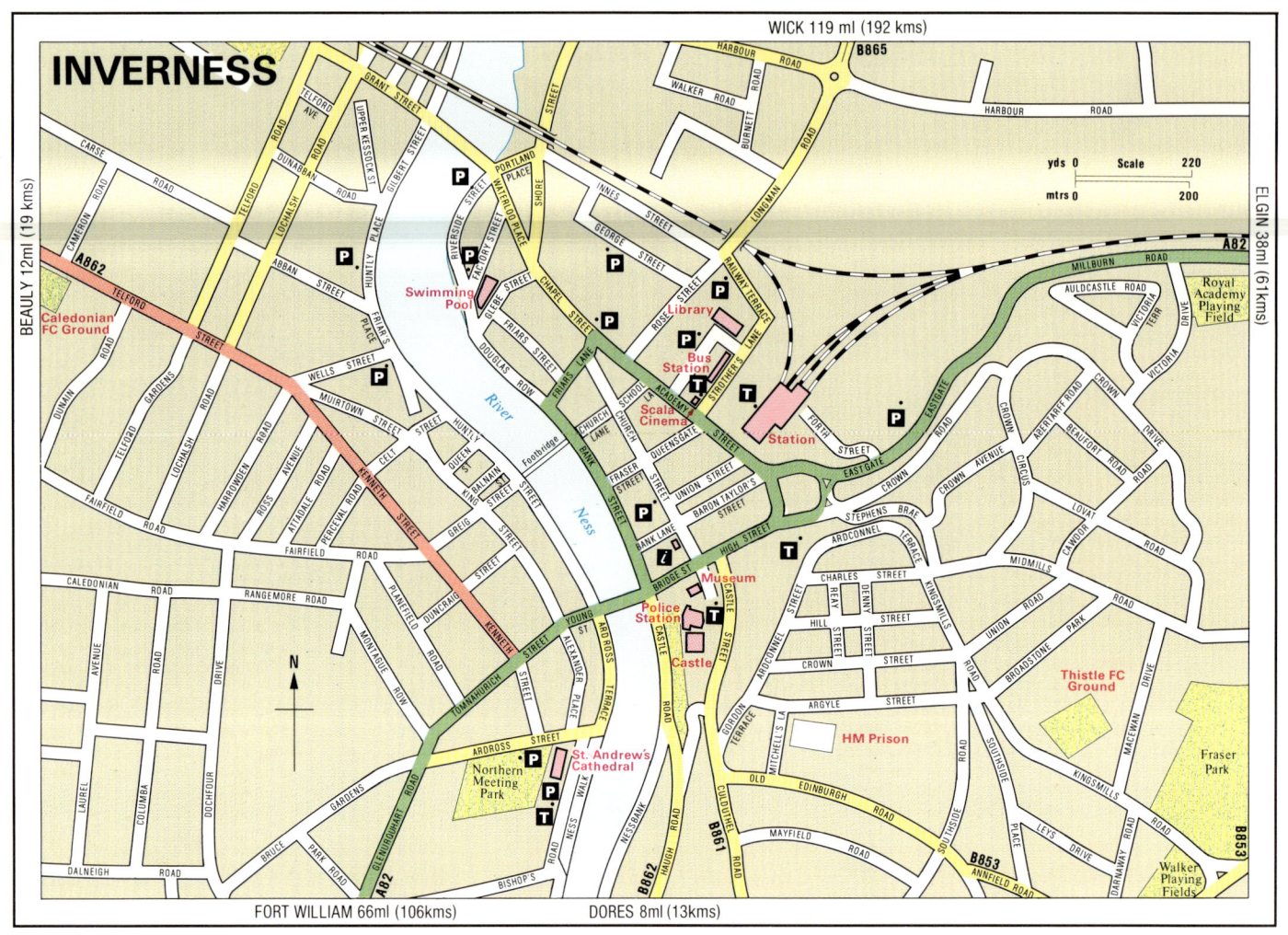

INVERNESS

WICK 119 ml (192 kms)

BEAULY 12ml (19 kms)

ELGIN 38ml (61 kms)

FORT WILLIAM 66ml (106kms)   DORES 8ml (13kms)

Kingsdown	**55**	10D	Kirkby Thore	**67**	9E			Larkhall	**72**	2D
Kingsfold	**54**	4D	Kirkcaldy	**72**	5F			Latchingdon	**55**	7G
Kingshouse	**71**	8G	Kirkcolm	**66**	1G	**L**		Latheron	**79**	9E
Kingside	**73**	7D	Kirkconnel	**72**	2B			Lauder	**73**	6D
Kingskettle	**72**	5G	Kirkcowan	**66**	2F	Laceby	**65**	7C	Laugharne	**56**	4C
Kingsland	**58**	3C	Kirkcudbright	**66**	4F	Ladock	**50**	3B	Launceston	**51**	6D
King's Langley	**54**	3G	Kirkham	**63**	7G	Ladybank	**72**	5G	Laurencekirk	**76**	5C
Kingsley (Cheshire)	**63**	8D	Kirkhill	**75**	9F	Ladykirk	**73**	8D	Laurieston	**66**	4F
Kingsley (Staffs)	**63**	10C	Kirkinner	**66**	3F	Lagg	**70**	3E	Lavant	**54**	2B
King's Lynn	**60**	5F	Kirk Langley	**59**	7G	Laggan Bridge	**75**	9D	Lavenham	**61**	7B
King's Somborne	**53**	7D	Kirk Michael	**66**	2C	Laide	**78**	3C	Laverstoke	**53**	7D
Kingstag	**52**	4C	Kirkmichael (Strath)	**71**	7A	Laindon	**55**	6F	Lawers	**75**	9A
King's Stanley	**52**	4G	Kirkmichael (Tays)	**76**	1B	Lairg	**79**	6D	Laxey	**66**	3B
Kingsteignton	**51**	8C	Kirknewton	**73**	8C	Lakenheath	**61**	6D	Laxfield	**61**	8D
Kingston	**76**	3G	Kirkoswald (Cumbria)	**67**	8E	Lamancha	**72**	4D	Laxford Bridge	**78**	4F
Kingstone	**58**	3B	Kirkoswald (Strath)	**71**	6A	Lamberhurst	**55**	6D	Laxo	**77**	10F
Kingswear	**51**	8B	Kirkpatrick Fleming	**67**	7G	Lambourn	**53**	7F	Layer-de-la-Haye	**61**	7A
Kingswells	**76**	5D	Kirktown of			Lamerton	**51**	6C	Lazonby	**67**	8E
Kingswinford	**58**	5E	Auchterless	**76**	5F	Lamington	**72**	3C	Lea	**58**	4A
Kingswood (Avon)	**52**	3F	Kirkwall	**77**	9B	Lamlash	**70**	5C	Leadburn	**72**	4D
Kingswood (Surrey)	**54**	4E	Kirriemuir	**76**	3B	Lamorna Cove	**50**	1A	Leadenham	**64**	5A
King's Worthy	**53**	7D	Kirtlebridge	**67**	7G	Lampeter	**56**	5E	Leaden Roding	**60**	5A
Kington	**58**	2C	Kirton	**60**	4G	Lamport	**59**	9D	Leadgate	**69**	6D
Kingussie	**75**	10D	Kirton-in-Lindsey	**64**	5C	Lanark	**72**	3C	Leadhills	**72**	3B
Kinlochbervie	**78**	4F	Kishorn	**74**	5F	Lancaster	**67**	8A	Leamington Spa	**59**	7C
Kinlocheil	**75**	6C	Kislingbury	**59**	9C	Lanchester	**69**	6D	Leatherhead	**54**	4E
Kinloch Hourn	**75**	6D	Knaresborough	**64**	2F	Lancing	**54**	4B	Lechlade	**53**	6G
Kinlochleven	**75**	7B	Knarsdale	**67**	9F	Landrake	**51**	6C	Leckmelm	**78**	4C
Kinlochmoidart	**74**	4B	Knebworth	**60**	3A	Land's End	**50**	1A	Ledbury	**58**	4B
Kinloch Rannoch	**75**	9B	Knighton	**57**	9F	Langford	**52**	2E	Ledmore Junction	**78**	4D
Kinloss	**76**	1G	Knockan	**78**	4D	Langham	**60**	1F	Leebotwood	**58**	3E
Kinmel Bay	**62**	5D	Knockandhu	**76**	2E	Langholm	**67**	7G	Leeds	**64**	2E
Kinross	**72**	4F	Knockando	**76**	2F	Langland Bay	**57**	6B	Leek	**63**	10C
Kintore	**76**	5E	Knockin	**63**	7A	Langport	**52**	2C	Leeming	**69**	6A
Kirby Cross	**61**	8A	Knottingley	**64**	3D	Langstone	**52**	2F	Leeming Bar	**69**	6A
Kirby Misperton	**64**	4G	Knowle	**52**	2D	Langtoft	**65**	6F	Lee-on-Solent	**53**	8B
Kirkbean	**67**	6F	Knowl Hill	**54**	2F	Langton Green	**55**	6D	Legbourne	**65**	7B
Kirkbride	**67**	7F	Knutsford	**63**	9D	Langton Matravers	**52**	5A	Leicester	**59**	8E
Kirkburton	**64**	1D	Kyleakin	**74**	5E	Langwathby	**67**	8E	Leigh	**55**	6D
Kirkby-in-Ashfield	**64**	3A	Kyle of Lochalsh	**74**	5E	Langworth	**65**	6B	Leigh-on-Sea	**55**	7F
Kirkby-in-Furness	**67**	7B	Kylerhea	**74**	5E	Lanivet	**50**	4C	Leigh Sinton	**58**	4C
Kirkby Lonsdale	**67**	9B	Kylesku	**78**	4E	Lanreath	**50**	5C	Leighton Buzzard	**60**	2A
Kirkbymoorside	**69**	8A	Kylestrome	**78**	4E	Lapford	**51**	8E	Leintwardine	**58**	3D
Kirkby Stephen	**68**	4B	Kynance Cove	**50**	2A	Larbert	**72**	3E	Leiston	**61**	9C
						Largo Ward	**73**	6G			
						Largs	**71**	6D			

Leith ... **72** ... 5E
Lelant ... **50** ... 2B
Lendalfoot ... **71** ... 6A
Leominster ... **58** ... 3C
Lerwick ... **77** ... 10E
Lesbury ... **73** ... 9B
Lesmahagow ... **72** ... 2C
Leswalt ... **66** ... 1F
Letchworth ... **60** ... 3B
Letter Finlay ... **75** ... 7C
Letterston ... **56** ... 2D
Leuchars ... **73** ... 6G
Leven (Fife) ... **72** ... 5F
Leven (Humber) ... **65** ... 6E
Levens ... **67** ... 8C
Lewdown ... **51** ... 6D
Lewes ... **54** ... 5B
Leyburn ... **69** ... 6A
Leysdown ... **55** ... 8E
Lhanbryde ... **76** ... 2G
Libberton ... **72** ... 3C
Lichfield ... **59** ... 6F
Lidgate ... **61** ... 6C
Lifton ... **51** ... 6D
Lightwater ... **54** ... 3E
Lilliesleaf ... **73** ... 6B
Limpley Stoke ... **52** ... 4E
Lincoln ... **64** ... 5B
Lindale ... **67** ... 8B
Lindfield ... **54** ... 5C
Lindford ... **54** ... 2D
Lingfield ... **54** ... 5D
Linlithgow ... **72** ... 3E
Linn of Dee ... **76** ... 1C
Linton (Cambs) ... **60** ... 5B
Linton (Kent) ... **55** ... 7D
Liphook ... **54** ... 2C
Liskeard ... **50** ... 5C
Liss ... **53** ... 9C
Lissington ... **65** ... 6B
Litcham ... **61** ... 6F
Little Brickhill ... **60** ... 2B
Little Bytham ... **60** ... 2F
Little Chalfont ... **54** ... 3G
Little Clacton ... **61** ... 8A
Little Compton ... **59** ... 7B
Little Gaddesden ... **60** ... 2A
Littlehampton ... **54** ... 3B
Little Hereford ... **58** ... 3D
Little Kimble ... **54** ... 2G
Little Langdale ... **67** ... 7C
Littleover ... **59** ... 7G
Littleport ... **60** ... 5D
Littlestone-on-Sea ... **55** ... 8C
Little Stretton ... **58** ... 3E
Littleton Drew ... **52** ... 4F
Little Torrington ... **51** ... 6E
Little Walsingham ... **61** ... 7G
Little Witley ... **58** ... 4C
Liverpool ... **63** ... 7E
Livingston ... **72** ... 4E
Lizard ... **50** ... 2A
Llanaber ... **62** ... 3A
Llanaelhaearn ... **62** ... 2C
Llanarmon Dyffryn
  Ceiriog ... **63** ... 6B
Llanarth ... **56** ... 5E
Llanarthney ... **56** ... 5C
Llanbedr (Clwyd) ... **63** ... 6C
Llanbedr (Gwynedd) ... **62** ... 3B
Llanbedrog ... **62** ... 2B
Llanberis ... **62** ... 3C
Llanbister ... **57** ... 8F
Llanbrynmair ... **57** ... 7G
Llanbydder ... **56** ... 5D
Llandaf ... **57** ... 8A
Llanddarog ... **56** ... 5C
Llanddewi Brefi ... **57** ... 6E
Llandderfel ... **62** ... 5B
Llanddulas ... **62** ... 4D
Llandeilo ... **57** ... 6C
Llandinam ... **57** ... 8G
Llandissilio ... **56** ... 3C
Llandogo ... **52** ... 3G
Llandovery ... **57** ... 6D
Llandre ... **57** ... 6G
Llandrillo ... **62** ... 5B
Llandrindod Wells ... **57** ... 8E
Llandrinio ... **63** ... 6A

Llandudno ... **62** ... 4D
Llandudno Junction ... **62** ... 4D
Llandwrog ... **62** ... 2C
Llandybie ... **57** ... 6C
Llandysul ... **56** ... 5D
Llanedwen ... **62** ... 3D
Llanegryn ... **62** ... 3A
Llanelli ... **56** ... 5B
Llanerchymedd ... **62** ... 2D
Llanerfyl ... **62** ... 5A
Llanfachraeth ... **62** ... 2D
Llanfair Caereinion ... **62** ... 5A
Llanfair Dyffryn Clwyd **63** ... 6C
Llanfairfechan ... **62** ... 3D
Llanfair P.G. ... **62** ... 3D
Llanfair Talhaiarn ... **62** ... 5D
Llanfarian ... **56** ... 5F
Llanfrothen ... **62** ... 3B
Llanfyllin ... **63** ... 6A
Llangadfan ... **62** ... 5A
Llangadog ... **57** ... 6D
Llangedwyn ... **63** ... 6A
Llangefni ... **62** ... 2D
Llangeler ... **56** ... 4D
Llangernyw ... **62** ... 4D
Llangollen ... **63** ... 6B
Llangorse ... **57** ... 8D
Llangranog ... **56** ... 4E
Llangurig ... **57** ... 7F
Llangynidr ... **57** ... 8C
Llangynog ... **62** ... 5B
Llanhamlach ... **57** ... 8D
Llanharan ... **57** ... 8A
Llanidloes ... **57** ... 7G
Llanilar ... **57** ... 6F
Llanrhaeadr ... **62** ... 5C
Llanrhaeadr-ym-
  Mochnant ... **63** ... 6B
Llanrhidian ... **56** ... 5B
Llanrhystud ... **56** ... 5F
Llanrug ... **62** ... 3C
Llanrwst ... **62** ... 4C
Llansannan ... **62** ... 5D
Llansantffraed ... **58** ... 2A
Llansantffraid ... **56** ... 5F
Llansantffraid-ym-
  Mechain ... **63** ... 6A
Llansawel ... **57** ... 6D
Llantarnam ... **52** ... 2G
Llanthony ... **57** ... 9D
Llantrisant ... **57** ... 8A
Llanuwchllyn ... **62** ... 4B
Llanvair Waterdine ... **57** ... 9F
Llanvapley ... **58** ... 2A
Llanvetherine ... **58** ... 2A
Llanwddyn ... **62** ... 5A
Llanwnda ... **62** ... 2C
Llanwrda ... **57** ... 6D
Llanwrtyd Wells ... **57** ... 7E
Llanymynech ... **63** ... 6A
Llanystumdwy ... **62** ... 2B
Llawhaden ... **56** ... 3C
Llay ... **63** ... 7C
Llechryd ... **56** ... 4D
Lloc ... **63** ... 6D
Llwyngwril ... **62** ... 3A
Llwynmawr ... **63** ... 6B
Llynclys ... **63** ... 6A
Llyswen ... **57** ... 8D
Lochailort ... **74** ... 5C
Lochaline ... **74** ... 4A
Locharbriggs ... **67** ... 6G
Loch Awe ... **71** ... 6G
Lochboisdale ... **78** ... 1D
Lochbuie ... **70** ... 3G
Lochcarron ... **74** ... 5F
Lochdonhead ... **74** ... 4A
Lochearnhead ... **71** ... 8G
Lochgair ... **70** ... 5F
Lochgilphead ... **70** ... 5E
Lochgoilhead ... **71** ... 6F
Lochinver ... **78** ... 4E
Lochlee ... **76** ... 3C
Lochmaben ... **67** ... 6G
Lochmaddy ... **78** ... 2E
Lochranza ... **70** ... 5C
Lochwinnoch ... **71** ... 7D
Lockerbie ... **67** ... 6G
Loftus ... **69** ... 9B

Logiealmond ... **76** ... 1A
Logierait ... **76** ... 1B
London ... **54** ... 4F
Longbridge Deverill ... **52** ... 4D
Long Buckby ... **59** ... 9D
Longburton ... **52** ... 3C
Long Compton ... **59** ... 7B
Long Crendon ... **59** ... 9A
Long Eaton ... **59** ... 8G
Longford ... **58** ... 5A
Longframlington ... **73** ... 9A
Longham ... **52** ... 5B
Longhorsley ... **69** ... 6F
Longhoughton ... **73** ... 10B
Long Itchington ... **59** ... 8C
Long Lawford ... **59** ... 8D
Long Marston ... **64** ... 3F
Long Melford ... **61** ... 6B
Longniddry ... **73** ... 6E
Longnor (Salop) ... **58** ... 3E
Longnor (Staffs) ... **64** ... 1A
Long Preston ... **67** ... 10A
Longridge (Lancs) ... **63** ... 8G
Longridge (Lothian) ... **72** ... 3D
Longside ... **77** ... 6F
Long Stratton ... **61** ... 8E
Long Sutton (Lincs) ... **60** ... 4F
Long Sutton
  (Somerset) ... **52** ... 2C
Longton ... **63** ... 10B
Longtown ... **67** ... 8G
Longville ... **58** ... 3E
Lonmay ... **77** ... 6G
Looe ... **50** ... 5B
Loose ... **55** ... 7D
Lopcombe Corner ... **53** ... 6D
Lossiemouth ... **76** ... 2G
Lostwithiel ... **50** ... 4C
Loughborough ... **59** ... 8F
Loughor ... **56** ... 5B
Loughton ... **54** ... 5G
Louth ... **65** ... 7B
Lowdham ... **59** ... 9G
Lower Dicker ... **55** ... 6B
Lower Peover ... **63** ... 9D
Lower Swell ... **59** ... 6A
Lowestoft ... **61** ... 10E
Loweswater ... **67** ... 6D
Lowick (Northants) ... **60** ... 2D
Lowick (Northumb) ... **73** ... 8C
Low Row ... **68** ... 5A
Lubenham ... **59** ... 9E
Ludborough ... **65** ... 7C
Ludgershall ... **53** ... 6E
Ludham ... **61** ... 9F
Ludlow ... **58** ... 3D
Ludwardine ... **58** ... 3B
Luib ... **71** ... 8G
Lulsgate ... **52** ... 3E
Lulworth ... **52** ... 4A
Lumphanan ... **76** ... 4D
Lumsden ... **76** ... 3E
Lundin Links ... **72** ... 5F
Lupton ... **67** ... 9B
Luss ... **71** ... 7F
Luton ... **60** ... 2A
Lutterworth ... **59** ... 8D
Lydbrook ... **58** ... 4A
Lydbury North ... **58** ... 2D
Lydd ... **55** ... 8C
Lydford-on-Foss ... **52** ... 3D
Lydham ... **58** ... 2E
Lydney ... **52** ... 3G
Lyme Park ... **64** ... 5B
Lyme Regis ... **52** ... 2B
Lyminge ... **55** ... 9D
Lymington ... **53** ... 7B
Lymm ... **63** ... 8E
Lympne ... **55** ... 9D
Lyndhurst ... **53** ... 6B
Lyneham ... **52** ... 5F
Lynmouth ... **51** ... 8G
Lynton ... **51** ... 8G
Lyonshall ... **58** ... 2C
Lytham St Annes ... **63** ... 7G
Lythe ... **69** ... 9B

Mablethorpe ... **65** ... 8B
Macclesfield ... **63** ... 10D
Macduff ... **76** ... 5G
Machrie ... **70** ... 5C
Machrihanish ... **70** ... 3B
Machynlleth ... **57** ... 6G
Mackworth ... **59** ... 7G
Macmerry ... **72** ... 5E
Maenan ... **62** ... 4D
Maentwrog ... **62** ... 3B
Maerdy ... **57** ... 7B
Maesteg ... **57** ... 7B
Maiden Bradley ... **52** ... 4D
Maidencombe ... **51** ... 9C
Maidenhead ... **54** ... 2F
Maiden Newton ... **52** ... 3B
Maidstone ... **55** ... 7E
Mainsriddle ... **66** ... 5F
Malborough ... **51** ... 8B
Maldon ... **55** ... 7G
Mallaig ... **74** ... 4D
Mallwyd ... **62** ... 4A
Malmesbury ... **52** ... 5F
Malpas ... **63** ... 7C
Maltby ... **64** ... 3C
Malton ... **64** ... 4G
Malvern (West) ... **58** ... 4B
Malvern Link ... **58** ... 4C
Malvern Wells ... **58** ... 4B
Mamble ... **58** ... 4D
Manchester ... **63** ... 9E
Manea ... **60** ... 4D
Manningtree ... **61** ... 8B
Manorbier ... **56** ... 3B
Mansfield ... **64** ... 3A
Mansfield
  Woodhouse ... **64** ... 3A
Manston ... **55** ... 10E
Marazanvose ... **50** ... 3B
Marazion ... **50** ... 2A
March ... **60** ... 4E
Marchwiel ... **63** ... 7C
Marden ... **55** ... 7D
Mareham-le-Fen ... **65** ... 7A
Maresfield ... **54** ... 5C
Margam ... **57** ... 7B
Margaretting ... **55** ... 6G
Margate ... **55** ... 10E
Marianglas ... **62** ... 3D
Mark ... **52** ... 2C
Mark Cross ... **55** ... 6C
Market Bosworth ... **59** ... 8E
Market Deeping ... **60** ... 3F
Market Drayton ... **63** ... 8B
Market Harborough ... **59** ... 9E
Market Lavington ... **52** ... 5E
Market Rasen ... **65** ... 6C
Market Weighton ... **64** ... 5E
Markfield ... **59** ... 8F
Markham Moor ... **64** ... 4B
Marksbury ... **52** ... 3E
Marks Tey ... **61** ... 7A
Marlborough ... **53** ... 6E
Marlow ... **54** ... 2F
Marlow Bottom ... **54** ... 2F
Marnhull ... **52** ... 4C
Marske ... **69** ... 8B
Martin ... **65** ... 6A
Martinstown ... **52** ... 3A
Martock ... **52** ... 2C
Marton ... **59** ... 8D
Maryculter ... **76** ... 5D
Marykirk ... **76** ... 4B
Maryport ... **67** ... 6E
Mary Tavy ... **51** ... 7D
Marywell ... **76** ... 4D
Masham ... **64** ... 2G
Matfield ... **55** ... 6D
Matlock ... **64** ... 2A
Matlock Bath ... **64** ... 2A
Mattingley ... **53** ... 9E
Mauchline ... **71** ... 8B
Maud ... **77** ... 6F
Maughold ... **66** ... 3C
Maulden ... **60** ... 2B
Mawgan Cross ... **50** ... 2A
Mawgan Porth ... **50** ... 3C

Maxwelltown 66 5G
Maybole 71 7A
Mayfield 55 6C
Mayford 54 3E
McInroys Point 71 6E
Meare 52 2D
Measham 59 7F
Meeth 51 7E
Meifod 63 6A
Meigle 76 2A
Melbourn 60 4B
Meliden 62 5D
Melksham 52 5E
Melling 67 9B
Mells 52 4D
Melmerby 67 9E
Melrose 73 6C
Melton 64 5D
Melton Constable 61 7G
Melton Mowbray 59 9F
Melvaig 78 2C
Melvich 79 8G
Memsie 77 6G
Memus 76 3B
Menai Bridge 62 3D
Menston 64 1E
Menstrie 72 3F
Mere 52 4D
Merrivale 51 7C
Merrymeet 50 5C
Merthyr Mawr 57 7A
Merthyr Tydfil 57 8C
Merton 51 7E
Meshaw 51 8F
Messingham 64 5C
Metfield 61 8D
Metheringham 65 6A
Methlick 76 5F
Methwold 61 6E
Mevagissey 50 4B
Mey 79 10G
Mickleover 59 7G
Mickleton (Durham) 68 5B
Mickleton (Glos) 59 6B
Middlebie 67 7G
Middleham 69 6A
Middle Rasen 65 6C
Middlesbrough 69 7B
Middleton 74 1A
Middleton Cheney 59 8B
Middleton-in-
Teesdale 68 5B
Middleton-on-Sea 54 3B
Middleton-on-the-
Wolds 64 5F
Middleton Stoney 59 8A
Middle Wallop 53 6D
Middlewich 63 9D
Middlezoy 52 2D
Midhurst 54 2C
Midsomer Norton 52 3E
Midtown Brae 78 2C
Mid Yell 77 10F
Milborne Port 52 3C
Mildenhall 61 6D
Milfield 73 8C
Milford 54 3D
Milford Haven 56 2C
Milford-on-Sea 53 6B
Millbrook 51 6B
Millhouse 70 5D
Millom 67 7B
Millport 71 6D
Milnathort 72 4F
Milnthorpe 67 8B
Milovaig 74 1F
Milton 60 4C
Milton Abbot 51 6D
Milton Common 53 8G
Milton Ernest 60 2C
Milton Keynes 60 1B
Milverton 51 10F
Minard 70 5F
Minehead 51 9G
Minster (Kent) 55 8E
Minster (Kent) 55 10E
Mintlaw 77 6F
Misterton (Notts) 64 4C
Misterton (Somerset) 52 2B
Mitchell 50 3B
Mitcheldean 58 4A
Mobberley 63 9D
Modbury 51 7B
Moffat 72 4A
Mold 63 6C
Molesworth 60 2D
Moniaive 72 2A
Monifieth 76 4A
Monkleigh 51 6F
Monkton 71 7B
Monmouth 58 3A
Montacute 52 3C
Montford Bridge 63 7A
Montgomery 57 9G
Montrose 76 5B
Monyash 64 1A
Monymusk 76 4E
Moorcock Inn 68 4A
Morar 74 4C
Morcott 60 2E
Mordiford 58 3B
Mordington 73 8D
Morebattle 73 7B
Morecambe 67 8A
Moretonhampstead 51 8D
Moreton-in-Marsh 59 7B
Morfa Nefyn 62 1B
Morpeth 69 6E
Morston 61 7G
Mortimer's Cross 58 3C
Morvah 50 1A
Morville 58 4E
Mossat 76 3E
Mossband 67 7G
Mosspaul 72 5A
Mosstodloch 76 3G
Mosterton 52 2B
Mostyn 63 6D
Motherby 67 8E
Motherwell 72 2D
Moulin 76 1B
Moulsford-on-
Thames 53 8F
Mound Station 79 7C
Mountain Ash 57 8B
Mountsorrel 59 8F
Mousehole 50 1A
Mouswald 67 6G
Moy 75 10E
Muchalls 76 5D
Much Birch 58 3B
Much Hadham 60 4A
Much Marcle 58 4B
Much Wenlock 58 4E
Muddiford 51 7G
Mudeford 53 6B
Muirdrum 76 4A
Muirhead 76 3A
Muirkirk 71 9B
Muir of Ord 75 8F
Muker 68 5A
Mullion 50 2A
Mumbles 57 6B
Mundesley-on-Sea 61 9G
Mundford 61 6E
Mungrisdale 67 7E
Munlochy 75 9F
Munslow 58 3E
Muthill 72 3G
Mybster 79 9F

N

Nacton 61 8B
Nafferton 65 6F
Nailsea 52 2F
Nailsworth 52 4G
Nairn 75 10G
Nantgarw 57 8A
Nantgaredig 56 5C
Nantwich 63 8C
Narberth 56 3C
Narborough 61 6F
Naseby 59 9D
Navenby 64 5A
Nayland 61 7B
Neath 57 6B
Needham Market 61 7C
Needingworth 60 4D
Nefyn 62 2B
Nelson 63 9G
Nenthead 68 4C
Nesscliffe 63 7A
Neston 63 6D
Nether Broughton 59 9G
Netherley 76 5D
Nethy Bridge 76 1E
Nettlebed 53 9F
Nevern 56 3D
New Abbey 66 5G
New Aberdour 76 5G
Newark-on-Trent 64 4A
Newarthill 72 2D
New Balderton 64 5A
New Barnet 54 4G
Newbiggin (Durham) 68 5C
Newbiggin (Strath) 72 3C
Newbiggin-
by-the-Sea 69 7F
Newbold-upon-Stour 59 7B
New Bolingbroke 65 7A
Newborough 62 2D
Newbridge (Dumf
& Gall) 66 5G
Newbridge (Gwent) 57 9B
Newbridge (Oxon) 53 7G
Newbridge-on-Wye 57 8E
New Brighton 63 7E
New Buckenham 61 7D
Newburgh (Fife) 72 4G
Newburgh
(Grampian) 77 6E
Newbury 53 7E
Newby 69 10A
Newby Bridge 67 8C
New Byth 76 5G
Newcastle Emlyn 56 4D
Newcastleton 73 6A
Newcastle-under-
Lyme 63 9C
Newcastle-upon-
Tyne 69 6D
New Cumnock 71 8B
New Deer 76 5F
New Elgin 76 2G
Newent 58 4A
Newgale 56 2C
New Galloway 66 4G
Newhaven 54 5B
New Holland 65 6D
Newick 54 5C
Newingreen 55 9D
New Luce 66 2F
Newlyn 50 1A
Newmarket 60 5C
Newmill 76 3G
Newmilns 71 8C
New Milton 53 6B
Newnham 58 4D
Newnham-on-Severn 58 4A
New Pitsligo 76 5G
Newport (Dyfed) 56 3D
Newport (Essex) 60 5B
Newport (Gwent) 52 2F
Newport (Humber) 64 5E
Newport (I. of W.) 53 7A
Newport (Salop) 63 9A
Newport-on-Tay 72 5G
Newport Pagnell 60 1B
New Quay 56 4E
Newquay 50 3C
New Radnor 57 9E
New Romney 55 8C
New Scone 72 4G
Newstead Abbey 64 3A
Newton Abbot 51 8C
Newton Ferrers 51 7B
Newtonhill 77 6D
Newtonmore 75 9D
Newton-on-the-Moor 73 9A
Newton-on-Trent 64 5B
Newton Poppleford 51 9D
Newton St Cyres 51 8E
Newton Solney 59 7F
Newton Stewart 66 3G
Newtown (Herefs
& Worcs) 58 4B
Newtown (Powys) 57 8G
New Tredegar 57 8B
Newtyle 76 2A
Neyland 56 2C
Nigg 79 7B
Ninfield 55 7B
Niton 53 8A
Nocton 65 6A
No Man's Land 50 5B
Norham 73 8D
Norman Cross 60 3E
Northall 60 2A
Northallerton 69 7A
Northam 51 6F
Northampton 59 9C
North Ballachulish 75 6B
North Benfleet 55 7F
North Berwick 73 6E
North Cave 64 5E
North Chapel 54 3C
North Coates 65 7C
North Creake 61 6G
North Dalton 64 5F
North Elmham 61 7F
North Erradale 78 2B
North Ferriby 64 5D
North Frodingham 65 6F
North Grimston 64 5F
North Holmwood 54 4D
Northiam 55 7C
North Kessock 75 9F
North Kilworth 59 9D
North Kyme 65 6A
Northleach 59 6A
North Muskham 64 5A
Northop 63 6D
North Petherton 52 1D
North Rigton 64 2F
North Somercotes 65 8C
North Stifford 55 6F
North Tidworth 53 6D
North Tolsta 78 3F
Northwaa 77 9C
North Walsham 61 8F
North Weald 54 5G
Northwich 63 8D
Northwold 61 6E
Norton 64 4G
Norton Fitzwarren 51 10F
Norton St Philip 52 4E
Norwich 61 8E
Norwick 77 10G
Nottingham 59 8G
Nuneaton 59 7E
Nunney Catch 52 4D
Nutfield 54 5D
Nutley 54 5C

O

Oadby 59 9E
Oakfordbridge 51 9F
Oakham 60 1E
Oakhill 52 3D
Oakley (Bucks) 59 9A
Oakley (Hants) 53 8E
Oare 53 6E
Oban 70 5G
Ochiltree 71 8B
Odiham 53 9E
Offord Darcy 60 3C
Ogbourne St George 53 6F
Ogmore-by-Sea 57 7A
Okehampton 51 7D
Old Dailly 71 6A
Old Deer 77 6F
Oldham 63 10F
Old Hurst 60 4D
Old Leake 65 8A
Old Meldrum 76 5E
Old Radnor 57 9E
Old Rayne 76 4E
Old Stratford 59 9B
Old Windsor 54 3E
Ollaberry 77 9F
Ollerton (Cheshire) 63 9D
Ollerton (Notts) 64 4A
Olney 60 1C
Ombersley 58 5C

Onchan	66	3B
Ongar	55	6G
Onich	75	6B
Ord	74	4D
Ore	55	7B
Orford	61	9B
Orgil	77	8B
Ormesby (Cleveland)	69	8B
Ormesby (Norfolk)	61	9F
Ormiston	72	5E
Ormskirk	63	7F
Orpington	54	5E
Orsett	55	6F
Orton	67	9D
Osbournby	60	2G
Osmington	52	4A
Ospringe	55	8E
Oswaldkirk	64	4G
Oswestry	63	6B
Otford	55	6E
Othery	52	2D
Otley	64	2E
Otterburn	68	4F
Otter Ferry	70	5E
Ottershaw	54	3E
Ottery St Mary	51	10D
Oulton Broad	61	10E
Oundle	60	2D
Outwell	60	5E
Over (Cheshire)	63	8D
Over (Glos)	58	5A
Overscaig Hotel	78	5E
Overseal	59	7F
Overstrand	61	8G
Overton	53	8D
Overton-on-Dee	63	7B
Overy Staithe	61	6G
Ower	53	7C
Oxford	59	8A
Oxted	54	5D
Oxton (Borders)	73	6D
Oxton (Notts)	64	4A

P

Padbury	59	9B
Paddock Wood	55	6D
Padeswood	63	6C
Padiham	63	9G
Padstow	50	4C
Paignton	51	8C
Pailton	59	9D
Painswick	58	5A
Paisley	71	8D
Palnackie	66	5F
Pandy	58	2A
Pangbourne	53	8F
Pannal	64	2F
Pant-y-Dwr	57	7F
Papworth Everard	60	3C
Par	50	4B
Parkeston Quay	61	8B
Parkgate	63	6D
Parkhurst	53	7B
Parkstone	52	5B
Patchway	52	3F
Pateley Bridge	64	1F
Pathhead	72	5D
Patna	71	7A
Patrick	66	2B
Patrington	65	7D
Patterdale	67	8D
Paulerspury	59	9C
Pave Lane	63	9A
Peacehaven	54	5B
Peakirk	60	3E
Peasedown St John	52	4E
Peasenhall	61	9C
Peasmarsh	55	7C
Peebles	72	5C
Peel	66	2B
Pelynt	50	5B
Pembrey	56	5B
Pembridge	58	2C
Pembroke	56	2B
Pembroke Dock	56	2B
Pembury	55	6D
Penally	56	3B
Penarth	57	8A

Pencoed	57	7A
Pencraig	58	3A
Pendeen	50	1A
Pendine	56	4C
Pendock	58	4B
Pengam	57	8B
Penhow	52	2G
Penicuik	72	4D
Penistone	64	2C
Penkridge	63	10A
Penmachno	62	4C
Penmaenmawr	62	4D
Penn	54	3F
Pennal	57	6G
Pennan	76	5G
Pennard	56	5B
Penpillick	50	4B
Penpont	72	3A
Penrhyn	62	2E
Penrhyndeudraeth	62	3B
Penrith	67	8E
Penryn	50	3A
Pensford	52	3E
Penshurst	55	6D
Pentcaitland	73	6E
Pentewan	50	4B
Pentraeth	62	3D
Pentrefoelas	62	4C
Penybont	57	8E
Penybontfawr	62	5B
Pen-y-groes	62	2C
Pen-y-gwryd	62	3C
Penzance	50	1A
Perranarworthal	50	3B
Perranporth	50	3B
Perrots Brook	59	6A
Pershore	58	5B
Perth	72	4G
Peterborough	60	3E
Peterchurch	58	2B
Peterculter	76	5D
Peterhead	77	7F
Peterlee	69	7C
Petersfield	53	9C
Petton	51	9F
Pentworth	54	3C
Pevensey	55	6B
Pevensey Bay	55	6B
Pewsey	53	6E
Pickering	64	4G
Picket Post	53	6B
Pierowall	77	9C
Pillerton Priors	59	7C
Pilling	67	8A
Piltdown	52	3D
Pinchbeck	60	3F
Pinhoe	51	9D
Pinwherry	66	2G
Pirbright	54	3E
Pirnmill	70	5C
Pitcaple	76	5E
Pitlochry	76	1B
Pitmedden	76	5E
Pitsea	55	7F
Pitstone	60	2A
Pittenweem	73	6F
Playing Place	50	3C
Pleasley	64	3A
Plockton	74	5E
Pluckley	55	8D
Plumpton	54	5B
Plusha	50	5D
Plymouth	51	6B
Pocklington	64	5F
Polbain	78	3D
Polbathic	51	6B
Polegate	55	6B
Polmont	72	3E
Polperro	50	5B
Ponders End	54	5G
Pont Aberglaslyn	62	3C
Pontardawe	57	7B
Pontardulais	56	5B
Pontefract	64	3D
Ponteland	69	6E
Ponterwyd	57	6F
Pontesbury	63	7A
Pontrhydfendigaid	57	6F
Pont-rhyd-y-groes	57	6F

Pontrilas	58	2B
Pont Yates	56	5C
Pontypool	57	9B
Pontypridd	57	8B
Poole	52	5B
Poolewe	78	2B
Pooley Bridge	67	8D
Pool-in-Wharfedale	64	2E
Porlock	51	8G
Porlock Weir	51	8G
Port Appin	74	5A
Port Askaig	70	2D
Port Bannatyne	71	6D
Port Charlotte	70	2D
Portchester	53	8B
Port Dinorwic	62	3D
Port Ellen	70	2C
Port Elphinstone	76	5E
Port Erin	66	2B
Port Errol	77	6F
Portesham	52	3A
Portessie	76	3G
Port Eynon	56	5B
Port Glasgow	71	7E
Portgordon	76	3G
Portgower	79	8D
Porth (Cornwall)	50	3C
Porth (Gwent)	57	8B
Port Henderson	78	2B
Porthcawl	57	7A
Porthcothan Bay	50	3C
Porthleven	50	2A
Porthmadog	62	3B
Porthtowan	50	2B
Portinnisherrich	70	5G
Portinscale	67	7D
Port Isaac	50	4D
Portishead	52	2F
Portknockie	76	3G
Portland	52	3A
Port Logan	66	1E
Portmahomack	79	8C
Portnacroish	74	5A
Portnahaven	70	1D
Port of Menteith	71	8F
Port of Ness	78	3G
Portpatrick	66	1F
Portreath	50	2B
Portree	74	3F
Port St Mary	66	2B
Portskerra	79	8G
Portslade-by-Sea	54	4B
Portsmouth	53	8B
Portsonachan	70	5G
Portsoy	76	4G
Port Sunlight	63	7E
Port Talbot	57	6B
Port William	66	2E
Postbridge	51	7D
Postcombe	53	9G
Potter Heigham	61	9F
Potterne	52	5E
Potters Bar	54	4G
Potton	60	3B
Poulton-le-Fylde	63	7G
Poundsgate	51	8C
Powburn	73	9B
Powick	58	5C
Poynton	63	10D
Praa Sands	50	2A
Prees	63	8B
Preesall	67	8A
Prees Green	63	8B
Prenteg	62	3B
Prestatyn	62	5D
Prestbury	63	10D
Presteigne	58	2C
Preston (Borders)	73	7D
Preston (Lancs)	63	8G
Preston Candover	53	8D
Preston Gubbals	63	7A
Prestonpans	72	5E
Preston Patrick	67	8B
Prestwich	63	9E
Prestwick	71	7B
Prestwood	54	2G
Priddy	52	3E
Princes Risborough	54	2G
Princethorpe	59	8D

Princetown	51	7C
Probus	50	3B
Prospect	67	6E
Prudhoe	68	5D
Puckeridge	60	4A
Puddletown	52	4B
Pudsey	64	2E
Puffin Island	62	3D
Pulborough	54	3C
Pulford	63	7C
Pulham	61	8D
Pumpsaint	57	6D
Purfleet	55	6F
Purley	54	5E
Purton	52	5F
Pwll	56	5B
Pwllheli	62	2B
Pyecombe	54	4B
Pyle	57	7A

Q

Quatt	58	4E
Queenborough	55	8E
Queensferry	63	7D
Quendon	60	5A

R

Rackenford	51	8F
Rackheath	61	8F
Radcliffe-on-Trent	59	9G
Radlett	54	4G
Radstock	52	3E
Radwinter	60	5B
Radyr	57	8A
Rafford	76	1G
Raglan	58	3A
Rainham (Essex)	55	6F
Rainham (Kent)	55	7E
Rake	54	2C
Rampside	67	7B
Ramsey (Cambs)	60	3D
Ramsey (I. of M.)	66	3C
Ramsgate	55	10E
Rannoch Station	75	8B
Rapness	77	9C
Ratcliffe-on-the-Wreake	59	9F
Rathen	77	6G
Rattray	76	2A
Ravenstonedale	68	4A
Rawtenstall	63	9F
Rayleigh	55	7F
Reading	53	9F
Rearsby	59	9F
Reay	79	8G
Redbourn	60	3A
Redbrook (Clwyd)	63	8B
Redbrook (Glos)	58	3A
Redcar	69	8B
Redditch	59	6D
Redgrave	61	7D
Redhill (Avon)	52	3E
Redhill (Surrey)	54	4D
Redland	77	8B
Redmire	68	5A
Rednal	63	7B
Red Roses	56	4C
Red Row	69	6F
Redruth	50	2B
Red Wharf Bay	62	3D
Reedham	61	9E
Reepham	61	8F
Reeth	68	5A
Reiff	78	3D
Reigate	54	4D
Reighton	65	6G
Reiss	79	10F
Rempstone	59	8F
Renfrew	71	8D
Resolven	57	7B
Retford	64	4B
Rettendon	55	7G
Rhayader	57	7F
Rhiwbina	57	8A
Rhosllanerchrugog	63	6C
Rhosneigr	62	2D
Rhos-on-Sea	62	4D

Place	Page	Grid
Rhossili	56	5B
Rhu	71	7E
Rhubodach	70	5E
Rhuddlan	62	5D
Rhunahaorine	70	4C
Rhyd-ddu	62	3C
Rhyd Owen	56	5E
Rhydspence	57	9E
Rhyl	62	5D
Rhymney	57	8C
Rhynie	76	3E
Riccarton	71	7C
Richard's Castle	58	3D
Richmond	69	6A
Rickmansworth	54	3G
Riding Mill	68	5D
Ridsdale	68	5E
Riggend	72	2E
Rillington	64	5G
Ringford	66	4F
Ringmer	54	5B
Ringwood	53	6B
Ripley (Derbys)	64	3A
Ripley (N. Yorks)	64	2F
Ripley (Surrey)	54	3E
Ripon	64	2G
Ripple	58	5B
Ripponden	64	1D
Risca	57	9B
Risegate	60	3F
Riseley	53	9E
Risley	59	8G
Roade	59	9C
Roadhead	67	8G
Roadside	76	5C
Roberton (Borders)	72	5B
Roberton (Strath)	72	3C
Robertsbridge	55	7C
Robeston Wathen	56	3C
Robin Hood's Bay	69	10A
Roborough	51	7C
Rocester	59	6G
Roch	56	2C
Rochdale	63	9F
Rochester (Kent)	55	7E
Rochester (Northumb.)	68	4F
Rockingham	60	1E
Rodel	78	2E
Rogart	79	7C
Rogate	54	2C
Rogerstone	57	9B
Rogiet	52	2F
Rollesby	61	9F
Rolvenden	55	7C
Romaldkirk	68	5B
Romanno Bridge	72	4D
Romford	55	6F
Romsey	53	7C
Rosebank	72	2D
Rosedale Abbey	69	9A
Rosehearty	77	6G
Rosemarkie	75	9G
Rosewell	72	5D
Rossett	63	7C
Ross-on-Wye	58	4A
Rothbury	73	9A
Rotherfield	55	6C
Rotherham	64	3C
Rostherne	63	9D
Rothes	76	2G
Rothesay	71	6D
Rothwell	60	1D
Rottingdean	54	5B
Rough Close	63	10B
Roughton	61	8G
Rowardennan	71	7F
Rowlands Castle	53	9C
Rowlands Gill	69	6D
Rowsley	64	2A
Rowstock	53	7F
Roxburgh	73	7C
Roxton	60	3C
Roy Bridge	75	7C
Royston	60	4B
Ruabon	63	7B
Ruan High Lanes	50	4B
Ruddington	59	8G
Rudgwick	54	3C
Rudston	65	6F
Rugby	59	8D
Rugeley	59	6F
Rumbling Bridge	72	3F
Rumney	57	9A
Runcorn	63	8D
Runswick	69	9B
Rushden	60	2C
Rushton Spencer	63	10C
Rushyford	69	6C
Ruskington	65	6A
Rustington	54	3B
Ruswarp	69	9B
Ruthin	63	6C
Ruthwell	68	1E
Ruyton of the Eleven Towns	63	7A
Rydal	67	7D
Ryde	53	8B
Rye	55	8C
Rye Foreign	55	7C

S

Place	Page	Grid
Saddell	70	4C
Saffron Walden	60	5B
St Abbs	73	8E
St Agnes	50	3B
St Albans	54	4G
St Andrews	73	6G
St Asaph	62	5D
St Austell	50	4B
St Bees	67	5D
St Blazey	50	4B
St Boswells	73	6C
St Briavel's	52	3G
St Budeaux	51	6C
St Buryan	50	1A
St Catherine's	71	6F
St Clears	56	4C
St Columb Major	50	4C
St Cyrus	76	5B
St Davids	56	1D
St Day	50	3B
St Dogmael's	56	3E
St Fergus	77	6G
St Fillans	72	2G
St Florence	56	3B
St Helens (I. of W.)	53	8A
St Helens (Merseyside)	63	8E
St Ives (Cambs)	60	4D
St Ives (Cornwall)	50	2B
St John's	66	2B
St John's Chapel	68	4C
St Jude's	66	3C
St Just	50	1A
St Just in Roseland	50	3A
St Keverne	50	3A
St Keyne	50	5C
St Lawrence (I. of W.)	53	8A
St Lawrence (Kent)	55	10E
St Leonards	52	5B
St Leonards-on-Sea	55	7B
St Margaret's-at-Cliffe	55	10D
St Margaret's Bay	55	10D
St Margaret's Hope	77	9B
St Mark's	66	2B
St Marychurch	51	9C
St Marys	77	9B
St Mary's Bay	55	8C
St Mawes	50	3A
St Mawgan	50	3C
St Monans	73	6F
St Neots	60	3C
St Owen's Cross	58	3A
St Paul's Cray	54	5E
St Stephen	50	4B
St Teath	50	4D
Salcombe	51	8B
Sale	63	9E
Salen (Highland)	74	4B
Salen (Strath)	74	4A
Salford	63	9E
Salfords	54	4D
Saline	72	3F
Salisbury	53	6C
Salle	61	8F
Saltaire	64	1E
Saltash	51	6C
Saltburn	79	7B
Saltburn-by-the-Sea	69	8B
Saltcoats	71	7C
Saltdean	54	5B
Saltfleet	65	8C
Saltford	52	3E
Salthouse	61	7G
Saltney	63	7D
Samlesbury	63	8G
Sampford Peverell	51	9E
Sanaigmore	70	1D
Sandbach	63	9C
Sandbank	71	6E
Sandbanks	52	5A
Sandford-on-Thames	53	8G
Sandgarth	77	9B
Sandgate	55	9D
Sandhaven	77	6G
Sandhead	66	1F
Sandhurst	54	2E
Sandiway	63	8D
Sandness	77	9F
Sandon	63	10B
Sandown	53	8A
Sandridge	60	3A
Sandringham	60	5F
Sandsend	69	9B
Sandwich	55	10E
Sandy	60	3B
Sanquhar	72	2B
Santon	66	2B
Sarclet	79	10F
Sarn	62	1B
Sarnesfield	58	2C
Sarre	55	9E
Saughtree	73	6A
Saul	58	4A
Saundersfoot	56	3C
Saunton	51	6G
Sawbridgeworth	60	4A
Sawley	59	8G
Sawston	60	4B
Saxby	60	1F
Saxilby	64	5B
Saxmundham	61	9C
Saxthorpe	61	8G
Sayers Common	54	4C
Scalasaig	70	2F
Scalloway	77	9E
Scarborough	69	10A
Scarinish	74	1A
Scawby	64	5C
Scole	61	8D
Sconser	74	3E
Scopwick	65	6A
Scotch Corner	69	6A
Scotforth	67	8A
Scotter	64	5C
Scoulton	61	7E
Scourie	78	4F
Scrabster	79	9G
Scunthorpe	64	5D
Seaford	54	5B
Seaham	69	7D
Sea Houses	73	9C
Seal	55	6E
Seamer	65	6G
Seamill	71	6C
Sea Palling	61	9F
Seasalter	55	8E
Seascale	67	6C
Seathwaite	67	7C
Seatoller	67	7D
Seaton	52	1A
Seaton Burn	69	6E
Seaton Sluice	69	7E
Seave Green	69	8A
Seaview	53	8B
Sedbergh	67	9C
Sedgeberrow	59	6B
Sedgebrook	60	1G
Sedlescombe	55	7C
Seend	52	5E
Seighford	63	9B
Selborne	53	9D
Selby	64	4E
Selkirk	73	6C
Sellindge	55	8D
Selsdon	54	5E
Selsey	54	2A
Selside	67	8C
Selston	64	3A
Selworthy	51	9G
Send	54	3E
Senghenydd	57	8B
Sennen	50	1A
Sennybridge	57	7D
Setchey	60	5F
Settle	67	10A
Sevenoaks	55	6E
Seven Sisters	57	7C
Shaftesbury	52	4C
Shaldon	51	9C
Shalfleet	53	7A
Shalford	61	6A
Shandon	71	7E
Shanklin	53	8A
Shap	67	8D
Shardlow	59	8G
Sharpness	52	3G
Shawbury	63	8A
Sheerness	55	8E
Sheffield	64	2B
Sheffield Green	54	5C
Shefford	60	3B
Shenfield	55	6F
Shepreth	60	4B
Shepshed	59	8F
Shepton Mallet	52	3D
Sherborne*	52	3C
Sherburn	64	5G
Sherfield-on-Loddon	53	8E
Sheringham	61	8G
Sherston	52	4F
Sherwood	59	8G
Shiel Bridge	74	5E
Shieldaig	74	5F
Shifnal	63	9A
Shildon	69	6B
Shillingford	53	8G
Shillingstone	52	4C
Shilton	59	7A
Shipdham	61	7E
Shiplake	53	9F
Shipley (Salop)	58	5E
Shipley (Sussex)	54	4C
Shipley (W. Yorks)	64	1E
Shipston-on-Stour	59	7B
Shipton (N. Yorks)	64	3F
Shipton (Salop)	58	3E
Shiptonthorpe	64	5E
Shipton-under-Wychwood	59	7A
Shoeburyness	55	8F
Shoreham-by-Sea	54	4B
Shorwell	53	7A
Shotley	61	8B
Shotley Bridge	68	5D
Shottisham	61	9B
Shotts	72	3D
Shrewsbury	63	7A
Shrewton	52	5D
Shrivenham	53	6F
Shurdington	58	5A
Shute	51	1B
Sibsey	65	7A
Sibson	59	7E
Sidcup	54	5E
Sidford	51	10D
Sidlesham	54	2B
Sidley	55	7B
Sidmouth	51	10D
Silk Willoughby	60	2G
Silloth	67	6F
Silsoe	60	2B
Silver End	61	6A
Silverstone	59	9B
Silverton	51	9E
Simonsbath	51	8G
Sinderby	64	2G
Singleton	54	2B
Sissinghurst	55	7D
Sittingbourne	55	8E
Six Hills	59	9F
Six Mile Bottom	60	5C
Skail	79	7F
Skaill	77	9B

INDEX

Skeabost Bridge......**74**......*3F*
Skegness......**65**......*8A*
Skelmersdale......**63**......*7F*
Skelmorlie......**71**......*6D*
Skelton-in-Cleveland......**69**......*8B*
Skene......**76**......*5D*
Skenfrith......**58**......*3A*
Sketty......**57**......*6B*
Skewen......**57**......*6B*
Skipness......**70**......*5D*
Skipsea......**65**......*6F*
Skipton......**64**......*1F*
Skirling......**72**......*4C*
Slaidburn......**67**......*9A*
Slamannan......**72**......*3E*
Slapton......**51**......*8B*
Sleaford......**60**......*2G*
Slebech......**56**......*3C*
Sledmere......**64**......*5F*
Sleights......**69**......*9B*
Sligachan......**74**......*3E*
Slindon......**54**......*3B*
Slingsby......**64**......*4G*
Slough......**54**......*3F*
Smailholm......**73**......*7C*
Smarden......**55**......*7D*
Smethwick......**59**......*6E*
Smithfield......**67**......*8G*
Snaith......**64**......*4D*
Snettisham......**60**......*5G*
Soham......**60**......*5D*
Solihull......**59**......*6D*
Solva......**56**......*2C*
Somersham......**60**......*4D*
Somerton......**52**......*2C*
Sompting......**54**......*4B*
Sonning......**53**......*9F*
Sonning Common......**53**......*9F*
Sorbie......**66**......*3F*
Sorisdale......**74**......*2B*
Sorn......**71**......*8B*
Souldern Gate......**59**......*8B*
Sourton......**51**......*7D*
Southam......**59**......*8C*
Southampton......**53**......*7C*
South Benfleet......**55**......*7F*
Southborough......**55**......*6D*
South Brent......**51**......*7C*
South Cave......**64**......*5E*
Southdean......**73**......*6B*
Southend......**70**......*4A*
Southend-on-Sea......**55**......*7F*
Southerndown......**57**......*7A*
Southery......**60**......*5E*
Southgate......**54**......*4F*
South Harting......**53**......*9C*
South Holmwood......**54**......*4D*
South Kessock......**75**......*9F*
South Kilworth......**59**......*8D*
South Kyme......**65**......*6A*
South Normanton......**64**......*3A*
South Mimms......**54**......*4G*
Southminster......**55**......*8G*
South Molton......**51**......*8F*
Southmuir......**76**......*3B*
Southport......**63**......*7F*
South Queensferry......**72**......*4E*
South Raynham......**61**......*6F*
Southsea......**53**......*8B*
South Shields......**69**......*7E*
South Stainley......**64**......*2F*
South Walsham......**61**......*9F*
Southwater......**54**......*4C*
Southwell......**64**......*4A*
Southwick (Hants)......**53**......*8B*
Southwick (Sussex)......**54**......*4B*
Southwold......**61**......*10D*
Spalding......**60**......*3F*
Spaldwick......**60**......*3D*
Sparkford......**52**......*3C*
Sparsholt......**53**......*7D*
Spean Bridge......**75**......*7C*
Spencers Wood......**53**......*9E*
Spettisbury......**52**......*5B*
Spey Bay......**76**......*3G*
Spilsby......**65**......*8A*
Spinningdale......**79**......*7C*
Spittal......**79**......*9F*
Spofforth......**64**......*2F*

Spratton......**59**......*9D*
Springholm......**66**......*5G*
Sprouston......**73**......*7C*
Sprowston......**61**......*8F*
Stableford......**63**......*9B*
Stadhampton......**53**......*8G*
Staffin......**74**......*3G*
Stafford......**63**......*10A*
Stagshaw Bank......**68**......*5E*
Staindrop......**69**......*6B*
Staines......**54**......*3E*
Stainforth......**67**......*10B*
Stair......**71**......*7B*
Staithes......**69**......*9B*
Stalham......**61**......*9F*
Stamford......**60**......*2E*
Stamford Bridge......**64**......*4F*
Stamfordham......**68**......*5E*
Standlake......**53**......*7G*
Standon......**60**......*4A*
Stanhope......**68**......*5C*
Stanley......**76**......*2A*
Stannington......**69**......*6E*
Stansted......**60**......*5A*
Stanton......**52**......*5F*
Stanton Harcourt......**59**......*8A*
Stanway......**59**......*6B*
Stanwix......**67**......*8F*
Stapleford......**59**......*8G*
Staplehurst......**55**......*7D*
Starbotton......**67**......*10B*
Starcross......**51**......*9D*
Staveley......**64**......*3B*
Staverton......**59**......*8C*
Staxton......**65**......*6G*
Steeple Aston......**59**......*8A*
Steeple Bumpstead......**60**......*5B*
Stein......**74**......*2G*
Stenness......**77**......*8B*
Stevenage......**60**......*3A*
Stevenston......**71**......*7C*
Steventon......**53**......*7G*
Stewkley......**60**......*1A*

Stibb Cross......**51**......*6E*
Stickford......**65**......*7A*
Sticklepath......**51**......*7D*
Stickney......**65**......*7A*
Stiffkey......**61**......*7G*
Stilligarry......**78**......*1E*
Stillington......**64**......*3G*
Stilton......**60**......*3D*
Stirling......**72**......*2F*
Stobo......**72**......*4C*
Stoborough......**52**......*5A*
Stobs......**73**......*6B*
Stock......**55**......*6G*
Stockbridge......**53**......*7D*
Stockport......**63**......*9E*
Stockton-on-Tees......**69**......*7B*
Stoer......**78**......*3E*
Stoke-by-Clare......**61**......*6B*
Stoke-by-Nayland......**61**......*7B*
Stoke Canon......**51**......*9E*
Stoke Ferry......**61**......*6E*
Stoke Fleming......**51**......*8B*
Stoke Goldington......**60**......*1B*
Stoke Mandeville......**54**......*2G*
Stoke-on-Trent......**63**......*9C*
Stoke Poges......**54**......*3F*
Stokesley......**69**......*8B*
Stone......**63**......*10B*
Stonebridge......**59**......*7D*
Stonehaven......**76**......*5C*
Stonehouse (Glos)......**58**......*5A*
Stonehouse (Strath)......**72**......*2D*
Stoneleigh......**59**......*7D*
Stonethwaite......**67**......*7D*
Stoney Cross......**53**......*6C*
Stoneykirk......**66**......*1F*
Stonnall......**59**......*6E*
Stonor......**53**......*9F*
Stony Stratford......**59**......*9B*
Stornoway......**78**......*2F*
Storth......**67**......*8B*
Stotfold......**60**......*3B*
Stoulton......**58**......*5C*

Stourbridge......**58**......*5D*
Stourpaine......**52**......*4B*
Stourport-on-Severn......**58**......*5D*
Stourton......**58**......*5D*
Stow......**73**......*6C*
Stowmarket......**61**......*7C*
Stow-on-the-Wold......**59**......*6A*
Strachan......**76**......*4D*
Strachur......**71**......*6F*
Stradbroke......**61**......*8D*
Stradishall......**61**......*6C*
Stradsett......**60**......*5E*
Straiton......**71**......*7A*
Stranraer......**66**......*1F*
Stratford St Andrews......**61**......*9C*
Stratford-upon-Avon......**59**......*7C*
Strath......**78**......*2B*
Strathaven......**72**......*2C*
Strathcarron......**74**......*5F*
Strathdon......**76**......*3E*
Strathkinnaird......**78**......*4C*
Strathmiglo......**72**......*4G*
Strathy......**79**......*7G*
Strathyre......**71**......*8G*
Stratton......**50**......*5E*
Stratton-on-the-Fosse......**52**......*3E*
Stratton St Margaret......**53**......*6F*
Streatley......**53**......*8F*
Street......**52**......*2D*
Strensham......**58**......*5B*
Strete......**51**......*8B*
Stretford......**63**......*9E*
Stretham......**60**......*5D*
Stretton......**60**......*2F*
Strichen......**77**......*6G*
Stromeferry......**74**......*5E*
Stromness......**77**......*8B*
Stronachlachar......**71**......*7F*
Strone......**71**......*6E*
Strontian......**74**......*5B*
Strood......**55**......*7E*
Stroud......**52**......*4G*
Struan......**74**......*2F*

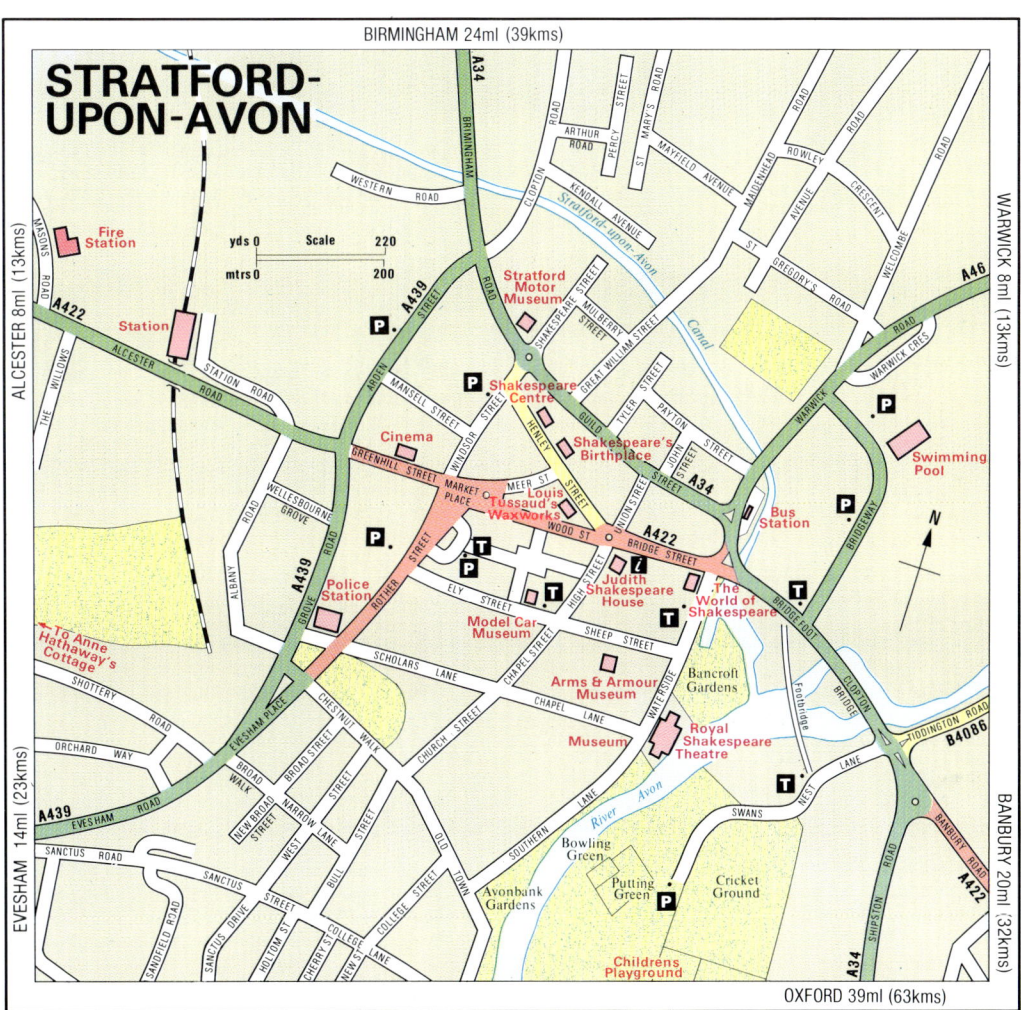

Place	Page	Grid
Stuartfield	77	6F
Studland	52	5A
Studley	59	6C
Sturminster Newton	52	4C
Sturry	55	9E
Sturton	64	5B
Sudbury (Derbys)	59	6G
Sudbury (Suffolk)	61	6B
Sulby	66	3C
Sullom Voe	77	9F
Sumburgh	77	10E
Summercourt	50	3B
Sunbury-on-Thames	54	4E
Sunderland	69	7D
Sunningdale	54	3E
Surfleet	60	3F
Sutterton	60	3G
Sutton	60	4D
Sutton-at-Hone	55	6E
Sutton Benger	52	5F
Sutton Bridge	60	4F
Sutton Coldfield	59	6E
Sutton Courtenay	53	8G
Sutton-in-Ashfield	64	3A
Sutton-on-Sea	65	8B
Sutton-on-the-Forest	64	3F
Sutton-on-Trent	64	4A
Sutton Scotney	53	7D
Sutton Valence	55	7D
Swadlincote	59	7F
Swaffham	61	6E
Swainswick	52	4E
Swalcliffe	59	7B
Swalecliffe	55	9E
Swallow	65	6C
Swallowfield	53	9E
Swanage	52	5A
Swanbridge	57	8A
Swanley	55	6E
Swansea	57	6B
Swanwick	53	8B
Swaton	60	3G
Sway	53	6B
Swimbridge	51	7F
Swindon	53	6F
Swineshead	60	3G
Swinford	59	8D
Swinton	73	7D
Swyre	52	3A
Symbister	77	10F
Symington (Strath)	71	7B
Symington (Strath)	72	3C
Symond's Yat	58	3A
Synod	56	5E
Syre	79	7F
Syresham	59	9B
Syston	59	9F

T

Place	Page	Grid
Tabley Superior	63	9D
Tadcaster	64	3E
Tadworth	54	4E
Tain	79	7B
Talacre	63	6D
Talgarreg	56	5E
Talgarth	57	8D
Talke	63	9C
Talkin	67	8F
Talladale	78	3B
Talley	57	6D
Talmine	79	6G
Talsarnau	62	3B
Talybont (Dyfed)	57	6G
Tal-y-Bont (Gwynedd)	62	3A
Tal-y-Bont (Gwynedd)	62	4D
Tal-y-Cafn	62	4D
Tal-y-llyn	62	4A
Tamworth	59	7E
Tankerton	55	9E
Tannadice	76	3B
Tanygroes	56	4E
Taplow	54	3F
Tarbert (Lewis)	78	2F
Tarbert (Strath)	70	5D
Tarbet	71	7F
Tarbolton	71	7B
Tarland	76	3D
Tarporley	63	8C
Tarrant Hinton	52	5B
Tarskavaig	74	4D
Tarves	76	5F
Tarvin	63	7D
Tattershall	65	7A
Taunton	52	1C
Tavistock	51	6C
Taychreggan	70	5G
Tayinloan	70	4C
Taynuilt	70	5G
Tayport	76	3A
Tayvallich	70	4E
Tealby	65	6C
Tebay	67	9D
Teddington Hands	58	5B
Teignmouth	51	9C
Telford	63	8A
Temple	72	5D
Temple Bar	56	5E
Temple Combe	52	4C
Temple Ewell	55	9D
Temple Sowerby	67	9E
Tempsford	60	3C
Tenbury Wells	58	3D
Tenby	56	3B
Tenterden	55	7C
Tern Hill	63	8B
Tetbury	52	4G
Tetney	65	7C
Tetsworth	53	8G
Teviothead	72	5A
Tewin	60	3A
Tewkesbury	58	5B
Thame	59	9A
Thamesmead	54	5G
Thankerton	72	3C
Thatcham	53	8E
Thaxted	60	5B
Theale	53	8F
Theberton	61	9C
Thetford	61	6D
Theydon Bois	54	5G
Thirlspot	67	7D
Thirsk	64	3G
Thornbury	52	3G
Thorne	64	4D
Thorney	60	3E
Thornham	61	6G
Thornhill (Central)	71	9F
Thornhill (Dumf & Gall)	72	3A
Thornton Cleveleys	63	7G
Thornton Dale	64	5G
Thornton-le-Street	69	7A
Thornton Rust	68	5A
Thorpe Bay	55	8F
Thorpe End	61	8E
Thorpeness	61	9C
Thorrington	61	7A
Thrapston	60	2D
Three Cocks	57	8D
Threekingham	60	2G
Threshfield	64	1F
Throckley	69	6E
Thropton	73	8A
Thrumster	79	10F
Thurmaston	59	9F
Thurnham	55	7E
Thursby	67	7F
Thursford Green	61	7G
Thurso	79	9G
Thurstaston	63	6D
Thwaite	68	4A
Tibbie Shiels	72	4B
Tibshelf	64	3A
Ticehurst	55	6C
Tichborne	53	8D
Ticknall	59	7F
Tideswell	64	1B
Tidworth	53	6D
Tigharry	78	1E
Tighnabruaich	70	5E
Tilbury	55	6F
Tillicoultry	72	3F
Tilshead	52	5D
Tilstock	63	8B
Tilton	59	9E
Tintagel	50	4D
Tintern	52	3G
Tiptree	61	6A
Tissington	64	1A
Titchfield	53	8B
Titchwell	61	6G
Tittensor	63	9B
Tiverton	51	9E
Tobermory	74	3B
Toddington	60	2A
Todhills (Cumbria)	67	7F
Todhills (Tayside)	76	3A
Todmorden	63	10F
Toft Hill	69	6C
Tollard Royal	52	5C
Tollesbury	61	7A
Tolleshunt D'Arcy	61	7A
Tolpuddle	52	4B
Tomatin	75	10E
Tomdoun	75	7D
Tomich	75	7E
Tomintoul	76	2E
Tomnavoulin	76	2E
Tonbridge	55	6D
Tondu	57	7A
Tong	63	9A
Tongue	79	6F
Tongwynlais	57	8A
Tonpentre	57	7B
Tonypandy	57	7B
Tonyrefail	57	8B
Topcliffe	64	3G
Topsham	51	9D
Torcross	51	8B
Tore	75	9F
Torgyle	75	7D
Torksey	64	5B
Torness	75	9E
Torphins	76	4D
Torpoint	51	6B
Torquay	51	9C
Torridon	74	5G
Torrin	74	4E
Torrington	51	6F
Torryburn	72	3E
Torthorwald	67	6G
Torver	67	7C
Totland	53	7A
Totnes	51	8C
Tottenhill	60	5F
Totton	53	7C
Towcester	59	9C
Tow Law	69	6C
Towton	64	3E
Tranent	72	5E
Traquair	72	5C
Trawsfynydd	62	4B
Trearddur Bay	62	1D
Trecastle	57	7D
Tredegar	57	8C
Treen	50	1A
Trefriw	62	4C
Tregaron	57	6E
Tregony	50	4B
Tremadog	62	3B
Trentham	63	9B
Treorchy	57	7B
Trer-ddol	57	6G
Tresillian	50	3B
Tretower	57	8C
Trevor	63	6B
Trewint	50	5D
Trimingham	61	8G
Trimpley	58	4D
Tring	60	2A
Troon	71	7C
Trossachs	71	8F
Trotton	54	2C
Troutbeck	67	8C
Trowbridge	52	4E
Trumpington	60	4C
Truro	50	3B
Tugby	59	9E
Tulloch Station	75	8C
Tummel Bridge	75	10B
Tunbridge Wells	55	6D
Tunstall	63	9C
Turnberry	71	6A
Turnditch	59	7G
Turnershill	54	5D
Turriff	76	5F
Turvey	60	2C
Tushielaw Inn	72	5B
Tutbury	59	7G
Tutshill	52	3G
Tuxford	64	4B
Twatt	77	8B
Tweedmouth	73	8D
Tweedsmuir	72	4B
Two Bridges	51	7C
Twycross	59	7E
Twyford (Berks)	53	9F
Twyford (Hants)	53	7C
Twynholm	66	4F
Tylorstown	57	8B
Tyndrum	71	7G
Tynemouth	69	7E
Tyn-y-Cefn	62	5B
Tytherleigh	52	2B
Tywyn	56	5G

U

Place	Page	Grid
Ubley	52	3E
Uckfield	54	5C
Uddingston	71	9D
Uffculme	51	9E
Ugborough	51	7B
Ugthorpe	69	9B
Uig (Lewis)	78	2F
Uig (Skye)	74	3G
Ulceby	65	6D
Uldale	67	7E
Uley	52	4G
Ullapool	78	4C
Ullenhall	59	6D
Ulpha	67	7C
Ulsta	77	10F
Ulverston	67	7B
Umberleigh	51	7F
Unapool	78	4E
Upavon	53	6E
Uplyme	52	2B
Upminster	55	6F
Upper Benefield	60	2D
Upper Brailes	59	7B
Upper Broughton	59	9G
Upper Largo	72	5F
Upper Swell	59	6B
Upper Tean	63	10B
Uppingham	60	1E
Upstreet	55	9E
Upton Cross	50	5C
Upton-on-Severn	58	5B
Upton Snodsbury	58	5C
Upwey	52	3A
Urchfont	52	5E
Usk	52	2G
Uttoxeter	59	6G
Uxbridge	54	3F

V

Place	Page	Grid
Valley	62	2D
Velindre	56	4D
Ventnor	53	8A
Verwood	52	5B
Vickerstown	67	7B
Virginia Water	54	3E
Voe	77	10F

W

Place	Page	Grid
Waddesdon	59	9A
Waddington (Lancs)	63	9G
Waddington (Lincs)	64	5A
Wadebridge	50	4C
Wadesmill	60	4A
Wadhurst	55	6C
Waenfawr	62	3C
Wainfleet	65	8A
Wakefield	64	2D
Walberswick	61	9D
Walgherton	63	8C
Walkerburn	72	5C
Walkern	60	3A
Walkington	64	5E
Wallasey	63	6E
Wallingford	53	8F

Walls	77	9E
Wallsend	69	6E
Walmer	55	10D
Walpole Cross Keys	60	5F
Walsall	59	6E
Walsall Wood	59	6E
Walsoken	60	4E
Waltham	65	7C
Waltham Abbey	54	5G
Waltham-on-the-Wolds	59	9F
Walton (Powys)	57	9E
Walton (Somerset)	52	2D
Walton (Surrey)	54	3E
Walton-on-the-Naze	61	8A
Wanlockhead	72	3B
Wansford	60	2E
Wanstrow	52	4D
Wantage	53	7F
Warboys	60	4D
Warcop	68	4B
Wardlow	64	1B
Ware	60	4A
Wareham	52	5A
Warenford	73	9C
Wargrave	53	9F
Wark (Northumb)	68	4E
Wark (Northumb)	73	7C
Warkworth	73	10B
Warlingham	54	5E
Warmington	59	8C
Warminster	52	4D
Warmley	52	3F
Warnford	53	8C
Warninglid	54	4C
Warrington	63	8E
Warsash	53	7B
Warsop	64	3B
Warwick (Cumbria)	67	8F
Warwick (Warwicks)	59	7C
Wasbister	77	8C
Wasdale	67	6C
Wasdale Head	67	7D
Washford	51	9G
Washington	69	6D
Watchet	51	9G
Waterbeck	67	7G
Watergate Bay	50	3C
Waterlooville	53	8B
Watermillock	67	8D
Watersfield	54	3C
Watford	54	4G
Watlington	53	8G
Watten	79	9F
Watton	61	7E
Watton-at-Stone	60	4A
Wearhead	68	4C
Weaverham	63	8D
Wedmore	52	2D
Wednesbury	58	5E
Weedon	59	9C
Weekley	59	10D
Weeley	61	8A
Weem	75	10A
Weeting	61	6D
Welbourn	64	5A
Weldon	60	2D
Welford	59	9D
Welland	58	4B
Wellesbourne	59	7C
Welling	54	5F
Wellingborough	60	1C
Wellington (Salop)	63	8A
Wellington (Somerset)	51	10F
Wells	52	3D
Wells-next-the-Sea	61	7G
Welney	60	5E
Welshampton	63	7B
Welshpool	63	6A
Welton	59	8C
Welwyn Garden City	60	3A
Wem	63	8B
Wemyss Bay	71	6D
Wendens Ambo	60	4B
Wendover	54	2G
Wendron	50	2A
Wentbridge	64	3D
Weobley	58	3C
Wereham	60	5E
West Auckland	69	6C
West Bilney	61	6F
West Bridgford	59	8G
West Bromwich	58	5E
Westbury (Salop)	63	7A
Westbury (Wilts)	52	4E
Westbury-on-Trym	52	3F
Westbury-upon-Severn	58	4A
West Byfleet	54	3E
West Calder	72	3D
West Coker	52	3C
Westcliff-on-Sea	55	7F
Westcott	54	4D
Wester Causewayend	72	4D
Westerdale	79	9F
Westerham	54	5D
West Felton	63	7B
Westfield	55	7B
Westgate-on-Sea	55	10E
West Haddon	59	9D
West Harptree	52	3E
West Horsley	54	3D
West Huntspill	52	2D
West Kilbride	71	6C
West Kirby	63	6E
West Lavington	52	5E
West Linton	72	4D
West Lynn	60	5F
West Malling	55	6E
West Meon	53	8C
West Mersea	61	7A
Westmill	60	4A
West Moors	52	5B
Westnewton	67	6E
Weston (Salop)	63	8B
Weston (Staffs)	63	10B
Westonbirt	52	4F
Weston Heath	63	9A
Weston-on-the-Green	59	8A
Weston Rhyn	63	6B
Weston Subedge	59	6B
Weston-super-Mare	52	2E
Weston-under-Lizard	63	9A
West Pennard	52	3D
West Quantoxhead	51	10G
West Runton	61	8G
Westruther	73	7D
West Tarbert Pier	70	5D
West Tarring	54	4B
West Town	53	9B
Westward Ho!	51	6F
Westwell	55	8D
West Wittering	53	9B
West Witton	68	5A
West Woodburn	68	4F
West Wycombe	54	2G
Wetheral	67	8F
Wetherby	64	3F
Wethersfield	61	6A
Wetwang	64	5F
Weybourne	61	8G
Weybridge	54	3E
Weyhill	53	7D
Weymouth	52	3A
Whaley Bridge	63	10D
Whalley	63	9G
Whalton	69	6E
Whaplode	60	4F
Whaplode Drove	60	4F
Whauphill	66	3F
Wheathampstead	60	3A
Wheddon Cross	51	9G
Whepstead	61	6C
Wherwell	53	7D
Whiddon Down	51	7D
Whippingham	53	8B
Whipsnade	60	2A
Whitburn	72	3D
Whitby (Cheshire)	63	7D
Whitby (N. Yorks)	69	9B

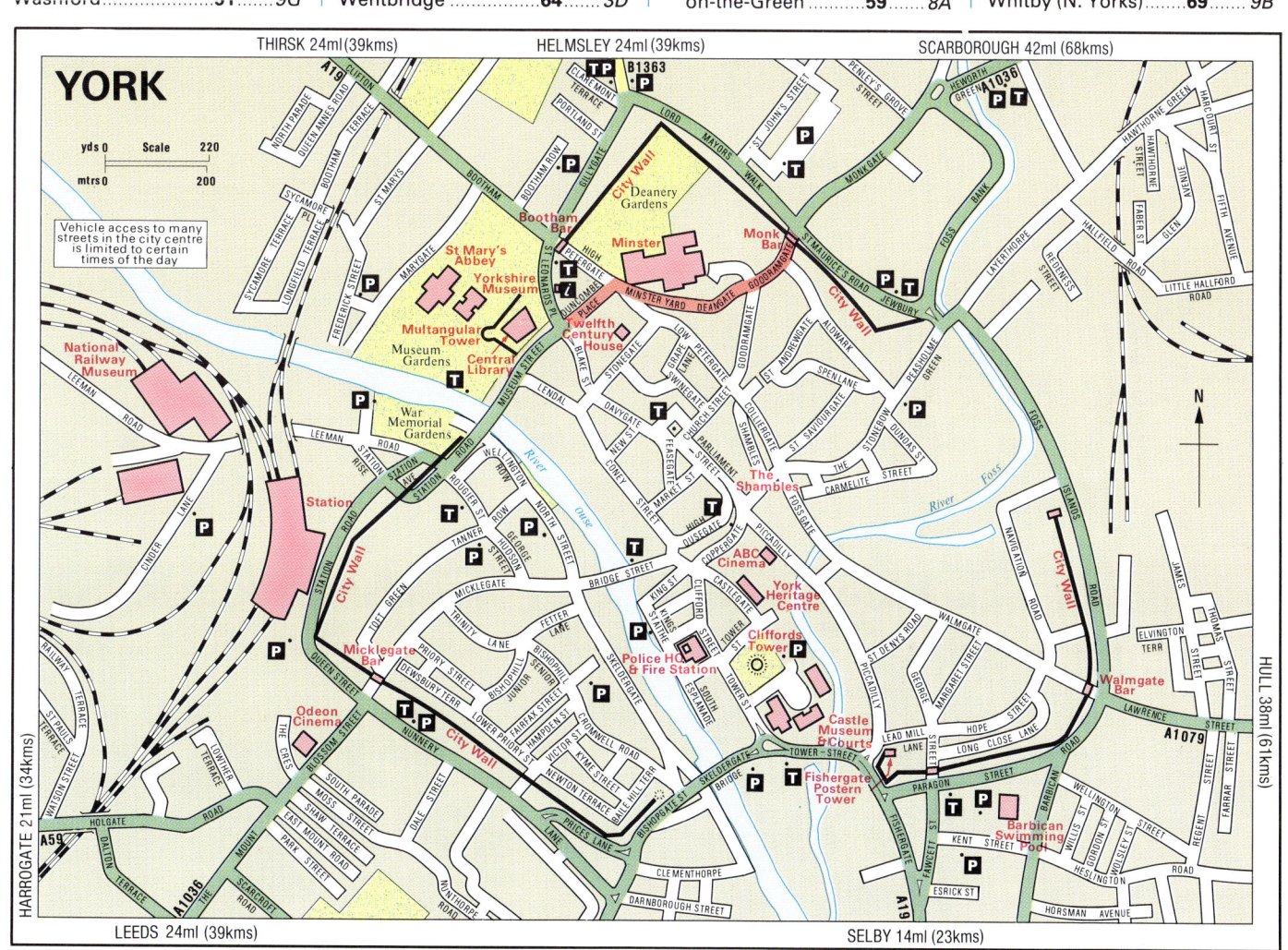

INDEX

Whitchurch (Bucks)	59	10A	Willingdon	55	6B	Witney	59	7A	Wrelton	69	9A
Whitchurch (Hants)	53	7D	Willingham	60	4C	Wittersham	55	7C	Wrentham	61	9D
Whitchurch (Salop)	63	8E	Willington	59	7G	Witton-le-Wear	69	6C	Wrestlingworth	60	3B
Whitebridge	75	8E	Williton	51	9G	Wiveliscombe	51	9F	Wrexham	63	7C
Whitebrook	58	3A	Willoughbridge	63	9B	Wivenhoe	61	7A	Writtle	55	6G
White Castle	72	3C	Wilmington	52	1B	Wix	61	8A	Wrotham	55	6E
Whitehall	77	9C	Wilmslow	63	9D	Woburn	60	2B	Wrotham Heath	55	6E
Whitehaven	67	6D	Wilshamstead	60	2B	Woburn Sands	60	2B	Wroughton	53	6F
Whitehill	53	9D	Wilsontown	72	3D	Woking	54	3E	Wroxall	53	8A
Whitehills	76	4G	Wilton	52	5D	Wokingham	54	2E	Wroxham	61	8F
Whitehouse	70	4D	Wimblington	60	4E	Wolf's Castle	56	2D	Wroxton	59	8B
Whitekirk	73	6E	Wimborne Minster	52	5B	Wollaston (Northants)	60	2C	Wychbold	58	5C
Whiteparish	53	6C	Wincanton	52	4C	Wollaston (Salop)	63	7A	Wyboston	60	3C
White Stone	58	3B	Winchcombe	59	6B	Wollaton	59	8G	Wych Cross	54	5C
Whithorn	66	3E	Winchelsea	55	8C	Wolsingham	68	5C	Wyke Regis	52	3A
Whiting Bay	70	5B	Winchester	53	7C	Wolverhampton	58	5E	Wylye	52	5D
Whitland	56	4C	Windermere	67	8C	Wonersh	54	3D	Wymondham	61	8E
Whitletts	71	7B	Windsor	54	3F	Woodbridge	61	8B	Wynds Point	58	4B
Whitley Bay	69	7E	Wing	60	1A	Woodchurch	55	8C			
Whitminster	58	4A	Wingham	55	9E	Woodfalls	53	6C			
Whitney-on-Wye	57	9E	Winkfield	54	3E	Woodford	52	3G	**Y**		
Whitstable	55	9E	Winkhill	64	1A	Woodhall Spa	65	6A			
Whittington	63	7B	Winkleigh	51	7E	Woodham Ferrers	55	7G	Yarcombe	52	1B
Whittlebury	59	9B	Winsford	63	8D	Woodland	68	5C	Yardley Gobion	59	9B
Whittlesey	60	3E	Winsham	52	2B	Woodstock	59	8A	Yardley Hastings	60	1C
Whitton	57	9F	Winslow	59	9B	Woodton	61	8E	Yarmouth	53	7A
Whitwell (Derbys)	64	3B	Winster	64	2A	Woofferton	58	3D	Yarrow	72	5C
Whitwell (Herts)	60	3A	Winston	69	6B	Wool	52	4A	Yarrowford	72	5C
Wick	79	10F	Winterbourne Abbas	52	3B	Wooler	73	8C	Yatton	52	2E
Wickford	55	7F	Winterbourne			Woolhampton	53	8E	Yatton Keynell	52	4F
Wickham	53	8C	Monkton	52	3A	Woolmer Green	60	3A	Yeadon	64	2E
Wickham Market	61	9C	Winterbourne Stoke	52	5D	Woolston	53	7C	Yealand	67	8B
Wickwar	52	4F	Winterbourne			Woore	63	9B	Yealmpton	51	7B
Widdrington	69	6F	Whitechurch	52	4B	Wootton	65	6D	Yelverton	51	7C
Widegates	50	5C	Winterton	64	5D	Wootton Bassett	52	5F	Yeovil	52	3C
Widemouth Bay	50	5E	Winterton-on-Sea	61	9F	Wootton Bridge	53	8B	Yetholm	73	7C
Widford	60	4A	Winton	52	5B	Wootton Wawen	59	6C	Yetts of Muchart	72	3F
Widnes	63	8E	Winwick	60	3D	Worcester	58	5C	York	64	4F
Wigan	63	8F	Wirksworth	64	2A	Workington	67	6E	Yoxall	59	6F
Wigmore	58	3D	Wisbech	60	4E	Worksop	64	3B	Yoxford	61	9C
Wigston	59	9E	Wisborough Green	54	3C	Wormit	72	5G	Ysbyty Ystwyth	57	6F
Wigton	67	7F	Wishaw	72	2D	Worplesdon	54	3D	Ystalyfera	57	6C
Wigtown	66	3F	Wisley	54	3E	Worstead	61	9F	Ystradgynlais	57	6C
Wilberfoss	64	4F	Wiston	72	3C	Worthen	58	2E	Ystrad Mynach	57	8B
Wilby	60	1C	Witham	61	6A	Worthing	54	4B			
Willand	51	9E	Witheridge	51	8E	Wotton-under-Edge	52	4G	**Z**		
Willenhall	58	5E	Withern	65	8B	Wragby (Lincs)	65	6B			
Willerby	65	6E	Withernsea	65	7E	Wragby (Yorks)	64	3D	Zeals	52	4D
Willersey	59	6B	Withyham	54	5D	Wrangle	65	8A	Zelah	50	3B
Willersley	58	2C	Witnesham	61	8C	Wrawby	65	6D	Zennor	50	1B

Answers to route planning puzzles on pages 41–45

Charlie wins the pools: Scarborough

True or false?: Perth and Berwick. The Forth Bridge. Primary route.

The jewel thief: Tenby

South to north: No. The motorway ends at Carlisle.

Acknowledgements

The publishers gratefully acknowledge the following for the use of material:

Photographs: the Metropolitan Police (pages 34–7), the Ordnance Survey (page 9), Wally Talbot (pages 2–3). All other photographs supplied by the Automobile Association Publications Division Photographic Library.

Original Artwork: Terence Dalley ARCA (pages 8, 16–17), KAG Design (pages 19–29), Joseph Wright (page 39).

Specimen road tax disc (page 32) reproduced with the permission of the Controller of HM Stationery Office. Crown copyright reserved.

PRINTED IN BELGIUM BY
proost
INTERNATIONAL BOOK PRODUCTION